Global
action

Global
action

A Personal Discipleship Manual for the World Christian

Editor:
Richard Briggs

FOREWORD BY
CHRIS WRIGHT

OM
publishing

Copyright © Operation Mobilisation 1997

First published 1997 by OM Publishing

03 02 01 00 99 98 97   7 6 5 4 3 2 1

OM Publishing is an imprint of Paternoster Publishing,
P.O. Box 300, Carlisle, Cumbria, CA3 0QS, U.K.

The right of Richard Briggs to be identified as the Editor of this Work has been asserted by him in
accordance with the Copyright, Designs and Patents Act 1988.

British Library Cataloguing in Publication Data

A catalogue record for this book is available from the British Library

ISBN 1–85078–271–7

This book is printed using Suffolk New Book paper which is 100% acid free.

Typeset by WestKey Ltd., Falmouth
Printed in the UK by Clays Ltd., St Ives plc

Contents

Foreword

The Apostle Paul insisted that self-sacrificial practical service should be accompanied by the transformation of our minds (Romans 12:1–2). OM has always stood for both, by calling people to offer themselves wholly to God's mission in living sacrifice, and by providing teaching and training along the way. In our long association with OM, we at All Nations Christian College have often observed that those who come to us for further mission training out of an OM background have an exciting and healthy balance of zeal for mission and appetite for the Scriptures. This study programme, *Global Action*, will enhance that happy combination. A number of features impress me greatly.

It is refreshingly *humble* in its claims and *open-ended* in approach. Unlike some distance learning packages, this one accepts that 'it will not tell you everything you need to know', and that 'we cannot always give answers to all the questions.' However, it lays solid foundations and constantly invites students to think things through, wrestle with their beliefs, work out how their Christian faith is to be expressed in different cultures and to grow in confidence and maturity.

It is thoroughly *biblical*, giving the trainee both a good survey of biblical content, and some excellent guidance on how to interpret the Bible and well, and pointing him or her to the range of resources available for additional help. For this alone we would have cause to be grateful.

It is wisely *balanced*. While setting out the strong foundations of the essentials of the biblical Christian faith, it acknowledges the differences among Christians over many issues and aims to help the trainee understand and assess the different positions. In a multi-denominational, multi-cultural organization like OM, this is of course essential for harmonious team-work, but it will also contribute to the theological maturity and judgement of their workers in any context.

It is strongly *missiological*, not just in motivating people for evangelism, but in teaching the biblical basis of mission (OT as well as NT), explaining the full breadth of holistic mission, introducing some of the key theological debates in mission, and familiarizing the trainee with a number of the contentious issues that arise in cross-cultural life and work. It has to be brief, of course, but as an introduction, it will be an eye-opener for many.

It is *realistic*. There is a strong vein of common sense running through the programme, which does not in the least undermine the spiritual zeal which it seeks to enhance. It is not afraid to nail a few old myths and excuses, some of which flow from distorted theology or spirituality ('Do not tell everyone you are "really under attack", if the actual problem is that you need to get more sleep'). And it concludes with some excellent advice for 'life after OM' (there is some, I'm told).

All of which means that when it comes to the acid test — would I recommend it to people coming to All Nations? the answer is, I could wish that everyone coming for mission training took the opportunity to work through this book. Anyone called by God into long-term crows-cultural mission will find that this programme provides them with a well-carved, well-laid, well-levelled foundation stone on which they can build subsequent levels of additional study and training, not just for work with OM, but in any field of service for the mission of Christ and the kingdom of God.

Chris Wright
Principal, All Nations Christian College

Editor's Foreword

This *Global Action* study manual has its roots in a new international Bible and mission training program lauched by OM (Operation Mobilisation) in 1997, under the title of *Global Action*. *Global Action* attempts to combine hands-on experience in Christian work with practical training and sold Bible study. This book is essentially the study part of that training, some of it reflecting tried and tested material used in various situations around the world over the years.

This background will help to explain some of the features of the book, such as its unapologetic focus on the need for Christian mission in today's world; its focus on evangelism; and its consideration of cross-cultural issues. It is our belief that these are increasingly relevant to everyone in our multicultural societies.

It also explains why several of the study exercises have been designed to work in a group format. Although you can use this book on your own, you may find it works best if you study it with friends. The introductory section of the book explains the overall design of the program, and offers practical suggestions on how to use it.

It is my pleasure to thank the many study program leaders, trainers and team members in OM who originally helped in the process of bringing this manual together, and particularly to thank Antony Billington, of the London Bible College, who read through a draft version of the manual and made several helpful suggestions. I have attempted to edit existing materials into a consistent overall package, and have on occasion added extra material where the syllabus demanded it. The views expressed in this manual do not therefore correspond entirely to the views of any particular person, nor to OM itself necessarily, nor even to my own views, but it is hoped that this program will reflect fairly the ethos and biblical understanding of many of those involved in international and interdenominational Christian work.

To God alone be the Glory.

Richard Briggs, editor
Nottingham, July 1997

Outline Syllabus

Section I   The Bible

Unit One   **Bible Survey**

A brief introduction to the study of the Bible, followed by an overview (or survey) of the contents of the Old and New Testaments.

Unit Two   **Introduction to Hermeneutics**

How to read, interpret and apply the Bible; and how to do different kinds of Bible study. This unit focuses on practical questions about method, since the particular interpretations and applications adopted will vary, according to many theological, cultural and personal issues.

Section II   God and His People

Calvin began his famous *Institutes* with the words: 'Nearly all the wisdom we possess, that is to say, true and sound wisdom, consists of two parts: the knowledge of God and of ourselves.'

Unit Three   **Knowing God**

The study of God is, by definition, the beginning of all theology.

Unit Four   Understanding Ourselves

This unit tackles questions of personal identity, and particularly looks at discovering our identity in Christ.

Unit Five   Discipleship

This builds on unit four, looking at the process of living out the Christian life (discipleship), and how these discipleship issues work out in relationship together.

Section III   Christian Mission

Unit Six   World Mission

A biblical look at mission, and a study of key issues and perspectives facing missionaries (World Christians) today.

Unit Seven   Evangelism

Evangelism is an essential part of mission, but what is it? This is a study of the essentials of evangelism, including many practical issues concerning how to use what you have learned.

Unit Eight   Communication

Building on several of the earlier units, this unit goes beyond the content of Christian understanding and looks at the issue of how we communicate, both personally and in public, with a particular focus on cross-cultural situations.

Appendix   Suggestions for Further Reading

Some pointers are given here of how to take further some of the topics covered in the manual. A few titles are suggested from different cultural backgrounds.

Note on Time Commitment

This study program is designed to take about **120 hours** of study. Each unit is designed to take **15 hours**, and in each case is divided into 5 sections. This would make it possible to consider each section as a 3 hour study if desired, although it will be found in practice that some sections take longer than others.

Notes on Recommended Reading

This study manual will not tell you everything you need to know. After much consideration we have decided to recommend a limited number of books as basic reading for the *Global Action* study program. If you do not have access to these books do not worry; you can do enough of the work without them to make it worth continuing.

The basic recommended reading which you will encounter as you go through the units is as follows:

Unit 2   *How to Read the Bible for All Its Worth* by Gordon D. Fee and
                Douglas Stuart (Grand Rapids: Zondervan and London:
                Scripture Union, 2nd edition, 1993)
                = *Effektives Bibelstudium* (Asslar: ICI, 1990)
                = *Nouveau Regard Sur La Bible* (Vida)
                or: *The BibleWith Pleasure: How to get the most out of
                Reading your Bible* by Stephen Motyer (Nottingham:
                Crossway Books, 1997)

Units 5 and 6   *Christian Mission in the Modern World* by John R.W. Stott
                (Downers Grove: IVP, 1975, reprinted 1995)
                = *Gesandt wie Christus: Grundfragen Christlicher Mission und
                Evangelisation* (Wuppertal: Brockhaus, 1976)
                = *Mission Chretien Dans Le Monde* (Groupe Missionaire
                en Suisse)
      or: Why Bother with Mission? by Stephen Gaukroger (Leicester:
                IVP, 1996) for non-English speakers.

The following reference books are also recommended, and will be of use throughout your study (they are introduced more fully in units 1 and 2):

New Bible Commentary, 21st Century Edition by D.A. Carson, R.T. France, J.A. Motyer and G.J. Wenham (eds.) (Leicester: IVP, 4th edition, 1994)

The NIV Complete Concordance by E.W. Goodrick and J.R. Kohlenberger III (eds.) (Grand Rapids: Zondervan, 1981)

The NIV Study Bible (general editor: Kenneth L. Barker) (London: Hodder & Stoughton, 1985)

In addition to these, lists of 'Further Reading' for each unit are given in the Appendix, enabling you to read more widely as you have the time and opportunity. You will note that some units have no required reading beyond this study manual.

Acknowledgements

Much of the material in the units that follow was originally developed in one format or another as part of study programs being run in OM around the world. It is possible that in editing these materials together it has not always been apparent where an OM study program has in turn developed material from an existing resource. If any reader should become aware of this having happened then the editor would be grateful to learn of this so that the appropriate permission can be sought. We apologise for any oversight in this area, and will seek to remedy any omissions in future editions.

OM Material

Many OM trainers and study leaders have developed material which has been used and modified here, and their kind permission to draw from their courses has been much appreciated. In particular:

The material for Unit 3 was contributed by John Hymus and Ian Orton from OM's Rhyl Leadership School.

The basic material for unit 4 was provided by Allan Adams.

In Unit 7 some of the outlines of evangelistic presentations were contributed by Mickey Walker from his privately distributed book, *The Cross and the Sketchboard.*

OM is also grateful for permission to draw upon the following non-OM sources for some material:

The outline for how to interpret a Bible passage in Unit 2 Section 1F is adapted from materials from Hans Finzel, *Opening the Book: Key Methods of Applying Inductive Study to all of Scripture,* (Wheaton, IL:

Introduction to
the *Global Action*
Study Program

Outline and Notes

This short section aims to introduce you to this manual and should be read before you start your studies.

Objectives

At the end of this section, you will be able to:

• describe the aims of the *Global Action* Study Program
• list some advantages and disadvantages of doing this program
• plan your use of the program to be effective as part of your ministry

Outline of this Section

1 The Aims of the *Global Action* Study Program

The *Global Action* Study Program aims to:

(1)   give you a foundation of biblical understanding

(2)   help you know God and know yourself

(3)   equip you for the task of Christian mission

These three aims correspond to the three main sections of the program. Of course, all three of these are areas which will take a lifetime to explore. Which leads us to:

2 What can this Program do for You?

There is tremendous diversity in the body of Christ; the church made up of all nations on the earth. What can unite such a diverse body?

We believe that the **gospel** unites us; that the person of **Jesus Christ** draws us together; and that the **God** who created us gives us all the same **Holy Spirit**. We desire to be *World Christians*, conscious of our role as part of a faith in a gospel which breaks down every dividing wall between fellow humans (see Ephesians 2:14-22 which describes the whole church, the world-wide body of Christ).

This program aims to *start* you on the process of finding your place in Christ's body, through basic studies in key areas. It touches on what we believe to be at the heart of being a Christian in today's world.

But we do not believe that this means we should ignore different **cultural backgrounds** and perspectives. And in an international study program there is a danger that we can do that.

Therefore you should realise as you begin this program that it cannot tell you what to believe: but it can tell you how to go about learning what you believe. It cannot necessarily tell you how to apply what you learn to your situation, but it can lay a foundation which you can then be applying yourself. Different people in different cultures will find different parts of the program more or less directly useful. But our hope is that it will be part of developing your Christian thinking, and will play a role in the essential goal of Christ-like living which the world today needs to see so much.

One of the results of this is that we cannot always give answers to all the questions: many of the exercises are simply to get you thinking about how the truths of the gospel apply where you are.

Additional Note

, What has just been said sounds straightforward, but actually raises some deep issues. You may or may not wish to think about them at the present time, and this note is just to alert you to some things to watch out for if you do decide to think about them.

What are the implications of arguing that different cultures understand the Bible differently? How does the gospel relate to cultures where shame is a stronger element of life than guilt, for example? Is evangelism the same thing in Christianised cultures as it is in places where the Bible has never been seen? These issues will all resurface later in this course. But in fact they go right to the heart of Christian study, and raise some questions about this study program.

It has tended to be argued in the past that theological truth is the same the world over, and that there is only one correct way of understanding the Bible. More recently, it has been widely noticed that this view was only really possible to hold when all the people doing the studying and thinking came from the same background. This has increasingly changed, and today different voices from around the world often argue strongly for different views of many issues.

This is not because they are being stubborn or illogical. It is

simply because different readers of the Bible bring their own questions to the text, and as a result are aware of different priorities in their reading. A classic example of this is the way in which some have taken the 'liberation' which Jesus speaks of in Luke 4:18-19 spiritually, and some have taken it politically. Those suffering from oppression have naturally seen Jesus as addressing that issue here, while others, still wanting to take the text seriously, have viewed it spiritually because that is what has made sense to them. Cross-cultural issues make all this particularly clear, but it occurs on a basic level just because the Bible itself comes to us from a different time and culture than our own (whatever our own is!).

Unit 2 will look at aspects of this discussion from the point of view of how to interpret the Bible, but it is worth pointing out that it actually affects your whole process of study. Very simply: every book comes with a point of view; every 'expert' has his or her own bias; every biblical author was trying to argue, defend or state something somehow for some reason. What will your point of view be? Will it be the same as any of these experts or biblical authors (especially if your situation is quite unlike any of theirs)?

This study manual itself combines many different

4

perspectives because it has drawn from many study courses developed in various contexts around the world. A certain amount of editing has tried to give it a clear approach throughout, but you should always feel free to challenge the views and ideas expressed here. When you do, ask yourself what elements of your culture or personality or church background or theological persuasion are making you challenge something. Be prepared to be open to new perspectives.

What strikes you as relevant may be totally irrelevant to someone else, and vice versa.

None of this needs to be a problem if you keep an **enquiring mind** and are open to re-evaluating what you believe in the light of new experience. Through the process of living out your faith you will work out your own response to God's sovereign call on your life. That should be an exciting process, however difficult it can be at times.

3 Using this Program

You *can* use this program without any extra resources, except a Bible. However, we sometimes recommend further reading, and it is always true that the program will function best when you have the chance to discuss what you are learning with others. For many of you, your local church situation may give you a chance to do that, and the material is divided into sections which may facilitate group discussion at regular intervals. It is also worth trying to build a small library of good reference books, even if it is only a few books. This will enrich your studies. (See the note on this at the beginning of this manual, as well as the suggestions for further reading in the Appendix.)

The program is designed to take approximately **120 hours** of study time. This includes reading this manual, answering the questions, and some group discussion time. Different people will work at different speeds. Do not worry if you cannot answer all the questions in the time suggested. Adapt to your own level.

For instance, if you want to complete this program in one year, you could aim to set aside **3 hours a week** for personal and/or group study. Of course you will not always find this possible, so this recommendation would mean that you need 40 weeks during your year in which you can find study time. The manual has been arranged so that most of the time you can, if you wish, study one section per week, and perhaps meet as a group with others to discuss that material on a weekly basis.

Practicalities

 You will find some sections of the text specially laid out like this. This writing symbol indicates that you should write an answer. *(Note: you should have a separate notebook for this: there will NOT be enough space in the manual for you to write all your answers).* **It is essential that you do these tasks.** You will get nothing out of this study program by just reading it and not responding to any of the questions. You may have to do some thinking, or praying, or discussing with a friend. Again, make sure you take the time to do this.

 Sections marked like this indicate suggested reading.

Some sections of the text are printed in smaller type and in 2 columns, like this. These generally contain more detailed discussions and more difficult questions.	Those who are struggling with keeping up with the course can leave out these sections, and it will not affect understanding the rest of the material.

For those with some study background, or with more experience in Christian ministry, the Appendix provides a few suggestions for further reading which may help you to think through issues more deeply and build on the core material.

Every unit (except Unit 2) contains brief suggestions for verses of the Bible to memorise.

If you have not already done so, think now about how you are going to plan your use of this program. How many hours a week do you intend to do? What group discussion or feedback times will you have? Who will you discuss your studies with?

If appropriate, make sure you discuss this as a team.

SECTION I:
THE BIBLE

Unit One
Bible Survey

Outline and Notes

This unit aims to give you an overview of the contents of the Bible. This will provide you with a framework for the following unit, on how to study different types of writing in the Bible in context.

Aim

The Global Action training program goals include the aim that at the end of their Global Action training the student will:

- have developed an attitude of trust in and obedience to God's word

Study Objectives

As well as laying the foundation for the above training goal, this unit will enable you to:

- explain what type of book the Bible is
- show how each Bible book fits into the overall biblical picture
- explain the different types of writing in the Bible and illustrate with examples

Recommended Reading

See the introductory note at the beginning of this manual on recommended reading for this unit. The Appendix will also recommend particular study books to use in Bible study.

Unit Outline

1 Introduction

1A   Introduction
        Using the Bible
        Reading in Context
        Humility

1B   Some Initial Questions
        The Big Picture

1C   Two Testaments
        The Theme of Covenant in the Bible

1D   The Biblical Canon
        The Old Testament Canon
        The New Testament Canon

2 The Old Testament (1)

2A   The Pentateuch
        The Law

2B   The Histories
        The Monarchy
        The Other Histories

3 The Old Testament (2)

3A   The Prophets
        Prophets and Prophetic Writings
        Apocalyptic Literature

3B   Poetry and Wisdom Literature
        Ecclesiastes

4 The New Testament (1)

4A   Between the Testaments

4B   The Gospels
        What is a Gospel?

4C   Acts

5 The New Testament (2)

5A   The Letters

5B   Revelation
        Interpreting Revelation

Glossary – A list of terms which are important for this unit.

1 Introduction

1A Introduction

We start with the Bible.

What is the Bible? This is a simple enough question, and yet we can answer it on many different levels. It is a book. It is also a collection of books. People call it the Word of God. Or is it better to call it the *words* of God? It is 'scripture': literally meaning 'writings'. It was written by people like King David and the apostle Paul. But it is clearly in some way the work of God. Who decided which books to include in it and which ones to leave out? Is it best to describe the Bible as history, truth, poetry, dreams and visions, laws, stories . . . ? Which version of the Bible are we talking about anyway? The English King James Version? The Greek and Hebrew originals? Do we have those? In fact, why start our course with the Bible at all? Shouldn't we start with God and who God is?

If you know the answers to all these questions then congratulations: you're the first person who does. There are a great many *opinions* about all of them. One of the purposes of this unit, in introducing you to the study of the Bible, is to help you develop your own convictions, as well as interact constructively with other viewpoints.

Using the Bible

One of the reasons for starting with the Bible is because of the unique importance it has for the Christian life. Sadly, many Christians are more enthusiastic about the Bible than knowledgeable about it. It features often in our discussions and disagreements, but do we really know what is in it and how to interpret it? To get an overview of what is in it we will be going on to a Bible *survey* in this unit. This will teach us to look at verses in context, which will become one of our main themes in Unit 2: how to interpret the Bible.

Reading in Context

We must underline the importance of reading verses in context, and compare it with an approach called **proof texting**. Proof texting is using biblical texts to 'prove' something which often does not in fact have much to do with those texts. The argument goes something like this: 'I already know exactly what I believe on this subject. I will find some verses which support my point, and then I will be able to show the biblical basis for my belief.' Notice the order here: the belief comes first and then the appeal to the Bible. This is why it is called 'proof texting'.

> What's wrong with this claim: 'The Bible says that women must not wear trousers'- it's right there in Deuteronomy 22:5'? Or this: a man says to a surprised woman 'God is telling us to get married: I prayed for it today and it says in the Bible that if you ask you will receive (Matthew 7:7) and I know that it is according to his will, so he promises it (1 John 5:15)'?

Quite a lot is wrong with these claims. The first one is a simple misunderstanding of the passage. The Hebrew, of course, has no reference to trousers. In fact, it doesn't even have a reference to men's clothing, but rather 'men's things'. It probably refers to objects used in fertility rites. The verse is probably a prohibition of this kind of magic practice. In any case, would verses 9–12 of the same chapter be applied with equal conviction today?

The second example is more complicated, and probably more serious. How does the man know that it is according to God's will? Would we not expect the woman to have some sense of this too? (And she might do, of course. We're not saying that God never works in this way: just that it is not settled by the confident announcement of the man). Furthermore, what if we applied Matthew 7:7 to just anything: e.g. $1,000,000 – even perhaps for building a new church car park, or world mission, or some equally worthy cause. Would it happen? Why doesn't Matthew 7:7 apply? . . . As you can see, this 'proof texting' approach leads us immediately into questions about reading in context; and about what makes for a responsible interpretation. There is no better preparation for dealing with these questions than to take an overview of what is in the Bible.

Humility

We must emphasise the constant need for humility in biblical interpretation. Learn from the mistakes of others. 'I beg you to consider the possibility that you may be mistaken' is a familiar cry from church history. Never lose sight of the fact that you too may be mistaken, and that certainly you do not know the whole truth about everything. This does not mean that you should not have confidence in the Bible, but that you should always be open to learning to see things in a new way. Growth in the Christian life depends on this.

Unit 2 will focus on questions of how to interpret the Bible. But the most basic requirement for good interpretation is an overall grasp of the content of the Bible. There is nothing wrong with a healthy enthusiasm for Scripture, but it needs to be part of a well-rounded confidence that we know the context of what we are reading.

This unit, therefore, will give a brief survey of what the Bible is and what it contains. Ultimately there is no substitute for picking up your own Bible and reading it regularly and systematically.

1B Some Initial Questions

It is good to start with some reflection on what you think *now*, before you study this unit. First we will outline briefly some of the assumptions which this whole course will make concerning some of the issues raised in our introduction above.

We start with the Bible because we believe it is **foundational** to all Christian living. We do not worship or idolise the Bible, since our worship is for God alone, but we believe that one of the ways, if not *the* main way, that we know God is through the Bible where God reveals himself. The Bible is the word of God in the sense that all its writers were inspired by the Holy Spirit. (This is a claim about the Bible as a whole. It is a slightly different claim to say that the Bible is God's words, which would refer to all the different sentences in the Bible.) It is the **original texts** that we put our trust in, although most of us will rely from day to day on the hard work that many people have done in translating and studying those originals (or at least, manuscripts which go back almost to the time of the originals, and which we can have confidence in as accurate copies of them).

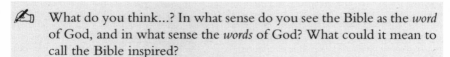 What do you think...? In what sense do you see the Bible as the *word* of God, and in what sense the *words* of God? What could it mean to call the Bible inspired?

One verse which is helpful for beginning to think about these issues is 2 Timothy 3:16. Is this talking about what the Bible *is*, or what it *does*, or what it *is useful for*, or some combination of these? (Note that the word used in 2 Timothy 3:16 to describe scripture is *theopneustos*, which comes from the words which mean 'God-breathed'.)

2 Timothy 3:16 is often quoted, and many people who know it in fact have no idea why Paul might have said it to Timothy at this point in his letter. If you have never thought of this, then take a look at what Paul is talking about in 2 Timothy 3 in general.

 Look in particular at verses 10-17. What is the relationship between the Bible and lifestyle which Paul is talking about?

We will be coming back to these topics later. The purpose at this stage is to make you think about your own assumptions. Do not worry if you find it hard to put into words what you think.

The Big Picture

Before going through the different parts of the Bible in detail it is good to stand back and try and get an overview. In this unit we can do no more than look briefly at the big picture, but there are sometimes some general observations about the content of the Bible which can help you as you work your way through it.

Did you know, for instance, that the great Old Testament story from Adam to the fall of Jerusalem is told twice? (sometimes called the Primary History, Genesis to 2 Kings; and the Secondary History, Chronicles-Ezra-Nehemiah). Or that some of Paul's letters tie in closely with key events in the book of Acts? (A good example of this is the relationship between Paul's collection as described from Paul's perspective in Romans 15:23-33 and from Luke's perspective in Acts 20 and 21- look these up if you want to pursue this example.)

The purpose of this introductory section is to help you towards this kind of 'big picture' overview of what is in your Bible, as well as introduce you to some terms which come up often in the study of the Bible. (*Note:* You may wish to refer to the Appendix at this point to get some help about books you could be using alongside this course.)

 How important is it to know the background of the biblical books?

In short: very important! But we will need to think more carefully about how and why it is important. We will return to this many times in later sections and units.

1C Two Testaments

The Bible contains 66 books arranged in two testaments. (Incidentally, recent research suggests that as many as two-thirds of non-Christians, even in relatively Christianised cultures (like America), do not know this. The fact that the Bible is a best-selling book may not mean that very many people have read it.)

✍ 'Testament' may be a familiar word, but what does it mean?

The English word comes from the Latin *testamentum* which is a translation of the Hebrew *berit* (Genesis 17:2) and Greek *diatheke* (Mark 14:22-5; 1 Corinthians 11:23-5, Hebrews 8:13). If you look up these references you will see that we normally translate it these days as '**covenant**'. In fact, some modern translations call the respective parts of the Bible the 'books of the Old Covenant' and the 'books of the New Covenant' (the New Revised Standard Version does this). The word was first applied to the two collections of books in the second century.

The Theme of Covenant in the Bible

If you study Genesis 17 you will find a good example of what is involved in God's covenants with humanity: God makes promises which require certain responses of obedience, but at the same time the promise is unearned, a reflection of God's grace: he did not have to offer it in the first place. For the people involved it is therefore both a privilege and a responsibility. It is sometimes difficult to grasp the significance of the covenant idea in biblical times. Perhaps the nearest we have to it in many modern cultures is the idea of marriage: an agreement that is entered into with various degrees of free will (depending on the culture), but which binds both parties to certain obligations, even though neither one 'deserves' the other's love or commitment.

✍ Do you think that marriage is a good modern day example of a covenant?

✍ Can you think of any other examples?

The idea of covenant is extremely important throughout the Bible, which makes it appropriate that we use the word 'testament' in describing the Bible contents. God makes covenants with Noah (Genesis 8-9), with Israel through Moses (perhaps the whole book of Deuteronomy is

---

best seen as a covenant, see especially chapters 4–28), with David and his descendants (2 Samuel 7), and ultimately with the whole of his chosen people (Jeremiah 31:31-34).

This last reference leads us into the New Testament as well where the new covenant is made through Jesus Christ and in some sense takes the place of the old one. The book of Hebrews could perhaps be seen as an extended reflection on this theme, in particular focusing on the superiority of Christ and the new covenant.

This immediately raises a key issue. The Old Testament is important, and is part of the Bible. But we have to remember that, as Christians, our perspective on it is determined by the way in which we see it through the eyes of the New Testament. Taking Old Testament teachings out of context can lead to misunderstandings. The most obvious example of this is 'prosperity theology', the idea that God guarantees financial prosperity to the faithful. We have to remember that *it is the life, death and resurrection of Jesus which gives us our framework for understanding the Bible.*

 Try to write a one sentence definition in your own words of what a covenant is.

1D The Biblical Canon

The word **canon** comes from an ancient word for 'reed', and since reeds were used to measure things, the word meant, among other things, an authoritative list or way of identifying important things. Thus the **biblical canon** is the collection of the 66 biblical books, 39 in the Old Testament, and 27 in the New Testament.

There are many issues concerning how the biblical books came to make up the canon which we do not have space to go into, although your other reference books will help you here if you are interested. It is clear that some books were disputed for a time: 2 Peter and Jude are examples of books which were debated by the early church: were they biblical or not? The final decision, in both testaments, was more of an attempt to say formally what was already believed by God's people (Israel, or the church) about which books were inspired, rather than a council decision which created any new understanding of the Bible.

Some parts of the Christian church adopt extra books (see the section later on the apocrypha) but in general few major issues are affected by this decision.

The Old Testament Canon

The first thing to note about the Old Testament is that it was not primarily a Christian book. Rather it was (and is) the authoritative collection of Jewish scriptures. As Christians we therefore have much to learn from how the Jews viewed their canon. They arranged it as 24 books in certain clear categories as follows:

The Law	The Prophets	The Writings
Genesis	**The Former Prophets**	**Poetical Books**
Exodus	Joshua	Psalms
Leviticus	Judges	Proverbs
Numbers	Samuel	Job
Deuteronomy	Kings	**'The Five Scrolls'**
	The Latter Prophets	Song of Songs
	Isaiah	Ruth
	Jeremiah	Lamentations
	Ezekiel	Ecclesiastes
	The Twelve	Esther
		Historical Books
		Daniel
		Ezra-Nehemiah
		Chronicles

The arrangement of the Protestant Old Testament canon, which is probably the order followed in your own Bible, dates from the 3rd century BC, from the earliest translation of the Hebrew Bible, called the **Septuagint**. The Septuagint is a Greek translation, made for Greek-speaking Jews. It arranges its 39 books as follows:

Law	History	Wisdom	Prophets
Genesis	Joshua	Job	Isaiah
Exodus	Judges	Psalms	Jeremiah
Leviticus	Ruth	Proverbs	Lamentations
Numbers	I Samuel	Ecclesiastes	Ezekiel
Deuteronomy	II Samuel	Song of Songs	Daniel
	I Kings		Hosea
	II Kings		Joel
	I Chronicles		Amos
	II Chronicles		Obadiah
	Ezra		Jonah
	Nehemiah		Micah
	Esther		Nahum

Law	History	Wisdom	Prophets
			Habakkuk
			Zephaniah
			Haggai
			Zechariah
			Malachi

Note: The 17 prophetic books are often divided into the **Major Prophets**, Isaiah-Daniel; and the **Minor Prophets**, Hosea-Malachi, which is equivalent to the Jewish book of 'The Twelve'.

 Study these two lists and note the major differences between them. In particular: how are the 24 books of the Hebrew canon related to the 39 of our Old Testament? For example, the books that make up the 'former prophets' are usually thought of as 'history' today: do we miss something by not thinking of them as 'prophets'? Is there a similar lesson (in reverse) concerning the book of Daniel?

 When Jesus confronts the Pharisees in Matthew 23 and denounces them as standing in a long line of wrongdoers, he predicts that upon them will come all 'the righteous blood that has been shed on earth, from the blood of righteous Abel to the blood of Zechariah son of Berekiah' (Matthew 23:35). The references are to Genesis 4 and to 2 Chronicles 24:17-22. Look these up. In the light of our discussion of canon, what is the significance of Jesus' remark?

The New Testament Canon

The order of books has never been quite so significant in the New Testament. Paul's letters, for instance, were simply arranged in order from the longest to the shortest, which is not a particularly helpful order. More pressing questions in the New Testament are why we have four gospels, instead of one, and why some other books (e.g. *The Gospel of Thomas*) are not included.

The first of these questions we may consider more fully in a later section. For a general discussion relating to this and many other relevant issues you could consult:

J. Harold Greenlee, *Scribes, Scrolls, & Scriptures* (Grand Rapids: Eerdmans, 1985 and Carlisle: Paternoster, 1996); or:

F.F. Bruce, *The New Testament Documents: Are They Reliable?* (Leicester: IVP, 5th edition, 1960).

2 The Old Testament (1)

This part of our unit, a survey of the Old Testament, can do no more than provide you with some basic things to look out for as you use Bible tools, and read the Old Testament yourself.

2A The Pentateuch

To understand a book it is often helpful to begin at the end, even if this might spoil the plot as you read through it! Although the **Pentateuch** (literally '5-volumed book', from the Greek) does not present itself as one book, it has always been regarded as a unit. Indeed the Jews accord a special place to it in their idea of God's revelation: this is the **Torah**, God's law which was revealed to Moses. This is in spite of the fact that much more than law is contained in it.

 How does the Pentateuch end? Read Deuteronomy 34. What is the major event which happens?

We cannot understand the Pentateuch without understanding the significant role which Moses plays in Israel's history. The 'law of Moses' is the standard against which Israel is judged. Moses is in fact portrayed as a prophet:

Read Deuteronomy 18:14-22. Note that verse 15, from a New Testament perspective, may be seen as a prophecy of Christ.

There is very little evidence about when the Pentateuch was written down, although there is no shortage of theories. The Bible itself does not seem concerned about this issue. What *is* it concerned about in these five books?

The great **theological themes** of Genesis (and to some extent the whole Pentateuch) are in many ways the great themes of the Bible:

- Creation   Genesis 1-2
- Fall   Genesis 3
- Sinfulness   Genesis 4-11, but not stopping there!

- Covenant   Genesis 12, 15, 17
- God's Grace   Genesis 12-50: God at work in the lives of undeserving individuals (often called the 'Patriarchs'– the 'father figures' of Israel)
- The Law   Exodus 19-23 and much of the rest of the Pentateuch

These themes could perhaps be summarised as Creation-Fall-Redemption. This is sometimes called **salvation history**, i.e. history viewed from the perspective of how humanity was relating (or not relating) to God. Although this is a useful way of looking at things, it is important to note that it is not the only concern of the Pentateuch. There is also a focus on how individuals struggled in difficult circumstances (Joseph, Moses) or on the joyful experiencing of God's miraculous intervention (the song of rejoicing in Exodus 15 for example: celebrating the crossing of the sea).

 Genesis tells its story through the lives of particular individuals. Draw out a 'family tree' from Abraham onwards showing who was related to who in the book of Genesis. You need only include major figures.

 A phrase which Genesis uses to divide up its story is 'these are the generations of...'. List the uses of this phrase and see if they help you build up a plan of the book. (See Genesis 2:4, 5:1, 6:9, 10:1, 11:10, 11:27. 25:12, 25:19, 36:1, 36:9, 37:2)

 There are many miracles in the account of Israel's exodus from Egypt to Sinai (Exodus 1-18). Make a list of them and analyse their effect upon the Israelites (and where appropriate the Egyptians). How would you account for the persistent grumbling (literally 'murmuring') of the Israelites towards the end of this journey? (see Exodus 15:22-16:12; the word occurs in 15:24, 16:2, 7, 8, 9, 12)

We have seen that **law** was not the only focus of the Pentateuch, and that in fact it presents itself as a story rather than a set of laws. The main **historical event** of the books is undoubtedly the **Exodus**. Two main dates are possible for this:

- 15th Century BC, in fact around 1440, based on reading 1 Kings 6:1 literally
- 13th Century BC, (1290-1250) based on archaeology and other considerations

The weight of evidence suggests the later date, with implications for other biblical dates (such as that the reigns of the judges in the book of Judges overlapped, which seems likely), and it is not really a problem to see the figure in 1 Kings 6:1 (480 years) as being a way of speaking of, for instance, 12 generations (at 40 years per generation) rather than an exact calculation of a number of years.

However, the date is not ultimately important. What matters is the significance of the event. The Exodus forms part of Israel's identity: many Psalms speak of how God saved his people out of slavery and brought them into their own land.

 Here is a question which people are still debating vigorously today: does the Exodus show that God is a God of liberation: always wanting to release people from slavery and imprisonment?

If the book of Exodus demonstrates very clearly that faith and politics cannot be kept separate, it also raises many questions concerning how precisely they may be related. History has seen strong claims made for the role of Christianity in both attacking and maintaining slavery; or calls to oppose Communism in the name of Jesus, or equally calls to oppose Capitalism in the name of Jesus. You will have to make up your own mind on these issues. The one option the Bible does not leave us is to say that our faith makes no difference to political and social issues.

The Law

We must look briefly at the **law**. It is essential to remember that the law came after the covenant (part of Paul's argument in Galatians, see 3:17) and has to be seen in that framework. God had graciously chosen Israel to be his people: the law indicated Israel's appropriate response to God within the covenant, not as a way of being good enough to please God in the first place.

Here is a good example of where, as Christians, we need to look at the Old Testament through the eyes of the New

Testament. In Matthew 23:23 Jesus says that the purpose of the law is justice, mercy and faithfulness. Romans 7:12-14 says that the law is 'holy and the commandment is holy, righteous and good' and that it shows us our sins and our need for redemption. In Galatians 3:24 Paul uses a word to describe the law which was used to describe the household slave who would take the children to school each day: in other words the law was part of the way in which God prepared the Jews to come to Christ.

The law was like a Jewish badge of identity for God's covenant community. Jesus' life, in a sense, showed the kind of God-pleasing life which the law was always pointing to (this is probably the meaning of 'fulfil' in Matthew 5:17).

 One of the classic 'problem questions' of Christianity is whether the law still applies today. Consider the 10 commandments (Exodus 20; Deuteronomy 5). Nine of these ten are reaffirmed in the New Testament. Does this suggest reasons why we still consider much of the law as morally binding today without needing it as our 'membership badge' as part of God's people?

2B The Histories

The histories are best seen in two distinct groups:

- the pre-exilic histories (sometimes called the 'Deuteronomic history')
- the post-exilic histories

The '**exile**' in question is the deportation of the remaining tribes of Israel under the Babylonian king Nebuchadnezzar in about 586 BC. This key event, known as the fall of Jerusalem since it occurred at the end of a two year siege of the city, is recounted at the end of 2 Kings.

Again, it is in fact useful to note where the books end, and the end of 2 Kings represents the end of one long narrative through the books of Joshua-Judges-Samuel-Kings. These 'former prophets' are often called today the Deuteronomic history, a term which simply refers to the way in which they tell history from very much the point of view of the theology of the book of Deuteronomy. This label does not necessarily imply any particular view of the date and authorship of these books: in fact we know very little about either. Perhaps more usefully it reminds us that all history is at the same time interpretation. Even in the basic choice of what material to include and what to omit the author makes a choice about what is and is not important. These books focus on events which generally show what happened to Israel as it either obeyed or disobeyed God in terms of the covenant which God set out in the book of Deuteronomy (see especially Deuteronomy 28 and 29).

One of the main issues raised in these histories is that of **kingship**.

 Read Deuteronomy 17:14-20. What are the warnings about having a king which Israel is made aware of in this passage? How well did they succeed in avoiding the problems listed here?

In fact, it is not as simple as saying that kingship was either a good or bad thing. While Moses' successor, Joshua, was alive, Israel prospered, and significantly the book of Joshua ends with a description of Joshua leading a covenant-renewal service to dedicate Israel's life in the promised land to God (see Joshua 24). But when the government of Israel passed into the hands of the judges things began to go wrong, and many of the stories in the book of Judges indicate serious moral and ethical problems in Israel. (Note: the Hebrew word *sopetim* often translated 'judges' may be better understood as 'saviours')

 Judges 17-21 forms a kind of epilogue to the book. What phrase is used as a way of passing judgement on events at this time? (see 17:6, 18:1, 19:1, 21:25). What does the writer of Judges 17-21 think of kingship?

A turning point in Israel's history is reached at the point where Samuel, the last judge, and a major prophetic figure, hands over the leadership to the first king, Saul. His public speech recalls many of the themes of Deuteronomy 17.

 Read this speech in 1 Samuel 8. Note that despite his attitude, Samuel does go on to bless Saul and anoint him (see chapters 9 and 10). And furthermore, despite the divine warnings about kingship, God himself chooses both Saul and his successor: David (1 Samuel 16:1).

It is David who secures Jerusalem as Israel's capital (2 Samuel 5), and then God makes a new covenant with him in 2 Samuel 7.

Although the word 'covenant' is not used itself, the idea is the same one of God's gracious commitment to humanity. This time there is no condition to be fulfilled: God makes an unconditional promise.

 An important verse here is 2 Samuel 7:16. What is the promise?

With Jerusalem established and this new covenant being unconditional, there is a sense that Israel has 'arrived' at the place where God intended it to be. This is the background for the building of the temple in Jerusalem in the reign of Solomon; often described as Israel's 'Golden Age.'

The Monarchy

 Why might Israel's attitude towards the monarchy contain both a positive and a negative evaluation?

This question touches on basic issues in understanding biblical history. Some have said that these different attitudes are the result of different writers (or 'sources') for different parts of the story. This of course may be true, although it is difficult to either prove or disprove it. More simply there may be a tension in the biblical account because it reflects the conflicting emotions or views of the people living at the time. Perhaps Israel could see the enormous benefits that had resulted from having David as king, or the early part of Solomon's reign, and yet recognise how easily the warnings about kingship going wrong could come true. On this view there would be no simple answer to the question of whether kingship was a good thing or not. We might say that it had the potential to be a good thing, but was frequently abused.

The event that seemed to set the monarchy on the irreversible road to ruin was the **division of Israel** into two kingdoms. This occurred during the reign of Solomon's son, Rehoboam in about 931-930 BC. The twelve tribes split into the Northern Kingdom, known as Israel, which contained the majority of the tribes, and the two tribes of Judah and Benjamin in the South, known as the kingdom of Judah, centred still at Jerusalem, which continued the Davidic line of kings. The books of Kings tell the stories of both kingdoms and how they went their separate ways to exile.

✍ You might think that the cause of such a catastrophic division would be some major event, but in fact, as with so many historical turning points, the division has its roots in bitter personal disagreement. Read 1 Kings 12 and summarise the reasons given. What do you think this passage tells us of God's way of working in unlikely circumstances?

Reading through the Old Testament, you might be surprised to jump from the exile at the end of 2 Kings back to Adam at the beginning of Chronicles.

Chronicles retells the story of Israel's history, starting in the form of genealogies (family lists) and then continuing right through the exile to the point where Israel is allowed to return (the decree of King Cyrus of Persia). It is significant that Chronicles ends on this positive note. In many ways the book chooses to focus on the positive lessons from Israel's history, with a particular focus on the role of worship and the temple.

The Other Histories

The books of **Ezra** and **Nehemiah** (originally one book) present a series of snapshots of activity surrounding the return to Jerusalem and the rebuilding of the city. These books are unique in the Old Testament because they both contain first-person accounts by the authors (Ezra 7-10 and Nehemiah 1-7, as well as other parts of Nehemiah). The use of eye-witness accounts like this becomes much more prominent in the New Testament. Some stories appear in both Ezra and Nehemiah.

Ruth and **Esther** are two stories which do not particularly fit into these historical sections, except that they are both clearly set in these times. The stories point to God's concern both for individuals (Ruth) and the way in which people are caught up in political struggles which have strong personal and emotional involvement (Esther).

✍ The biblical culture was very male dominated. What lessons could we draw from the way in which these two books focus in detail upon the role and significance of these two women?

3 The Old Testament (2)

3A The Prophets

The Old Testament prophets were primarily people who spoke the word of God to others, usually to the people of Israel, but occasionally to other nations as well.

Sometimes a prophet would be called a 'man of God' or a 'servant of God'. It is good to note that when we talk of a biblical prophet we primarily mean someone who presents God's verdict on a situation. This would sometimes involve predicting an event before it happened (as, for example, if God's word was one of coming judgement due to the people's sins), but in general 'prophecy' does not mean 'predicting'. We should also remember that, as we noted in our section on the Pentateuch, Moses is considered as the great Israelite prophet (Deuteronomy 18:14-22).

 We find many passages focusing on how God called the prophets to their ministry, notably Isaiah 6:1-14, Jeremiah 1:4-19 and Amos 7:10-15. Would you say in any of these cases that the person *wanted* to be a prophet? Why did they become prophets? (In this connection you could look at Exodus 3 and 4 also).

The chief characteristic of most of the prophets was the complete conviction that they spoke the word of God. If it was difficult to do this, as frequent opposition demonstrated, and the temptation was there to run away (e.g. Jonah), it was even more difficult to hold back from proclaiming God's message. A good passage to consult for this is Jeremiah 20:8-9. Jeremiah himself had a hard time understanding this, as is shown by the way that verse 13 is followed by verse 14!

Prophets and Prophetic Writings

Prophecy developed from the model of Moses (and even Abraham, Genesis 20:7) and we find periods both where the prophets were concerned with personal morality (as with the judges and Samuel) and with wider moral issues in society (Elisha, Elijah). Schools of prophets were a common feature of the monarchy.

It is important to distinguish between the prophecies given and

---

the written messages which have become the books of the Bible. The earlier prophets often did not write down their messages, e.g. Elisha and Elijah, whose prophecies are recorded in 1 and 2 Kings. Jeremiah, on the other hand, appears to have written them down himself sometimes, but also used a secretary, Baruch, at other times (Jeremiah 29:1 and chapter 36).

The Bible places emphasis on the *source* of the prophetic writings (they all came from God), but very little is said about the *way* in which this message came to the prophet. Sometimes God gave the message to the prophet by means of a dream or vision. Sometimes the prophet was actively aware of God's communication: 'the word of the Lord came to me'.

If we think of the *oracle* or *prophetic saying* as the basic prophetic message then it helps to explain why the long books of **Isaiah**, **Jeremiah** and **Ezekiel** are so difficult to follow as whole books. In each case they contain many disconnected passages, probably collected together at a later date than the original prophecies. Most of the prophets speak into pre-exilic situations, although Ezekiel in particular addresses the problems of being in exile. The threat of exile loomed over Israel, and we find the

following themes occurring many times in these books:

1. A call to faithfulness for Israel
2. A focus on certain sins, particularly idolatry, which was seen as the root of many other sins
3. A warning of punishment for these sins and a call for repentance
4. A promise that if they repented, Israel would be restored to their land.

The last three books of our Old Testament (Haggai, Zechariah and Malachi) date from the post-exilic period, and are concerned with issues surrounding the rebuilding of the temple (especially **Haggai**) or Israel's future hope. It is not difficult to see why, for instance, **Zechariah** collects together visions of the future: for so long Israel's hope had been centred on returning to the land from exile, yet when they came back and rebuilt the temple there was a realisation that it was nothing like the previous temple (see Haggai 2:1-9). Thoughts turned now to what God might have in store for Israel at the day of the Lord, the expected day when God would intervene in history and prove once and for all that Israel's true worship of their own God had been correct. This, for instance, is the theme of Zechariah 14, and can also be found in the closing chapters of Isaiah.

Apocalyptic Literature

Zechariah 9-14 also hints at a new kind of writing which was developing at this time, and which is probably best thought of *not* as prophecy but as **apocalyptic**. In its full-fledged form, this writing was common between the Old and New Testaments (and forms some of the background to the bizarre stories mentioned in the book of Jude, which quotes from several apocalyptic books). However we find it taking shape in Daniel 7–12, which describes a series of visions about national and international events from God's perspective.

The main idea of apocalyptic is that despite the terrible times being lived through, God really is in control. It is not particularly concerned with providing timetables for what God will do, despite the best efforts of several interpreters to see here detailed predictions of modern events. Rather it is a message which promotes hope and perseverance.

3B Poetry and Wisdom Literature

The remaining five books in our Old Testament are a collection of assorted material, all drawn from the 'writings' section of the Hebrew Bible. We look first at the **Psalms**, Israel's inspired songbook. Here, where deep emotion and thinking are combined, we find perhaps the most revealing theology of the whole Old Testament: here we find David and others grappling with what they *know* of God and with how it relates to what they have experienced. Sometimes the two are in wonderful harmony (Psalm 103) and sometimes they are in conflict (Psalm 22, where the psalmist is finally able to declare God's praises despite his suffering; or more remarkably Psalm 88, where he is unable to do so).

 How would you account for finding Psalm 88 in the Bible? What would be an appropriate 'use' for it?

It is the context of Psalm 88 in the whole Bible which is important. The believer will generally understand God's message to be one of hope in times of distress, but this does not mean that they will not at times *feel* an overwhelming sense of distress. It would be a mistake to say that a Christian is never allowed to express themselves in this way. Perhaps there is an important counselling lesson here: it is tempting to try and get people to suppress these kinds of feelings as somehow not being glorifying to God. Many cultures struggle with letting people express their suffering. Having said this, it is fair to note also that there would be evidence of some real problems if Psalm 88 were always the passage that you related best to. And even here, verse 1 contains an affirmation of the character of God: the God who saves.

The books of Proverbs and Ecclesiastes are unusual in the way that they present wisdom without much reference to the great history of God's involvement with Israel. **Proverbs** clearly has some kind of background in the sayings of the royal court (note its link with Solomon, which may mean that Solomon wrote it or that a group of 'wise men' linked with his royal establishment were responsible for it). We should perhaps think of the proverbs as reflections on aspects of Israelite life which take for granted certain key truths about covenant and grace. Otherwise it is easy to quote Proverbs out of context.

Ecclesiastes

Likewise with **Ecclesiastes**, we are reminded of the need to set a book in its biblical context. The situation is complicated here because the last six verses of the book seem to present the philosophy: 'Life makes no sense so let's just get on with it and do the best we can'. This philosophy, of course, is familiar in the twentieth century in many modern forms of secularism in the West. However, although this may at times be a practical step to take, it does not reflect the view of those parts of the Bible which argue for a meaning for life based on God's creation of humanity, for instance, and shown in the death and resurrection of Jesus. Perhaps we should instead see Ecclesiastes as an example of what happens when we forget the framework of creation, covenant and grace.

But it is important to remember that this is an *interpretation* of Ecclesiastes, and certainly not the only interpretation which Christians have held. Many, for instance, have quoted Ecclesiastes 4:9-12 at weddings: and not to say that a wedding is meaningless!

 What do you think? What would you say to someone who said 'I've been reading Ecclesiastes and it expresses my own view that life is meaningless'?

This is a very personal question, designed to make you think. We will probably never know the full story about a book like Ecclesiastes, so perhaps that should remind us of the need for *humility* in our interpretations. You should be careful about responding to this kind of remark by just quoting a verse, such as Ecclesiastes 12:1, which might seem to support a more optimistic view. If you look at 12:1-8 it would be difficult to defend the argument that here we have a confident return to a more positive attitude towards serving God. Remember that the biblical picture is not really in favour of a 'it doesn't make any sense but I'll do it anyway' faith as a basic understanding of why we 'remember our Creator'. You would probably do best to respond to this remark by showing the person some other parts of the Bible.

The book of **Job** is one long poem with a prologue and an epilogue
which set the scene. The book comes with no obvious historical
setting, and again does not mention things like covenant or any of the
great historical figures of Israel who were often so important in Israelite
understanding. Even among the earliest Jewish scholars there is no
agreement about where the book came from. So again we do best to
look at its message instead. It is often said that the book deals with the
question of suffering, but perhaps more accurately we should say that
it shows how awful suffering is and offers no simple solution or
explanation.

The **Song of Songs** is a poem which celebrates sex and sexuality,
reminding us that the biblical attitude to sex within a loving and
committed relationship is both positive and joyful. This can be a useful
corrective to some negative attitudes which have sometimes become
quite established within Christianity.

4 The New Testament (1)

4A Between the Testaments

In our survey of the Old
Testament we have frequently
looked at major themes and
spoken of the need to view them
from the perspective of the New
Testament. This is already a helpful
first step towards bridging the gap
between the Testaments. We
should note two other points.

(1) As Jewish tradition
developed and different schools of
thought grew up, the Jews began
to expect a definite answer to the
Old Testament prophecies about a
'**Messiah**' figure. In fact, there was
more than one way in which this
was expected: we should see a
variety of messianic hopes. Perhaps
a good illustration of this is the way
today in which almost every
Christian believes in the Second
Coming of Christ, but there is

wide disagreement about how this
will happen. It was similar with the
Jewish Messianic hope. Different
groups like Pharisees, Sadducees
and Zealots would have had
different hopes.

But the important thing was that a
Messiah was expected. Similar
developments can also throw
helpful light on other New
Testament ideas, such as the
development of the idea of the
Spirit of Prophecy between the
Testaments. This shows how the
gift of prophecy speaking through
the illumination of the Holy Spirit,
was not an idea which appeared
out of nowhere, but has its roots in
Jewish thinking which is based on
the Old Testament

(2) It is also helpful to remember
that in about the third century
B.C. a Greek translation of the Old

Testament was made (the **Septuagint**) and that this may often have been the source of New Testament quotations of the Old Testament, which sometimes explains why the quotes we have in the New Testament do not always match up to the text of the Old Testament as we have it. In fact, it was a common practice to put together selections of quotations for the purpose of public readings or teaching, and this may explain why in many places in the New Testament we have long strings of quotes together, almost as a text for a sermon (the book of Hebrews has many examples of this, as does Romans 3, or Romans 9-11).

You could also consult some of the suggested reference books about basic background to the New Testament concerning events in the period between the end of the Old Testament and the coming of John the Baptist. (For instance, the *New Bible Commentary* (by D.A. Carson *et al* *(eds.),* see details in the Appendix) has an excellent short survey of this period on pp.890-95.)

More daring readers can read some of the original documents in the **Apocrypha**, a collection of Jewish books not accepted into the Protestant canon, which deals with events and ideas around this time. (It is printed in some Bibles.) The apocryphal book of **1 Maccabees** contains some reliable historical information. Many of the other apocryphal books mix history and fiction in a more imaginative way!

As with the Old Testament it is helpful to start by breaking down the New Testament into different types of writing. Here the division is much more straightforward: all the books fall naturally into certain categories, even if with Acts and Revelation they are the only books in their categories. But first, a preliminary question:

Which New Testament book was written first?

Don't worry if you didn't know. In fact we cannot be sure of the answer, although it is probably one of Mark, Galatians or 1 Thessalonians. Even then there is always some fashionable new theory asserting that such and such a book was the earliest. The point is this: we often assume that the gospels tell the beginning of the story, and then Acts and the letters build on them. But in all likelihood most of the letters were written without having access to the written gospels as we have them, and certainly some of the letters were written before all four gospels were complete. This may help to explain why some of the prominent features of the gospels, e.g. the parables, are never mentioned in the letters - had you ever wondered why Paul, for instance, never settles an argument by saying 'As Jesus put it in the parable of . . . '. All the New Testament writing is a product both of observing events, but equally of thought and reflection about those events. This observation should be enough to equip us for an overview of the various New Testament writings

4B The Gospels

We tend to draw our picture of Jesus from the four gospels taken together. This is no bad thing. However, it is worth noting that each gospel provides a slightly different view of him. **Mark**'s Jesus is a man of action; a man of the people. **Luke**'s Jesus is concerned about the poor and the outcast, the people marginalised in first century Palestine, including women. **Matthew**'s Jesus fulfils the law: he is the ultimate figure of Jewish righteousness. The Scribes and the Pharisees come in for a particularly hard time in Matthew (see e.g. chapter 23). John's gospel is different again.

These first three are usually called '**synoptic**' gospels. This means, literally, 'seen together': they all present accounts of Jesus' ministry, and there are many passages where they overlap significantly. We do not know who copied who, or how much they relied on each other, but these three gospels are clearly interdependent.

John's gospel starts, in contrast, with an abstract prologue about eternal truth and light, and focuses a lot on a few major miracles, with quite long comments about their significance. There is comparatively little narrative (simply telling the story of what Jesus did). Even the section on his last week on earth is very different, beginning with five chapters called his 'farewell discourse' (chs 13-17), which we do not have in any other gospel. (A *discourse*, in this sense, is a passage which reports spoken words.)

We might want to say that John is more concerned to provide an *interpretation* of certain key events, but this is to overlook the fact that all the gospel writers interpret Jesus' ministry. The choice of what to include is a choice of interpretation. They all include the feeding of the 5000, but no other miracle apart from the resurrection occurs in all four gospels. Why not? What was it, for instance, that prompted Mark and Matthew to include a second miraculous feeding story, of the 4000 (Mark 8:1-10 and Matthew 15:29-39) but persuaded Luke and John to leave it out?

What is a Gospel?

In fact, we may have assumed too much already in our discussion. In particular we may have assumed that we knew what a **gospel** is.

 What kind of a writing is a gospel? What does the word mean?

A gospel is obviously a bit like a biography. But it is not the same thing. In a biography we expect to find more of a general account of what the person did. Almost all the gospels are devoted to Jesus' short public ministry, and only two of them mention his birth, with only one story about his childhood or early adult years (Luke 2:41–52). There is not much focus on Jesus' position in wider Israelite religion: in fact you might assume from reading the gospels that he was widely regarded as the central figure in Judaism at the time, but this is unlikely. John the Baptist was a much more prominent figure.

To answer our question we need to look at the word *gospel*. It is a translation of the Greek *evangelion*, which means literally 'good news'. When Mark uses the word in Mark 1:1 it has the sense of 'an account of the good news'. It is described by Paul as *being* the power of God (Romans 1:16), and so it is clearly active: good news with a purpose, perhaps. Thus, although the use of the word 'gospel' to describe the books of the New Testament is not itself a biblical term, we are probably justified in seeing the description this way: a gospel is an account of the message of Jesus, God's message, as lived out by Jesus, with the purpose of encouraging faith (see, for example, John 20:31).

The gospels, then, are designed to provoke a response in us. They are not just 'a good read', or an object of study, but they reveal God to us, and so make a difference in our lives.

It is interesting to note that we do not find anywhere in the gospels a 'gospel presentation' (such as 'four things to know about God, or life . . .' etc.). Jesus spoke in language that made sense to his listeners. For instance, he uses a lot of farming imagery (e.g. the parable of the seed and the sower, in Mark 4:1–20).

 Can you think of examples of language that makes sense to you and your listeners more than farming imagery might do? For example, how would you explain this parable to someone who has never experienced seed sowing? Is there a principle which can be expressed in different ways?

This leads to another question. Was Jesus' message just for his culture? Can we actually say that there is *a gospel message* which is the same in all cultures?

These are questions of interpretation, which we cannot answer fully yet. Keep them in mind for later units, such as those on mission and evangelism. We should probably say that *sinfulness* is the same in all cultures, even though the particular sins which are problems may vary. The gospel is about how God deals with sin, through Jesus' death and resurrection. At its heart the gospel challenges all cultures at this point. We pick up these issues later. The idea of re-expressing Jesus' words in ways more appropriate to today's situations is known as **'recontextualisation'**.

Consider the following example, based on the passage in Mark 4:

A man moved into a new house and decided to hang some pictures. He got out his hammer and nails and went up to the wall. The first nail he banged in didn't go well: it started to bend as he hammered and soon fell out of the wall and landed on the carpet. Finding a new spot he banged in a second nail. This one went in, and he quickly hung up the picture, but as he stood back to admire it, it came crashing down and landed, broken, at his feet. Determined to keep going, he tried again.

He tested out several places which he thought might be good, and finally tapped a third nail in cautiously. But after trying a few different pictures on it, and being concerned each time that it wouldn't take the weight, he just left it there in the wall and put nothing on it. Finally he banged in a fourth nail, which went in with no problems, and he hung a picture on it just where he wanted it, and over the years several of his favourite pictures hung from that spot. He who has a hammer, let him use it.

 What are the advantages and disadvantages of this kind of exercise? How would *you* retell the story?

Further Exercises

 Make a chart of major events in the gospels, to familiarise yourself with their contents. Include events such as baptism, particular areas visited, particular collections of teaching (especially in Matthew), miracles (especially in John), entry into Jerusalem, teaching in Jesus' final week, death, resurrection and ascension. Some of these events will not occur in every gospel.

Consult reference books to help you in this.

 In what particular ways does the picture of Jesus in John's gospel provide new or different perspectives on Jesus? Do you find this helpful?

John's gospel is much more focused on teaching, and is less 'Jewish' than the others. Jesus speaks in more general terms, using images such as light and darkness, or truth and life. John also takes time to explain the significance of the miracles at length. This may be more easily understood by some cultures than Jesus' more specific illustrations and parables in the other gospels. Alternatively, you may find it unhelpful because John's gospel may appear abstract and philosophical in comparison with the accounts of Jesus' personal ministry elsewhere. These are the kinds of issues you would need to consider in making a decision about which gospel to read with someone who wanted to start finding out about Jesus.

4C Acts

Acts is 'Luke's Gospel – Part Two'. Written by Luke, it picks up the story of Jesus where the gospel of Luke left off, at the ascension, and tells of how the group of disciples left behind went on to become a world-wide church. 'World-wide' in this context needs explaining.

The centre of the world in the first century, in economic and political terms, was Rome. Nothing could be more significant for Christianity than that it should shed its image of being a regional Jewish faith located in Palestine and establish a stronghold in the main city of the world. And so in Acts, Luke shows first how Peter and the others spread the gospel around Jerusalem and the surrounding areas. And then the focus shifts to the apostle Paul and his great 'missionary journeys' as the gospel spreads ever wider until, in the last chapter, Paul comes to Rome.

Clearly the book of Acts has a special relevance for those involved in missionary work and evangelism, and we will be coming back to it in later units with these topics in mind.

 Does the first verse of Acts suggest how Luke saw the relationship between what is included in Acts and the ministry of Jesus as recorded in his earlier gospel?

The key phrase is 'all that Jesus began to do and teach', implying that what follows is a direct continuation of *Jesus'* ministry, even though carried out by others. Just as we have stressed the importance of viewing the Old Testament from the perspective of the New, so here we find a reminder that in Acts we must keep in mind the focus on Jesus, and how his life, death and resurrection is the central point of our understanding of any other part of the Bible. Some have suggested that although the book is called 'The Acts of the Apostles' it could just as easily be called 'The Acts of the Holy Spirit'. What do you think of this suggestion?

Acts ends at a rather unexpected point: Paul is awaiting trial in Rome, but we do not learn of the result of the trial. Probably Acts ends where it does because that is when Luke wrote it: he had brought the story up to date. This is a further reminder that we have here a first-hand record of events from someone who, in this case, was involved in them himself from time to time (see the 'we' passages where Luke includes himself in the story, e.g. the sudden change in 16:5-10).

 The main figure in Acts 1-12 is Peter. Make a chart of the major events in his story. Paul takes over in Acts 13-28, having been introduced in 8:1 as Saul. With the aid of a map follow his journeys around the ancient world. Which chapters relate to which journeys?

Use a reference book to help you with this. Many Bibles print maps of Paul's journeys at the back.

5 The New Testament (2)

5A The Letters

A lot of the theology of the New Testament is developed in the letters which form the majority of the books. Many are written by Paul, often to whole churches and almost always dealing with some pressing problem of the time. (Ephesians and Philippians are possible exceptions to this: they do not seem so concerned to attack any particular error.) This is important because we tend to imagine that they were written somehow for us today and address our own needs and concerns. It is usually necessary, however, to go back to the original contexts and work out why Paul (or whoever) was writing in the first place. This raises questions of interpretation which we shall consider in the next unit. For now it is worth noting that most of the New Testament offers its insights and wisdom in this 'engaged' form, i.e. that the writers are generally engaging with a particular issue or viewpoint. This obviously has major implications for our own understanding of it.

It also helps us understand why some of the letters take the form they do. For example, Paul had never been to Rome when he wrote **Romans** (see Romans 1:8-15 and 15:23-33) and so very likely there were a lot of believers in Rome who were wondering who exactly he was, and what his message was. In fact, we might see much of Romans as Paul's explanation of the gospel, which he mentions in 1:16, and which then takes over the letter until he returns to his initial theme in chapter 15. He would have included it here in order to let the Romans know what exactly he preached.

In fact, this is probably a simplification. Most likely he expresses the particular thoughts which he does here in Romans because they led directly to the answers he wanted to give to certain questions, such as 'stronger' and 'weaker' brothers, or the relationship between Jews and Gentiles, in chapters 9-11. These questions were probably the ones being asked in Rome, and Paul knew that to answer them properly would take some serious thinking about God and his people. Most of us read Romans as if it were timeless, and to some extent this is true, but it helps to explain the

overall shape of the book to see why Paul chose this particular moment to give us these particular thoughts on the gospel.

On the other hand, in a letter like **1 Corinthians** we find a lot of issues being taken up by Paul arising from his earlier communication with them (notice the opening verses of chapters 7, 8, 12, 13 and 15, as well as other verses, which all suggest that he is responding to something). Here we need to be very careful before saying that what Paul said to the Corinthians is directly applicable to us.

Other letters are not particularly like letters at all. The book of **Hebrews** is possibly best thought of as a sermon, with its series of warnings against falling away; **James** reads a lot like a series of 'notes from the pastor's desk'- perhaps from actual sermons that James had preached in Jerusalem, and this might explain why it is quite hard to follow the letter through in one go. **1 John** lacks many of the standard characteristics of a letter: perhaps it is more of an official warning document against heresy. None of these suggestions are more than guesses, but they remind us that we need to look at each book carefully and see what kind of writing to expect.

Pick a letter we have not discussed and go through it looking for clues about who wrote it, who they wrote it to, what kind of situation you think they might have been confronting, what kind of relationship they already had with the recipients, etc. Some of these will be easy questions to answer, and some more difficult. Check your answers with a reference book. Which features of the background to the letter may or may not make it relevant to your situation?

The question which all this raises, of course, is how we may arrive at an overall understanding of the New Testament, if it is concerned with so many different, historical issues. But this does not need to be a problem. It simply reminds us that we do not expect to find every New Testament writer explaining his whole 'systematic theology' every time he addresses one particular issue. This doesn't mean that if we could somehow sit them all down together and ask them the same questions they wouldn't all give the same answer. (On the other hand, we know that Paul and Peter didn't exactly see eye to eye on everything. Paul is quite aggressive against Peter in Galatians 2, and Peter's comment about finding Paul's letters difficult to understand in 2 Peter 3:15-16 may perhaps suggest that he wasn't Paul's biggest fan.)

Some passages give particularly clear statements of essential themes in understanding the gospel, and perhaps not surprisingly some of these are old Christian hymns which were incorporated into the letters. As with the Psalms we find that poetry and music bring out deep reflection on the meaning of our relationship with God. The Philippians and Colossians passages below are both hymns:

 Study the following passages and note some of the most important features of the gospel:

1 Corinthians 15 (esp. v.15-19)	What does the resurrection demonstrate?
2 Corinthians 5:16-21	What does God think now of our sin?
Philippians 2:6-11	How is Jesus' life a model for us?
Colossians 1:15-20	How is creation linked with the gospel?

Titus 3:3-9	This passage is perhaps the nearest we have to a 'gospel presentation' in the Bible. Paul wanted Titus to 'stress these things' (v.8).

Write out how you would explain these things to someone who was asking you what the gospel was.

Many other passages could be used. This is an important exercise and one which you should go through regularly. Expect your understanding to grow.

5B Revelation

The last book of the Bible is also one of the least understood. Written in a situation of intense persecution (1:9 is probably a reference to imprisonment for the writer's faith), the book starts with some letters to struggling churches and then goes on to a series of great visions which seem to be saying that, whatever the appearances to the contrary, God really is in control.

Interpreting Revelation

Some of the characteristics of **apocalyptic** were discussed when we looked at Daniel earlier. Here the style reaches its fullest expression in the Bible. The imagery involved in these dramatic visions is perhaps a result of John struggling to put into words what he has seen. Although some of the imagery is indeed fantastic, we should not get too mystical about it all. It is good to remember that 'apocalypse' was simply the Greek word for 'revelation' (Revelation 1:1). In fact, the book of Revelation as a whole is presented not as 'an apocalypse' (which as we noted before was a kind of writing common between the testaments) but as a *letter*. This may save us from some of the more fanciful interpretations of the book: if it was a letter then it must have meant *something* to the people it was written to, which rules out interpretations which see things like helicopters and electronic bar codes all over the book.

The book's great message is one of hope: a hope based on Jesus the risen Lord, in the midst of terrible suffering and persecution which makes it look as though other, evil powers may be in control. The book insists: no, God is in control, and Jesus has shown us how. Here eternal truths are conveyed in pictorial fashion.

It is difficult to separate an introduction to Revelation from an interpretation of Revelation.

✍ Why do you think the book starts with a dramatic and glorious appearance of the risen Jesus to the writer? (1:12-18) What does the book teach us about worship? (1:12-18, 4:6-11 and elsewhere)

In the face of persecution we need more than ever the experience and knowledge of who God is, and his greatness, to cope with the situations we experience. It is no coincidence that this book teaches us much about *worship*: the amazing privilege of having access to a holy and majestic God. It also suggests that our worship is part of the way in which the message of hope is kept alive in times of trouble. There is certainly no hint here of worship reflecting the way we feel — rather it changes the way we feel.

Glossary

This is a list of terms which may be unfamiliar, but are important for this unit, and which you can refer to during your work as a reminder of some key definitions. Most of them are explained in more detail at the appropriate place in the unit.

Apocalyptic   a type of writing which developed towards the end of the Old Testament, and is found most notably in Daniel and Revelation, where symbolic language is used to express great social, political and religious upheaval, and a message of hope is delivered to the faithful.

Canon   the collection of books comprising the Bible

Covenant   a relationship between God and humanity. The idea is difficult to express clearly — see the discussion in section 1B.

Deuteronomic History   the name sometimes given to the books from Joshua to 2 Kings which tell one continuous story of Israel's history, using the perspective of the book of Deuteronomy, and particularly its views on obedience and kingship.

Divided Kingdom   a title referring to the fact that from the time of Solomon's son Rehoboam onwards, the kingdom of Israel was in two parts, called Israel in the North and Judah in the South.

Epistle a letter, such as the ones written by Paul in the New Testament. Sometimes a distinction is made between more or less formal letters, and epistles are considered to be more formal, but this distinction is not recognised by everybody.

Pentateuch the first five books of the Bible, sometimes called the books of Moses

Salvation History this is a translation of the German word *Heilesgeschichte*, and refers to the way that history can be viewed from the perspective of how God relates to humanity, and particularly the progress of God's activity of redemption in human history.

Septuagint the earliest translation of the Old Testament, in Greek, from about the 3rd Century BC.

Testament from the Latin word for 'covenant', used to refer to the two main parts of the Bible

Torah the Hebrew word for 'law', specifically referring to the law of Moses contained in the Pentateuch.

Memory Verses

2 Timothy 3:16
2 Peter 1:20-21

Unit Two
Introduction to Hermeneutics

Outline and Notes

'Hermeneutics' here means 'interpretation'. This unit builds directly on Unit 1, and aims to equip you with tools for interpreting and studying the Bible.

Aims

The Global Action training program goals include the aim that at the end of their Global Action training the student will:

• have developed an attitude of trust in and obedience to God's word

Study Objectives

As well as laying the foundation for the above training goal, this unit will enable you to:

• study a passage in its original context to answer the question 'What did it mean when it was written?'
• demonstrate how such a study can lead on to answering the question 'What does it mean today?'
• show how different types of passage require different types of interpretation
• use Bible study aids and reference books competently

Recommended Reading

See the introductory note in the manual on recommended reading for this unit.

Unit Outline

1 Introduction to Hermeneutics
 1A Introduction
 1B Some Terms and Assumptions
 1C Why Do We Need Interpretation?
 1D What does it mean? and What did it mean?
 1E Genre: Different Types of Writing
 1F How to Study a Passage
   Observation, Interpretation and Application
 1G Sample Passage Study – 1 Corinthians 13

2 How to Study a Passage (1)
   OT Study Exercise

3 How to Study a Passage (2)
 3A Introduction
   Study Aids Available
   NT Study Exercise

4 Character Studies
 4A Introduction
 4B An Example: Lot
 4C Observation
 4D Interpretation
 4E Application
 4F Study Examples

5 Topical and Word Studies
 5A How to do a Topical Bible study
   Features of a Topical Study
   Study Exercise
 5B How to do Word Studies
   Study Exercise

Additional Note on Preparing and Leading Bible studies

Glossary – A list of terms which are important for this unit.

Note: Section 1 of this unit contains more reading than usual, in order to allow you to concentrate on the exercises in later sections.

1 Introduction to Hermeneutics

1A Introduction

Let's begin at the beginning: Genesis chapter 1. Here is a straightforward account of how God made the world in six days. True or false?

Perhaps we could choose a less controversial example, but immediately we see the issues raised clearly. Some would see Genesis 1 as a literal six days and some as a figurative account.

What is less often considered, but is probably more important, is that in all likelihood this chapter was written in the context of people believing in polytheism: many gods. Sun worship, for instance, was very common. It becomes obvious, if you read Genesis 1 against this background, that it has very little time for sun worship: it states very firmly that God made the sun and put it in its place. And likewise the moon, and in fact everything else around. Seen this way the chapter is a very powerful attack on all those belief systems which involve worshipping creation. It is highly unlikely that the author was at all concerned with the length of time the creation took, or when it happened.

Of course, if you were already a monotheist (a believer in one god only) you might not have seen this point as very important.

This debate, along with countless hundreds of others concerning the Bible, centres on questions of **interpretation.** The technical term for this is **hermeneutics**, from the Greek *hermeneuo*, to interpret or explain, as used in Luke 24:27, when Jesus walks to Emmaus with the disciples, and Luke records: 'Beginning with Moses and with all the prophets, he explained (*hermeneuo*) to them the things concerning himself in all the scriptures'.

1B Some Terms and Assumptions

Our main assumption, as we noted in Unit 1, is this: we approach the Bible with **humility**. History is full of confident pronouncements about how the Bible is to be interpreted which have been shown to be wrong, varying from statements about when the world will end, to who wrote which bits of Genesis, to what kind of communist group Jesus belonged to.

On the other hand, we should not get discouraged and give up trying to understand. For many years people puzzled over why Jesus wanted the Laodicean believers to be hot or cold rather

---

than 'lukewarm' (Revelation 3:15-16). What was so good about being cold? All kinds of spiritual sounding interpretations were offered. But archaeological and historical investigation of the area has shown that the point here is to do with Laodicea's water supply. Those first hearing the letter read out would have known of the two nearby towns: Hierapolis with its hot water for healing; and Colossae with its cold refreshing drinking water. In contrast, Laodicea's water was only good for being spat out! In other words, the church in Laodicea was failing either to be refreshing (cold) or healing (hot). Jesus was drawing on the details of the situation which the original readers would have understood. So, sometimes we can make real advances in our understanding of the Bible.

Our second assumption concerns the role of the **Holy Spirit**. The Spirit was involved in the writing of the Bible, as we noted in Unit 1. This is the idea behind the word **inspiration**. We believe that the Bible was written by human beings at particular points in time in various situations, but we also believe that that is not the whole story. God used those situations to bring about the writings that he wanted, or to put it another way, God *inspired* the human writers.

This does not mean that every statement in the Bible reveals God's will: sometimes the point is to notice that what is described is *not* what was wanted. Remember the stories of Judges 17-21? Or the stories of how Abraham lied about his wife (Genesis 12 and 20). If we just assumed that what Abraham did was all right because he was Abraham and it's in the Bible then we would get a very strange picture of events. Rather we should see that what is happening in a situation like this is a description of what someone did wrong, and yet *God used them anyway*. Again, interpretation is the key issue here.

But a second point about the Holy Spirit is equally important: he did not just inspire the original Bible, but he helps readers today to grasp its message. This is sometimes called **illumination**. It is important to see what we are *not* saying here: we do not mean that whatever you think the passage means is OK because that's what the Spirit is saying to you. Rather we are saying that there is a *spiritual* aspect to understanding what God is trying to communicate through the Bible. Just *knowing* a passage is not usually the major issue.

If we combine our two points so far, humility and inspiration, then we arrive at a third point: **authority**. If we are humble before an inspired Bible then God's revelation through the Bible will have authority in our lives. We do not have the option of saying, for example, 'The Bible is clearly teaching us to forgive those who sin against us, but I don't accept that for my life today'. This is not the same as saying that every verse out of context, or every interpretation of a controversial passage, has authority. Abuse of spiritual authority is a real problem in today's Christian world. In contrast we are invited by a gracious God to submit to his authority, by the witness of his Spirit in our hearts.

Finally, **truth**. It is sometimes said that 'the Bible is true'. This is not always a very helpful statement, since it can obscure the fact that much of the Bible is not in the form of statements which are either true or false (e.g. poems, laws, greetings and letters in general, parables . . .). It is better to say that what the Bible **affirms** is true. Then of course we may have differing interpretations about what a passage actually affirms, but at least we are using the word 'true' in a potentially accurate way. However, since all scripture is useful for teaching and correcting (2 Timothy 3:16 again) we can have confidence that the Bible is not designed to mislead us, even if experience suggests that the same cannot be said of all Bible interpretations . . .

1C Why Do We Need Interpretation?

(Some of what has been said on the role of the Spirit in the above section is relevant here.) Paul obviously saw no conflict between the understanding given by the Spirit, and the hard work of studying.

 Look up 1 Corinthians 2:6-16 on the one hand, and 2 Timothy 2:15 on the other hand. As we have noted before, even Peter needed some help! (2 Peter 3:16).

How would Paul answer the question 'Why do we need interpretation?' do you think?

The New Testament itself gives plenty of examples of false teaching. The ability to read and teach the Bible is not enough to save us from error.

 How to Read the Bible for All Its Worth, chapter 1: 'Introduction – The Need to Interpret'.

1D What Does it Mean and What Did it Mean?

A frequent question which people ask of a Bible passage is 'What does it mean?'. But this is often the wrong question to start with. What does it mean to whom? To me? To the original reader?

It is good to get into the habit of distinguishing between these two things. We would not want to build a whole theology on this, but on a practical level it is helpful to distinguish between two different questions:

(1) What *did* the passage mean when it was written and first read or heard?

(2) What *does* the passage mean to me today?

The first of these questions relies on *observing* the passage closely to see what it is actually saying: i.e. what actual words are in it. It also involves *interpreting* the passage so that we feel we could express what the original hearers understood. It is the second of these two questions which is perhaps more interesting, and certainly more important for our day-to-day Christian living, but this second question can only really be answered *after* the first one. It is a matter of *applying* the understanding gained in answering the first question to our present situation. We will return to these three steps below: they are very important in learning how to handle the Bible correctly:

> Observation, Interpretation, Application

Memorise them now. (One way to memorise them is as follows: See it! Know it! Do it!)

1E Genre: Different Types of Writing

Our final introductory topic is **genre**. This word comes into English from the French. It refers to the different types of writing we find in the Bible. Some examples of genre are *story, parable, psalm, letter, gospel, apocalyptic, prophecy* . . . These will hopefully be familiar to you from our survey of the Bible, where, without concentrating on it, we were already learning to distinguish different genres.

Sometimes we have genres within a genre: in the Psalms for instance we find Psalms of praise (e.g. Psalms 146-150), of lament (Psalms 3, 80), or of thanksgiving (Psalms 30, 32). Within a prophecy we find oracles of woe, words of praise, or apocalyptic visions. Within a letter we find praise sections (doxologies), hymns, introductory greetings, and sections where truths just described are applied in new ways (e.g. Romans 12-15; the technical term for this is *paraenesis*).

It is very important to look at *what kind of writing* you are dealing with when you study the Bible. For instance, if we have to make a decision about whether a passage is using pictorial language (or imagery) or is to be taken literally, it will make a difference to our decision whether that passage is part of a historical account (e.g. in the gospel of Luke) or an apocalyptic dream (e.g. the visions of Daniel 7-12). Failure to take seriously the *genre* of a passage has led to some over-literal interpretations and consequently a wrong understanding of God.

Good Bible interpretation may take hard work, but it is the duty of every Christian to be on guard against those who distort the word of God, and in turn to make sure that you handle it correctly.

> 📖 Look up 2 Corinthians 4:2, 2 Peter 3:16 and 2 Timothy 2:15. Do these verses support the above claim?

As evangelicals we believe that it is possible to handle the Bible correctly and hear it speak to our present day situations. We turn now to some basic tools for doing this.

1F How to Study a Passage

Observation, Interpretation and Application

We introduced these terms in the above section on 'What does it mean? and What did it mean?'. Here we will set out some principles to follow in interpreting a passage of scripture which you need to work with and develop until they become your standard way of approaching a passage. In this way, it is the Bible which sets your agenda: you learn how to accept the priorities and emphases of the biblical authors rather than impose your own set of priorities on the Bible. Much as you might like to be able to go to the Bible and get your particular question answered ('Which party should I vote for? What job should I take? Who should I marry? Is democracy Christian? Where should I be a missionary? . . . '), you will probably end up with a distorted view of the biblical teaching on the topic in question unless you first learn to listen patiently to *what the text is saying.*

Learn to *ask questions* as you go through a passage. Learn to think in the way the original authors thought. Accept that they did not come from your culture and may use arguments which you might not have thought of using, or alternatively might fail to use arguments which you wish they would have used ('if only he had explained what kind of baptism was permitted . . . ').

We could note here the advantage of reading the Bible as part of a community (e.g. your church, or a small Bible study group . . .).

Especially in cross-cultural situations you have the chance to see how other people are listening to the biblical text, and in the process to refine and correct your own understanding. *Learning from others' interpretations* is all a part of hermeneutics.

The following model is adapted from Hans Finzel, *Opening the Book* (Wheaton, Ill: Victor Books, 1987) where it is described as **an inductive approach**.

The 3 Steps:
1. **Observation**
2. **Interpretation**
3. **Application**

---

1. Observation

Principle 1: Determine what the original author actually wrote.

A. Establish Historical Context
   1. Where does it fit in biblical history?
   2. What were the prevailing political, social and economic conditions behind the text?
   3. Who wrote the passage? What was their situation?
   4. To whom was it written? What was their situation?

B. Determine Biblical Context
   1. Read through the entire book, if possible.
   2. What comes before and after the text?

   Before   *After*

   Paragraphs
   Chapters
   Books
   3. How does the passage fit into this context? What does it contribute to the whole?
   4. Which literary genre is the passage (or which genres are in the passage)? Adjust your analysis accordingly.

C. Read the Text
   Your goal = an overview, the 'big picture'
   1. Read the text in two different translations, noting differences.
   2. After the second reading, make brief notes on your major impressions, problems, questions, and any related passages that come to mind. Also note the tone or mood of the author.

---

3. Skim through again and record the following:
   a. *Who?* are the major characters involved? Their traits?
   b. *Where?* does it take place?
   c. *When?* does it take place?
   d. *What?* are the topics of concern? Or the events that occur? What repeated/key words, phrases, ideas are used? What is the main subject?
   e. *Why?* is this being discussed? Why did the author write this passage?
4. What literary forms are used in the text and what is their function?

D. Breakdown of the Text

Answer 'what's the point?'
1. Break down the passage into logical thought units or paragraphs
2. Re-read, paragraph by paragraph, asking of each 'what is the point?'
   a. Record briefly the content of each: What is said?
   b. Write out briefly the point of each: Why is it said? Or, stated another way, how does it contribute to the overall argument or story?
3. Re-write these points, making them into titles for each paragraph.
4. Make an outline of the passage, including the paragraph titles, a passage title, and major and minor divisions.

2. Interpretation

Principle 2: Seek the meaning of the text in its original setting. The correct interpretation must be something the original author could have intended and the original recipients could have understood.

A. Summarise Observations
   1. What is the subject/need/problem that the text addresses?
      a. How is this addressed or solved?
   2. What does this passage mean? What's the main point?
      a. What are the subpoints that contribute to this overall meaning?

B. Determine Spiritual Principles

> 1. What are the moral and spiritual principle(s) which serve as the basis for the above-stated message and solution?
>> a. How would the original readers have understood this?
> 2. What does the text tell us about God?
> 3. What does the text tell us about human beings?
> 4. What does the text tell us about God's relationship with humanity?

3. Application

Principle 3: Apply the basic moral, spiritual and theological principles operative in the passage to the contemporary world. The practical applications and theological implications of a passage must be something the original author could have intended and the original readers understood if they were transported into the contemporary situation.

A. Past

> 1. How did the above stated principles apply then?
>> a. To whom?

B. Present

> 1. How do the above stated principles apply now?
>> a. To whom?
> 2. Is there anything in the text that doesn't apply now?
>> a. Why?
> 3. How do your findings compare with other Scripture passages?

C. Personal

> 1. To what areas of my life does each principle apply?
> 2. How can I act on this now? (write out one or two specific actions)
> 3. Relate these principles to your life with: (as applicable) God, the Church, yourself, others, Satan . . .

(Note: depending on the passage, some of these questions will be more relevant than others. Some questions will not apply to some passages.)

1G Sample Passage Study - 1 Corinthians 13

The main purpose of this study is only secondarily to analyse 1 Corinthians 13. It is primarily to look at *how we study* 1 Corinthians 13. This should help you as you do your own passage studies. We choose this chapter because it is very familiar, and yet we can learn a lot from approaching it with clear hermeneutical guidelines. How often have you heard this chapter read or quoted without any reference to its context? We will analyse it in some detail, because it is intended as a model for you to follow when you study other passages.

1 Observation

The Historical Context:
The letter to the Corinthians is part of Paul's on-going relationship with that church, and judging by the letter it is not an entirely peaceful relationship. Corinth was a lively and multi-cultural port town, which would have had a lot of people passing through, and an active religious life. It was buzzing with energy and enthusiasm. Much of what Paul writes to Corinth is concerned to correct excesses which have developed out of that enthusiasm.

The letter was probably written around AD55, as Paul was on his third missionary journey. It was written before he had visited them on that journey, and draws on his relationship with them which he established on his second missionary journey (see Acts 18).

How would you know all this? This kind of information is readily available in study Bibles, commentaries, introductions, etc. It is worth looking up this kind of thing before your detailed study of the passage (which you have *not* yet looked up anything about!).

The Biblical Context
1 Corinthians begins with Paul writing about divisions and disorder within the church (chapters 1-6), and then taking up several points which have clearly already been raised in a previous letter from the Corinthians to Paul (look for the clues for this in 7:1; 8:1; 11:2, 12:1 and 15:1). In fact these verses are significant for our study, suggesting that the section from 12:1 to 14:40 forms a unit. This is a very important point, and comes not from detailed study but from taking the broader overview.

Pursuing this insight, we note that chapter 12 (immediately before our passage) concerns spiritual gifts, and so does chapter 14 (following our passage). What does this suggest is the biblical context for 1 Corinthians 13? It suggests that Paul is discussing love in the context of spiritual gifts. This is further suggested by the last half verse of chapter 12 (which should really be taken with chapter 13, as many Bible translations show by the way they divide the paragraphs).

The more immediate biblical context can be understood from

seeing that 12:12-31 discuss the spiritual gifts as they relate to the church being a body. We are therefore prepared for our passage to focus on how we relate to the variety of gifts we find in the church, perhaps concerning our attitude to those with different gifts. We are on the right track!

We should note, more specifically, that chapter 14 picks up in particular the gifts of prophecy and tongues. These are in our chapter too: why? Perhaps the contrast or comparison between love and these gifts is going to be particularly important. We can see here that reading this passage in context, treating it as part of a *letter*, helps us to see why Paul says what he says.

Reading the Text

We are *now* ready to read the passage! Yes, we have made some preliminary observations already, but only now do we get into the details of the passage. Hopefully we will be better equipped to see what we are looking for now that we have the context in view.

In this particular passage there are not too many major discrepancies between translations, and even where there are variations (e.g. should verse 3 be 'surrendering my body to the flames' or 'that I may boast'?) they reflect problems with understanding the Greek text which do not significantly affect our analysis. (Note: this is true on a reassuring number of occasions: a great deal of debate about correct translations is concerned with

details like this and is not of life-changing importance).

What are our major impressions?

The first seven verses are clearly about the greatness and wonderfulness of love, but at first sight it is not so clear why Paul starts talking about child/adult and perfect/imperfect contrasts. In particular, what is the 'perfection' (or 'perfect') which is coming (v.10)? And when will that be? What does 'remain' in v.13 mean? and does the 'now' in that verse refer to when perfection comes, before then, or just to the fact that we've reached the end of the passage (as in 'now, let me conclude . . . ')? We are now equipped with these questions to know what we need to be looking out for as we go through the passage in detail.

Who? It is very personal. Paul keeps saying 'I'. He includes himself in his comments.

Where? is not a very relevant question this time. The passage is general.

When? This is significant: there is a comparison or contrast between the *now* of v.1-7, and the future of v.8 (and v.9-10 repeat this contrast, as do later verses). Something will be different. When does the change take place? When perfection comes!

What? (We look here especially for repeated words or phrases.) The main topic is love, but the goal of the passage seems to be more a comparison between love and prophecies, tongues and knowledge. Love remains (v.13) but these others will not last for ever (v.8).

One emphasis that is clear in translation, but even more striking in the Greek, is the verb *katargeo*, which occurs four times in v.8-11, and in English is translated as *cease*, *pass away, disappear*, and *put behind* (NIV, v.8 twice, v.10 and v.11).

Why? In fact, this repetition is such a strong emphasis that we would do better to say that this is a passage about how love will never pass away, but prophecies, tongues and knowledge will. This makes sense too in the context we discovered earlier: if the Corinthians were arguing or dividing over the use of these gifts, then Paul here is trying to restore a sense of perspective. (Another *what* observation: although the word *know* or *knowledge* could just be a general way of talking about study or intellect, the context suggests that it is a particular gift of knowledge which is being discussed. In fact in v.12 the now/then contrast does *not* say that we will one day know nothing, but on the contrary that we will know fully. This makes sense if Paul means that the *gift* of knowledge will pass away, but not if he means that knowledge in general will pass away.)

The *literary forms* of the passage are not in this case too significant, although we can note that v.12 is obviously an image rather than a literal description, and we suspect that v.3 is an exaggeration!

Breakdown of the text
If we have done our observational work well so far then this should be straightforward. A good outline might be:

v.1-3 Love: its value (as demonstrated by its absence)
v.4-7 Love: its characteristics (as demonstrated by its presence)
v.8-12 Love: it always remains (as demonstrated by comparisons with gifts)
v.13 Conclusion: love is the greatest (which is what Paul promised for this passage: see the end of chapter 12).
The third of these sections could be broken down further:
v.8-9 A comparison between love and things which pass away
v.10 When these things will pass away
v.11-12 Two illustrations of the comparison

2 Interpretation

We now know the outline of what Paul says, and we have a fair grasp of why he is addressing this issue. But we have only *observed* the passage, because there is still some *interpreting* to do. (Note: we did in fact do some interpretation, when we argued that 'knowledge' refers to a *gift* of knowledge, because there we were trying to make things fit together). If you now work through the 'interpretation' section of our passage analysis outline, you will find in fact that we have done enough work to make most of the interpretation straightforward.

✍ Do this now.

Our concern is still with the *original context* and what it meant *then*. For example, we should interpret this passage to say that if the Corinthians were arguing over spiritual gifts, and doing so without love, then they had missed the whole point: in fact their gifts were worthless because of their lack of love.

But interpretation is not always settled by observation. In particular, a major interpretative question hangs over our passage: we have shown that Paul contrasts the eternal nature of love with the temporary nature of the gifts, but *when* do these gifts pass away? We have *observed* when this happens: it happens 'when perfection comes' (v.10). But we have not *interpreted* this.

This is an interesting and important point. Note that while we may already have an opinion on this issue in general, our concern here is to let this passage speak first before deciding in advance what we are going to allow it to say! And here you probably need some help. For instance, you need to know that the Greek word translated 'perfection' (NIV) is *teleion*, which has a more literal meaning of *totality* (the *end* of something, in the sense that it has arrived at its goal). 'Perfection' isn't a bad translation but it loses this sense of completeness, of arriving at a goal. In particular it loses the connotation which this Greek word has of the fulfilment of all things which we expect at the second coming of Christ. This is only a connotation, not the actual meaning, but it is strengthened by its association in v.12 with the words 'then we shall see face to face'. This common expression for meeting with God draws on a rich Old Testament background, e.g. Genesis 32:30, Judges 6:22, Deuteronomy 5:4, 34:10 and Exodus 33:11, and further suggests that the contrast Paul has in mind here is with the time when we shall see *God* face to face. (Note this is an *interpretation*, you cannot *observe* this in the passage, but rather it is implied by a careful study of the passage).

We should therefore say that in this passage, Paul is comparing eternal love with the gifts which, though important, are invalidated if used without love, and which are not the ultimate aim of any Christian anyway, as shown by the fact that they will disappear when Christ returns. (To be rigorous, we should note in turn that this passage says nothing about how those gifts may or may not be experienced between then and now).

Now would be a good time to look up some commentaries or reference books, if you want to see what other people make of this passage, and in particular note *why* they say something different if they do.

3 Application

Past

Seeing what the application was in the past is almost the same as *interpreting* the passage in its original context. You should by now have a clear grasp of why Paul is discussing this subject with the Corinthians. You should also be able to see why he chose this particular point to describe how great love is: it is not just a piece of teaching about love which he decided to put in this letter rather than another letter.

Present
Is the application the same today? To some extent. *If* we have these same arguments about gifts then we could say that yes, the application is exactly the same today. Otherwise, we should probably say that what the passage says about love is still true today, and that should affect our attitude to one another. But we could *not* say, for instance, that only love is important and the gifts don't matter (which would not represent Paul's attitude in the wider context of this passage, see the next verse, 14:1), or even more vaguely that 'love is the only important thing: it doesn't matter what we do as long as we love each other'. That would be to ignore completely the context of the passage (as well as many other Bible passages). You might like to ask: what kind of application is in view when this passage is read at a wedding? Is it a good one?

If our interpretation is correct then the passage still applies today. Those who would say that the 'perfect' has already come (e.g. that it referred to the completion of the Bible) would answer this differently. They would also have to say that we now see face to face, and are thus in a better position than the apostle Paul, who only saw things poorly; and that we now know fully. While this application is problematic, the real problem with it is that it relies on an interpretation which finds little

support in the passage. This is a good example of the dangers of applying the passage before interpreting it carefully (or to put it another way: the dangers of starting a Bible study by saying 'what does it mean to me?').

Two other passages that you should find support our conclusions, which is always an encouraging sign, are Galatians 5:6 and Ephesians 3:17-19.

Personal
How much of what you do, think or say is correct in theory but lacking in love? Ultimately the application of this passage concerns attitude and not action. The passage should change who we are, and our attitude to others (particularly those we disagree with), and the Bible suggests that when that happens then what we *do* will change too. This is a message which badly needs teaching and preaching in a church which is so consistently divided over such a wide variety of issues.

Prayer
Lord, help me to have my attitude tested and changed by the standards of this passage. Forgive me when I fail to love those I disagree with. Thank you for giving Paul the courage to say these words to a divided church. Change my heart so that I can love with the love that Paul describes. Amen.

Note: This opening section of the unit has involved more reading than usual. The only 'exercise' is to make sure you work through the 1 Corinthians 13 study properly. The unit is organised this way to help you have the tools you need for the studies of the remaining sections.

2 How to Study a Passage

Study Exercise

Now over to you. If possible use reference works to help you at various stages of these studies. Some notes are included in section 3 below on this topic.

Using the suggested method of studying a passage, and taking into account the different *genres* of these passages, make a detailed study of as many of the following Old Testament passages as time allows you to. Everyone should try a minimum of two passages.

Genre	*Passage*
Narrative	Joshua 1:1–18
Poetry	Psalm 7
Prophecy	Amos 5:18–27
Wisdom	Proverbs 2:1–11
Law	Leviticus 16

These passages have been chosen because they are examples of where the *principles* of interpretation should help you make clear distinctions between appropriate and inappropriate interpretation. But feel free to choose different passages if you have a particular reason to do so.

Note: Most books on hermeneutics contain sections on how to read different types of literature. Stuart and Fee's *How to Read the Bible for All Its Worth* does this too. If you can, consult the relevant sections of this book for your different passage studies.

3 How to Study a Passage

3A Introduction

We have been focusing on how to help you do your own work with the Bible. Now we look briefly at the question of how to make the best use of the resources around us. Depending on your situation, there can be quite extensive resources available: the fruit of hard work by scholars from which we can all benefit.

Once you have done your own work on a passage, it is good to check your insights against those of other people. But make sure you do not only read people who share your own views! This is especially important if you are considering some controversial issue where there is more than one common viewpoint. Try and listen to (and read) arguments from either side.

Study Aids Available

A **concordance** is a reference work listing major words in the Bible and usually giving you the verses in which every occurrence of the word can be found. This is very useful for compiling a list of passages to study, and for locating that half-remembered verse about being innocent as doves, or whatever. If the concordance is based on a translation, then you may need further help about where the idea you are studying occurs when it is not translated in the same way.

The best concordances will indicate the link between the word you are studying (in your language) and the Hebrew and Greek originals. Some go further, and concentrate on the derivations of words, and allow you to look at what the Hebrew and Greek originals meant at different times. These books are sometimes called **lexicons**. You can even get entire **theological dictionaries** organised by the Hebrew and Greek words, which can give you enormous depth in your understanding of some terms. However, there are some cautions about word studies below which you should bear in mind.

A **commentary** should do a variety of things, but most importantly it should answer the question 'What did it mean then?'. A good commentary will hopefully give you some guidelines on what it means now, but of course this will only make the commentary more specific to the culture and time it was written in. Try to avoid just using a commentary to look up what one verse means without considering what the author thinks in general of the passage or book in question. A good commentary should also provide you with the information you need about the historical background to the book, and things like difficult translation issues which you can probably not tackle yourself.

A **one-volume commentary** will do all these things a little, but is most useful for providing you with an overall view of the book in question. Use it especially for these overview type studies.

A **Bible dictionary** will give you basic information about a variety of biblical topics, varying over individual books, names of people or places, ancient customs, main theological ideas, archaeological information, issues like chronology or authorship or maybe even ethical issues. This can be an invaluable tool as long as you are prepared to supplement it with your own study.

Another useful help is to have more than one Bible **translation** available, if possible, which will help you avoid building your interpretations on some unusual perspective of the translator. It is

---

good to have one quite literal translation for study purposes, even if you find it easier in general to read a more simply written translation in a modern version of your language.

Many modern **study Bibles** combine quite a lot of these features, and can be very useful references, as long as you remember that it is only the biblical text that is inspired, and the reference material is not!

Note: Specific titles are recommended for many of these types of book in the Appendix. You may like to consult this appendix now.

We will return in the next section to some other ways of doing Bible study which make use of these tools. For now, see if you can use them alongside your passage study.

Study Exercise

This is similar to the exercise for section 2.

Using the suggested method of studying a passage, and taking into account the different *genres* of these passages, make a detailed study of as many of the following New Testament passages as time allows you to. Everyone should try a minimum of two passages.

Genre	Passage
Narrative	Acts 1:1-11
Gospels	Matthew 18:23-35
Letter	2 Timothy 3:10-17 (remember this passage?)
Apocalyptic	Revelation 4:1-11

4 Character Studies

4A Introduction

There is a particular reason for studying individuals from the Bible. God has given us accounts of men and women living through victories, defeats, second chances, struggles, elation and depression . . . men and women, in fact, a lot like us in the way they went up and down. In studying their lives we are able to identify with their humanity: realising that failure is not final, and that even the strong have weaknesses. In showing us how God dealt with them, the Bible enables us to see his holiness and sovereignty not in some theoretical set of statements about God, but in the applied day-to-day outworking of living with God. In studying the biblical characters we have an insight into how God may deal with us.

You do not need to choose a major character in order to draw some interesting conclusions. The key thing is to let all the relevant passages speak in their contexts, and *only then* attempt the task of putting them together. A good example of this is Lot.

4B An Example: Lot

Lot, one of Abraham's nephews, is quite a major character in Genesis 12-19, but apart from a few scattered references to his descendants he is only mentioned twice elsewhere in the Bible, one of these being a general reference by Jesus to his story (in Luke 17:28-32). If you study the passages concerning Lot you will find little to inspire you as a role model.

> ✍ What are the major events in the biblical story which involve Lot? (See Genesis 11:27 - 14:16, and chapter 19)

But if you take into account Abraham's prayer for the righteous in Genesis 18, and the only other biblical reference to Lot (2 Peter 2:7), you are left with an interesting insight into how God viewed a man with such obvious failings as Lot had.

> ✍ In what way does 2 Peter 2:7 cause you to reassess some of the Genesis stories?

> ✍ What particular features of a character study make it differ from the kind of passage study we have looked at?

4C Observation

When you have decided on a particular character, you need to build up a list of relevant verses and passages. Often passing references will not be directly relevant (as e.g. with the Luke passage in our Lot study above), but it is best to look up everything. The simplest way to do this is with a concordance, although a good study Bible may contain references, or even a character profile, which will help you on your way. To get the most out of this stage you need to work carefully through the different passages as outlined in the section on passage study.

Some things are particularly worth looking out for:

1. *Meaning of name.* Often Old Testament names were significant for their meaning. Even in the New Testament we find this occasionally (e.g. Simon whom Jesus names 'Peter', see Luke 6:14, which meant 'rock'. This was clearly significant: see Matthew 16:18).

2. *Ancestry.* The person's father, mother or tribe may be significant. (Paul's background was clearly significant to him, see Acts 26:4-5, although his view is modified in his new perspective as a Christian: Philippians 3:4-6 and especially verse 7).

3. *Background, training and conversion.* Sometimes information which becomes important to our understanding of the story is given in a way that would not cause us to notice its significance if we were not considering the person and their development (e.g. the last sentence of Nehemiah 1, which turns out to explain how Nehemiah came to have an audience with the king, and also shows that he was a trusted man before the story really starts).

4. *Times lived in, years lived, periods of life.* It is helpful, for instance, to see Moses' life in three periods of forty years, against quite different backgrounds.

5. *Shortcomings and accomplishments.* Even the great people of the faith in Hebrews 11 have many of their shortcomings revealed in the stories about them in the Old Testament. Why do you think this is?

6. *Spiritual life.* What can we see about the way they pray, or praise God, or exercise wisdom, impartiality, boldness, faith . . . . What are their attitudes, responses, reactions . . ?

7. *Effect on other people.* Who else was particularly influenced by them, and how?

8. *Death.* How is their death recorded? How were they mourned? What happened after they died and does the narrator link later developments with the fact that they have died?

4D Interpretation

There is more than one way to organise your material once you have gathered it.

1. *Chronologically*: the order in which events happened, from birth to death.

2. *Major events*. Sometimes we do not actually know the order of events, but it is still possible to group our observations around key events. This is probably better, for instance, with characters like the disciples in the gospels.

3. *Principles*. We may be helped by examining one of the principles at work in someone's life: e.g. studying Moses and looking at how he chose who to serve, and had to keep coming back to that commitment.

4. *Ministry*. Likewise it may be helpful to study someone from a particular angle of ministry: e.g. Moses the intercessor, or Moses the leader.

The potential danger with these last two methods is in forcing the evidence to fit some theory. If, for instance, you start to develop an idea of Paul as a church planter, you may find it too easy to fit the evidence in Acts into this theory without looking carefully to see what the writer of Acts may have thought was the most important thing Paul was doing at various stages of his life. The focus is certainly not *always* on starting a church. So caution is needed with these approaches.

Only after you have attempted to organise the biblical material should you really turn to something like a Bible dictionary to see how someone else has organised it, and to check on whether you are overlooking something major.

4E Application

It is just as easy to abuse the application stage of the study! If Elijah was faithful and believed in God for miracles and was then lifted bodily into heaven in a fiery chariot, we should not jump to the conclusion that if we are faithful we too will receive such an invitation to heaven.

In considering how to apply what you have learned it is usually better to focus on what the study shows you about *attitudes* and *thinking*. As a result of studying Elijah, what kind of attitude would you have to miracles? Do you see how even a great man like him suffered intense depression after performing a great miracle? (1 Kings 19 tells this story).

The application is less something to *do*, but more a new resource that you have for dealing with times of depression if they come along. You are strengthened in your character. Seeing how God dealt with Elijah changes who you are, and your view of the world, and your appreciation of God. It might be nice to have some concrete things you can tick off on a list as an application, but the Christian life is rarely as neat and ordered as that (which should not be much of a surprise, if you do some character studies, e.g. Abraham, Moses, David . . . , etc.).

4F Study Examples

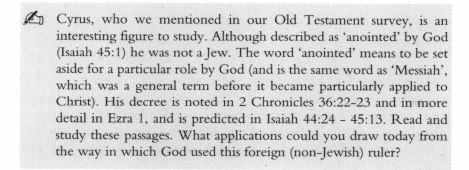

Cyrus, who we mentioned in our Old Testament survey, is an interesting figure to study. Although described as 'anointed' by God (Isaiah 45:1) he was not a Jew. The word 'anointed' means to be set aside for a particular role by God (and is the same word as 'Messiah', which was a general term before it became particularly applied to Christ). His decree is noted in 2 Chronicles 36:22-23 and in more detail in Ezra 1, and is predicted in Isaiah 44:24 - 45:13. Read and study these passages. What applications could you draw today from the way in which God used this foreign (non-Jewish) ruler?

Good characters to examine, with more material for study than Lot or Cyrus, would be **Jonah** or **Barnabas**. Work through the above guidelines on doing a character study for these two people.

Note: not all of the points raised in the above outline will be applicable in each case. For **Jonah** you should note that your focus is not on the many interesting points which the book of Jonah raises about God, cities, its historical setting, or even about whales. Rather your aim is to see what the character of Jonah in the book may teach you. You will not really need to look outside the book of Jonah for this study.

For **Barnabas**, you will need to think about the kind of relationships which existed in the early days of the church, and how Barnabas did or did not contribute to helping them. You may need to pursue one or two of the references outside Acts, but your focus will be on a limited number of passages in Acts.

5 Topical and Word Studies

5A How to do a Topical Bible Study

A topical study is a study of what the Bible has to say regarding a specific topic. As such, it is a lot like a word study (see below), but more comprehensive. The advantage of a topical study is that it gives a total picture about the subject you are studying, which a word study does not necessarily do. The corresponding disadvantage is that it takes an enormous amount of preparation, and in particular it takes a lot of integrity to listen carefully to such a wide variety of passages without prejudging what you will let those passages say.

We should actually be grateful that the Bible is not just God's word to you in your culture and at your time. If it were then everyone else would be very frustrated! But of course this means that frequently we ourselves are frustrated because the Bible does not immediately answer the questions we want it to. One possibility that you have to bear in mind in a topical study is that perhaps it does not answer your question at all (consider for example if you have a burning question about how often you should take communion, or whether you should stand or kneel to pray: these are perfectly good questions but unfortunately the Bible does not answer them. Even a Christian attitude to abortion is something which has to be inferred from other principles, since the Bible does not address the issue directly).

Features of a Topical Study

You should again use reference works to **locate passages** without getting 'answers' from them about your topic. Be sure to look up words related to your topic. For example if you are studying prayer then you should also look up *ask, intercession, supplication,* and *petition*.

See if there is a particular key passage where the subject is addressed as the main focus, rather than being mentioned in passing when the focus is really on something else. For example, you would not want to focus your prayer study on 1 Timothy 2:8 and conclude that the key thing in prayer is lifting up hands (and for men only?!). The passage is focusing on worship, and a better idea of prayer could be got from studying, say, Ephesians 3:14–21. Incidentally, lifting up hands in prayer was normal then, so the emphasis in the Timothy verse must be on the word holy. In contrast, kneeling was very rare, which makes Ephesians 3:14 quite striking. This is a good example of where not being in tune with the biblical cultures may lead you to the wrong conclusions.

Are some of your major passages in the Old Testament? Here you need to be particularly careful to study both what it meant in its original setting and how it applies today. For instance, are the Old Testament promises linked to the Old Covenant? (For example, the promise of long life was one of the ways that God's blessing was experienced under the Old Covenant. You might want to contrast this with New Testament teaching on life after death, which is hardly ever a focus in the Old Testament).

Do not build your doctrines on unclear or **obscure teachings**. For example, Paul definitely mentions the practice of baptising for the dead (1 Corinthians 15:29): in fact it appears to play a role in his argument about resurrection. But whatever Paul meant then is certainly obscure now. Don't pretend to understand what is simply no longer clear! He *might* have meant many different things, but you would be very unwise to let any interpretation of this verse play a major role in your thinking (which is precisely what the Mormons do with this verse).

Pay attention to the **biblical emphasis**. A good example of this is the comparison of Jesus with the angels in Hebrews 1. It is not that angels are not important, but our focus is not to be on them, but on Jesus. This point could not be put more forcefully than it is in Hebrews 1. If you have to study angels (and why not?!) then don't get carried away with all the interesting things you can find out: keep this focus on Jesus as your main perspective. Wrong emphasis is a common failing in much Christian teaching these days.

Finally, be prepared to **learn new things** every time you study the same topic. Don't just take out your old notes and rely on them. For example, you could do a thorough study of the biblical idea of suffering, and then think you have grasped that teaching. However, if you subsequently go through difficulties, or depression, or bereavement, you will probably find that the next time you come back to those passages they speak to you in new ways. Many people have found this with the book of Job, for example, or Lamentations. (This has even become a major area of modern hermeneutics: the study of how the reader's experience affects their interpretation).

Study Exercise

You could pursue any of the examples mentioned above: e.g. prayer (or even angels!). There will probably be many questions you have yourself which you would like to study. Perhaps it is better at this stage not to aim for something as major as 'God's sovereignty and human free will', or any topic like that which has been debated at great length and with many different views on either side.

Ask questions. For prayer, for instance, look at the prayers recorded in the Bible. Are they for believers or unbelievers? What is the role of praise and thanksgiving in these prayers? Are they short or long? Who are they addressed to? Do they focus on practical details or God's larger purposes or people's responses or what?

Another good topical study, if you feel that prayer is a bit ambitious, is *giving*. To what extent does the Bible teach tithing? What and how should we give? Are there biblical principles in, for instance, Paul's collection for Jerusalem, which we can apply today?

5B How to do Word Studies

Word studies can be very revealing about key terms used in the Bible, but there are some problems which have to be avoided as you do them. The first question is: what language will you look at the word in? It is best to study a Hebrew or Greek word, and you will need reference tools to help you do so.

Secondly, it is a difficult issue to say exactly how we know what a word means, but clearly one important issue is how we use the word in general. If you always use the word 'incredible' to mean 'amazing, brilliant, fantastic' then you are in good company, but you are not using that word to mean 'it cannot be believed', which is where the word comes from: 'credible' means believable, so 'incredible' is the opposite. (You might equally use the word 'unbelievable' to mean 'amazing, brilliant . . . ' too.) So it would be entirely wrong to analyse the sentence 'Jesus performed incredible miracles' by saying that what it really meant was that Jesus' miracles should not really be believed. You would have to know how the word was being used.

Believe it or not ('incredibly'!) this type of mistake is frequently made in word studies. For example: Paul says that women will be 'saved' through childbirth (1 Timothy 2:15). What does 'saved' mean here? Is it referring to spiritual salvation, or to being saved from physical pain, or even death? Is it that through-*out* the process of childbirth, women will be kept safe? All of these are *interpretations*, because we may simply not know exactly how Paul was *using* the word at the time. (You can look up this verse to see how these different options are treated in commentaries, etc.)

So with these cautions in mind, consider the following guidelines:

1. Look up the derivation of the word - where it comes from (its 'etymology')

2. To see how it is used, look at several passages where the author uses it, if possible. Look at the overall use of it in the Bible. Does the New Testament draw on an Old Testament understanding of the word, for example?

3. Check the grammatical features of the word. For instance, in 1 John 3:9-10 we read that if we are born of God, we cannot go on sinning. This is a translation of a present tense verb (to sin) which in this verse carries the sense of a continuous action: i.e. it is referring to habitually sinning. It is not therefore saying that once we are Christians we never sin. Careful grammar is important in Bible study.

4. Look at other words related to the word you are studying (this clearly links our present section with the preceding one on how to do topical studies). In fact, it is obvious once you think about it that a word study may not include a passage where your topic is discussed but uses a different word (e.g. the *word* 'unity' is rare in the Bible, but the *theme* is a common one).

5. Check your translation! You may commence a word study only to find that the word is a poor translation in some key verse, whereas a better translation does not use it.

Concordances, dictionaries and word study books will all help you in gathering information, and hopefully will also guide you through some of the pitfalls outlined above.

Study Exercise

A good word study you might try is on *leadership*. You will find that the Bible makes very few direct points about leadership: can you think of any before you start? What related words would you need to look up if you were to expand this into a topical study? (You should probably look up *leader, leading* . . . etc. anyway).

Another interesting study could look at the word *immortal* (and *immortality*). There are only a few occurrences of this, but they may be thought-provoking if you have never studied it before.

Additional Note on Preparing and Leading Bible Studies

One practical implication of this unit concerns the leading of Bible studies, whether in a church, in a small group, one-to-one, and with Christians or non-Christians. Since many of you will be doing this, it is good to say something concerning it here.

> ✍ Would you say that there are any problems with the following approach: 'I don't need to prepare for this study. I'll just rely on the Holy Spirit to lead me to say the right things'?

Note that appealing to Matthew 10:19-20 to defend a view like this would be a classic case of failing to read a passage in context. The context is given by v.18, and by the phrase 'when they arrest you' in v.19.

We should probably say that there is a difference between someone who genuinely does not have time to prepare and someone who simply does not bother. What follows are some thoughts designed to help you the next time you are preparing.

Preparing a Bible study is like doing one of the different kinds of study we have outlined above: whether on a passage, a topic, a word, a character, or whatever. However, if you are leading a study (and remember this is not the same as preaching) then you should especially note the kind of questions you are asking yourself because it will be good to ask those in the study. This does not mean that you should ask *everything* which you yourself have considered. For instance, you may need to do a lot of background work on one particular point, but only sometimes will you need to share all this in the study. Rather, you are now prepared in case that topic proves to be one which causes discussion.

Returning to our example of the angels in Hebrews 1: your purpose in the study should really be to focus on Jesus, as the passage does, rather than let the study wander off into speculation about all the things which angels may or may not do, or be like. Just as in your own study you need to be disciplined about finding the right emphasis, so in a group study you need to help others to do so.

Secondly, you should keep a clear mental distinction between what you have *observed* in the passage, and what you have *interpreted*. Make sure you help other people to observe what is really there: be prepared to push people until they too observe it. Don't let them think something is in the passage when it isn't. However, when it comes to interpretation, you need to be much more cautious: allow others to pursue different ways of interpreting the passage. A sure sign of maturity in a Christian is that they do not feel the need to make everyone interpret every passage in the same way that they do. This is even more true of the *application* section. Think very carefully before telling someone what God is saying to them through the passage. (Note: we are *not* saying that you should let *any* interpretation stand, or that *no* applications should be mentioned. Instead, prompt people to work through their interpretations to see if there really is value in them, but always be open to different views. And perhaps make suggestions about applications, but encourage people to think of their own too.)

Your goal in leading the study is not to make people hear your voice, but to let them hear God's voice. As with all biblical interpretation, it may require hard work, but the effort is worth it, as God speaks to us today through his inspired word, and continues the process of changing us to be more like the people he wants us to be, and more like his son Jesus Christ.

Optional Exercise

 If you are preparing a study for the near future, work through it now and see how much this unit helps you to organise your thoughts in a useful way.

Glossary

This is a list of terms which may be unfamiliar, but are important for this unit, and which you can refer to during your work as a reminder of some key definitions.

Commentary   a commentary is a book written about the Bible text or passage which helps you to understand it.

Concordance   a book which lists the words appearing in the Bible.

Context   the setting in which a word or verse or passage appears. This can be its *historical* context or its *literary* context.

Genre   a type of writing, or literary style, such as poetry, parable, apocalyptic, etc.

Hermeneutics   the activity of interpreting or explaining something, particularly used to refer to the science (or art?) of interpreting the Bible. This is sometimes broken down into **exegesis**, a word from the Greek which means literally to 'read out of', i.e. to see what the passage said when it was written; and **application** which looks at how the original meaning applies today.

Illumination   the activity of the Holy Spirit in helping readers to understand the words of the Bible. This is different from, but related to, **inspiration**.

Inspiration   from the Greek word meaning 'breathing', this term is used to explain the nature of the Bible: that it is 'breathed out' or 'inspired' by God, i.e. it has a divine authorship (as well as a human one).

Lexicon   a type of concordance giving information about the words listed and their development.

Memory Verses

There are no memory verses for this unit. Instead here is an exercise for you: when you are learning the memory verses for all the other units then check first: am I taking these verses out of context and would I feel confident that I could explain why they were written in their own contexts? If not, then study them carefully before memorising them.

SECTION II:
GOD AND HIS PEOPLE

Unit Three
Knowing God

Outline and Notes

This unit focuses not just on knowing about God, but also on knowing God. (In Greek, the words for *knowing* and *God* combine to give us the word *theology*). We do this through the framework of how God revealed himself to Moses, as recorded in Exodus 34:6-7.

Aims

In this unit you will be learning how to know God better through a careful study of different passages where he has revealed Himself, especially in Exodus 34:6-7.

Study Objectives

As well as laying the foundation for the above aim, this unit will enable you to:

- explain the ways in which God reveals himself through the Bible.
- give a brief account of the doctrine of the Trinity.
- describe the characteristics of God as revealed in Exodus 34:6-7.
- explain the connection between having a correct view of God and knowing God better.

Unit Outline

1 Introduction to the Name of God

1A Introduction
    A Correct View of God
1B The Name of God
    Exodus 34
    Into the New Testament
1C Who Do We Worship?

2 The Lord, The Lord

2A The Lord, The Lord
    Yahweh, Yahweh
2B Jesus is Lord
    Lordship
2C The Trinity
    Is Jesus God?
    For Further Study
    Three Persons, One God . . . ?

3 The Compassionate and Gracious God, Slow to Anger

3A Studying the Attributes of God
3B The Compassionate God
3C The Gracious God
3D Slow to Anger

4 Abounding in Steadfast Loving Kindness and Truth, Maintaining Love to Thousands

4A The God of Love
    What is *Love*?
    Hesed
4B Truth and Faithfulness
4C Maintaining Love for Thousands

5 Forgiving Wickedness, Rebellion and Sin and by no means Clearing the Guilty

5A Sin and Its Consequences
    The Old Testament Sacrificial System
    Forgiveness
5B By No Means Clearing the Guilty

Resolution
The Third and Fourth Generation
5C   Summary

Note: Throughout this unit we use the male pronoun 'He' or 'His' or 'Him' when referring to God. This is for convenience only and is not meant to imply that God is male. It is more a reflection of the fact that no agreed alternative has been found to this linguistic usage.

1 Introduction to the Name of God

1A Introduction

[A note on how this unit works: in section 1 we basically take an overview of the whole subject, including a look at God's self-revelation in Exodus 34 in context, and showing how the main themes of our study can be traced through to the New Testament and our own devotional lives. In the remaining sections, we go over this ground much more thoroughly, including a detailed look at Exodus 34 word-by-word.]

What do we expect to cover in a unit entitled 'Knowing God'? We might think that we will be learning a lot *about* God, and in that way we will know God. But in the Bible, the idea of *knowing* goes much deeper than understanding certain facts (*cognitive* knowledge). And in this unit we will be trying to do much more than know about God. *We actually want to know God.* How can we do that in a study?

We are helped by the way that in the Bible we see people who know God. We see God revealing himself in different ways at different times. We see how people's experience of God transformed their lives.

As we allow the biblical record of God's self-revelation to change us; to change our expectations and hopes; our worldview and our understanding; so we can do much more than know about God. We can, through our study of the Bible, actually know God. Our study and our thinking will play a part in changing who we are as we grow in our spiritual lives.

This is the perspective we must have as we come to our study.

A Correct View of God

At the same time it is important that what we know *about* God is correct. If our understanding of God is wrong then we will grow up as distorted Christians. Many of us have an unbalanced view which is false or incomplete in some way, and spiritual difficulties can often be traced directly to this. Hence the importance of careful Bible study as we come to this topic.

1B The Name of God

What is God like? This is a question about the *character* of God, but it will help us at this point if we realise that in the Old Testament someone's character was very tied up with their *name*. Unfortunately most modern translations of the Bible obscure the significance of this, and use familiar words like 'Lord' which actually do not mean very much to many people. The word 'Lord' is certainly not thought of as a name today, rather as a title.

To know somebody's name was to know something deeply important about them. We lose the significance of this in cultures where often the first thing we do is introduce ourselves by our name. Old Testament names often had a meaning which meant that people did not just tell everyone their name.

 A good example of this is the story of Jacob wrestling with a man (Genesis 32:22-32). See especially vv.27, 29. In the setting of the story it would have been impossible for the man to bless Jacob without knowing his name.

Exercise

Look up three or four of these Bible names to see their significance. You can do this most easily with a translation like the NIV, which usually footnotes the meaning of a name where it is relevant.

Abraham	Naomi	Jesus
Jacob	Christ	Beth Aven
Israel	Jonathan	Beersheba
Ruth	Bethlehem	Bethel

 Would you agree that a name in the Bible is often significant in terms of character?

Look up 1 Samuel 25:25 for a particularly clear example.

Many English translations use a special way of writing LORD to indicate one of God's names, which, when copied from the Hebrew into English letters, is represented by the letters YHWH. (The classical Hebrew which makes up most of the Old Testament did not record vowel sounds, and these were added centuries later by the Masoretes, which gives us the Masoretic text used by translations like the NIV. A problem with the word YHWH is that we do not really know what vowels were used with it, since the Jews did not speak God's name in later centuries for fear of misusing it. One early modernisation of the word YHWH borrowed the vowels from another word for Lord, and made the word 'Jehovah' out of it. Today, most would agree that 'Yahweh' is a more useful way of writing this name of God. Many Bible translations discuss this in more detail in their introductions.)

✍ Look up Exodus 6:2-3. Which names does God use to reveal himself to which people?

These verses have been at the centre of many disputes about our understanding of God, and it is helpful to look at them in some detail. Here they are taken from the useful *Jerusalem Bible* translation:

> God spoke to Moses and said to him, 'I am Yahweh. To Abraham and Isaac and Jacob I appeared as El Shaddai; I did not make myself known to them by my name Yahweh.'

This translation uses the actual Hebrew words that God uses. The term *El* is a general word for 'God' (and is used to apply to other gods when appropriate). When we combine this Exodus 6 passage with Exodus 3:14 we find that not only is Yahweh revealing himself to Moses in a new way, but that the name Yahweh is also a new revelation to Moses.

This is straightforward enough, although it is complicated by the fact that the word 'Yahweh' appears often in Genesis. (In fact all three people mentioned in Exodus 6:3 appear in passages which use it: see Genesis 15 where Abram and Yahweh both use the name 'Yahweh' in their discussion; and Genesis 26:2, where 'Yahweh appeared to Isaac';

and Genesis 30:30, where Jacob refers to 'Yahweh'.) This observation was once the basis of an entire approach to the study of the Old Testament which broke it down into different 'sources' on the basis of which of God's names were used. Few today agree with this approach except for a general acceptance that ancient books often were compiled out of different sources.

The particular point which is relevant for our study is that if we take the Exodus verses at face value then we have not just a revelation of who God was, but in particular a revelation of God's name which was a significant part of him revealing who he was. In other words: to learn that God was Yahweh was a major step forward for Moses, and in the passage we look at below it was a key part of his understanding of who God was and what he was like.

We should briefly offer one possible solution to the various difficult issues this may raise for our understanding of the early parts of the Old Testament. In a helpful book called *The Old Testament of the Old Testament* (Minneapolis: Fortress Press, 1993), Walter Moberly argues that all of these passages mean exactly what they say, and the reason that the name 'Yahweh' appears in Genesis is because these so-called patriarchal stories (i.e. stories about the patriarchs, the great father figures of Israel) are being told by a later author who *does* know that God's name is Yahweh. Moberly therefore sees Genesis as a bit like an Old Testament for the rest of the Old Testament itself: it depicts humans relating to God in a slightly different way to the rest of the Old Testament; a way that is no longer the case for those who lived at or after the time of Moses. This approach would seem to be a satisfactory way of understanding the various 'name of God' passages in Exodus.

Exodus 34

We can now look at what will be the key passage for our study in this unit: Exodus 34. Here we take an overview of it in its biblical context.

First read Exodus 32-33 as background.

After the giving of the law there is a ceremony where Moses and all the people commit themselves to obey the words of Yahweh (see Exodus 24). Chapters 25-31 represent Yahweh speaking to Moses about some of the details of the tabernacle and the priesthood, but when chapter 32 begins we read that because Moses was such a long time talking with Yahweh the people grew restless and were led into sin. In particular they made a golden calf and worshipped it (idolatry). Moses, grieved, decides to stand in the place of the Israelites (32:32), and then, *since he knows God's name* (33:12) he asks Yahweh to show that he will treat his people with favour. As Moses calls on the name of Yahweh we read:

> Yahweh passed in front of Moses, proclaiming, 'Yahweh, Yahweh, the compassionate and gracious God, slow to anger, abounding in love and faithfulness, maintaining love to thousands, and forgiving wickedness, rebellion and sin. Yet he does not leave the guilty unpunished; he punishes the children and their children for the sin of the fathers to the third and fourth generation'. Exodus 34:6-7

We will be returning to this passage regularly in the unit. The major elements of this revelation of who God is recur throughout the Old Testament. It is of central importance for our understanding of God.

Briefly look up the following to see how this is true:

2 Chronicles 30:9; Nehemiah 9:17, 31; Psalm 86:15; 103:8; 111:4; 145:8; Joel 2:13 and Jonah 4:2.

We will study some of these passages later in this unit.

In particular here we see again the link between a name and the character of the one who has the name (in this case: Yahweh). It is also significant that God's revelation of himself in these terms comes after such apostasy (failure and turning away from the truth) as we see in Exodus 32. It was certainly not the case that the Israelites earned the right to have God reveal himself (or his Name) to them: it was an act of God's grace.

 What effect did God's revelation have on Moses? (See Exodus 34:29ff)

As we study the character of God and come to know him more, can we hope that we too will radiate the glory of his character?

Into the New Testament

The theme of God revealing his name is not just an Old Testament one. Jesus uses exactly this phrase in his prayer at the end of his life on earth, perhaps as a summary of a major part of his ministry.

 Look up John 17:6, 26. The NIV obscures this by not translating the word 'name'. If you can, find a translation which does use the word. What is the significance of this phrase in the light of our Old Testament discussion?

(Note: Of course, the fact that the NIV translates John 17:6 the way it does is itself an example of the wider meaning of the phrase 'name of God' which we are considering in this study.)

 Hebrews 1:2-3, like Exodus 34:29ff , expresses a link between the revelation of who God is and the radiance of his glory. What is the link?

1C Who Do We Worship?

We said in our introduction to this unit that our image of God plays a major part in our spiritual growth. In a sense we become like the God we worship. In the Bible this can be both a positive and a negative idea.

The implication of this is that we need to be strict with ourselves in our understanding of God.

 In Romans 1:21-23 it is negative. What link does Paul express here between false worship and the development of the false worshippers?

In 2 Corinthians 3:7-18 it is positive. Study this passage to see the link between our relationship with God and the way in which we are changed (v.18). Note here how Paul draws a parallel between us and Moses in the passage we studied earlier.

Time for Reflection

Consider the following quote from A.W. Tozer and then spend time reflecting on your view of God.

Satan's first attack upon the human race was his sly effort to destroy Eve's confidence in the kindness of God. Unfortunately for her and for us he succeeded too well. From that day, men have had a false conception of God . . . Nothing twists and deforms the soul more than a low or unworthy conception of God. . . .

Much Christianity . . . has been grim and severe. And the cause has been the same — an unworthy or an inadequate view of God. Instinctively we try to be like our god, and if He is conceived to be stern and exacting, so will we ourselves be.

From a failure properly to understand God comes a world of unhappiness among good Christians even today. The Christian life is thought to be glum, unrelieved cross-carrying under the eye of a stern Father who expects much and excuses nothing. He is austere, peevish, highly temperamental and extremely hard to please. The kind of life which springs out of [this] must of necessity be but a parody on the true life in Christ.

. . . If we hold Him to be kind and understanding our whole inner life will mirror that idea. . . . He is just, indeed, and He will not condone sin; but . . . toward the trusting sons of men His mercy will always triumph over justice. . . . . How good it would be if we could learn that God is easy to live with.

From A.W. Tozer, *The Root of the Righteous*, ch.3 'God is Easy to Live With', pp.17-19.

Self-examination

Where does your view about God come from? How much have you made the God of the Bible your God?

In what ways do you think of God as 'stern and exacting', in fact as impossible to live with? Do you have deeply held views of God's nature which you perhaps need to rethink and correct?

For the remainder of this unit we will use the framework of God's self-revelation in Exodus 34 as a way of looking at the character of God.

2 The Lord, The Lord

2A The Lord, The Lord

This opening phrase of the divine revelation of Exodus 34:7 makes us immediately aware of some of the difficulties involved in studying the Bible and hearing its original voice. This is especially true when a phrase like this has developed all kinds of meanings through its repeated use in prayers and songs, for example, down through many centuries.

It will be helpful to start by examining some of the basic ideas that the word 'Lord' brings to mind for you, which will help us when we come on later to look at what the Hebrew word is.

A good way to do this is to do a word-web, or a spider-diagram, around the word LORD, just noting down quickly thoughts that come to mind.

Yahweh, Yahweh

You may recall from section 1, or have noted from looking at Exodus 34 in your Bible, that the divine revelation of 34:7 begins 'The

LORD, the LORD. . . ', which reminds us that the text actually says 'Yahweh, Yahweh. . . '. So what does the word 'Yahweh' mean?

In Exodus 3:14 God says something to Moses which at first sight looks very odd, and which is certainly difficult to translate. He appears to say 'I AM WHO I AM'. Again, many translations print this in capitals, as a way to signal that there is more to this than the words being used. In this verse, God is saying to Moses that he is to tell the Israelites that 'I AM has sent me to you'. The suggestion here is that God's name is linked with the concept of God being the one who *is*, i.e. who exists. (The Hebrew for 'I am' here is *'ehyeh*, which seems linked to *Yahweh*).

This all sounds quite abstract, but its basic point is simple and important. When God reveals himself as Yahweh to Moses, he is making a revelation about the fact that He is a God who always exists, and is always the same God: 'I AM the God who always IS', we might say.

 In some ways, then, we need to unlearn the ideas that come with the word 'Lord' in a verse like Exodus 34:7, and refocus our thinking around the phrase 'I AM WHO I AM'. Meditate on this and do a new spider diagram:

Returning now to Exodus 34:7 we can see that it is easy to bring into this self-revelation all kinds of ideas associated with the modern word 'Lord' which were not part of what God intended when he said it. This is all part of the process of learning to let the Bible set the agenda for our correct understanding of God.

 Review briefly any differences between your two word-webs in this section. Summarise what you find from this comparison.

Equally significant for understanding this verse is to realise the importance of the repetition of 'Yahweh' at the beginning. To repeat a word like this is to emphasise it greatly. (We find straightforward examples of this with the repetition of 'pits' in the Hebrew of Genesis 14:10 and of 'gold' in 2 Kings 25:15. If you look up these verses you will see how translators have tried to capture this emphasis in various ways.) The highest form of emphasis in Hebrew was a triple repetition, which was such an emphasis that it was extremely rare.

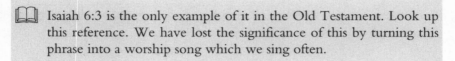 Isaiah 6:3 is the only example of it in the Old Testament. Look up this reference. We have lost the significance of this by turning this phrase into a worship song which we sing often.

What then do you see as the significance of the repetition in Exodus 34:7, given its context?

How would you express in your own words the link between our understanding of the word 'Yahweh' and our general understanding of the word 'Lord'? (Another way of asking this is to say: in what sense does the character of God described by the name 'Yahweh' overlap with the meaning of 'Lord'?). It is important that you take time to reflect on this before going on.

2B Jesus is Lord

The link between our use of the word 'Lord' and our understanding of the name 'Yahweh' can help us as we come to God through the New Testament. We recognise that Jesus is our Lord, but again we have to think about how we understand that term.

One verse which in particular helps us to understand Jesus better is John 8:58. Again this sounds odd in English, but its oddness should remind you of Exodus 3:14.

 What is the significance of Jesus using the phrase 'I am' to describe himself? What point would this make to the Jews he was talking with in John 8? (This should also make sense of the violent reaction his words caused: see v.59.)

For Further Study

Jesus uses the phrase 'I am' also in vv.24 and 28 in John 8, both of which are very important verses. We should note that this phrase would probably have been understood in Jesus' time in the context of its use in Isaiah 40-55. If you look up the following verses you will find Yahweh using this description of himself, obviously drawing on the idea of the Exodus passages too. See Isaiah 41:4, 43:10-13, 43:25 and 48:12. We could therefore say that already before the time of Jesus it was understood that this phrase referred to Yahweh, and that to use it of oneself was to make a claim to deity.

Lordship

We should now be able to understand God as Lord in a helpful way: a way that fits with the biblical idea behind the use of the word rather than with the various meanings that 'Lord' has acquired down through history, and which we often subconsciously read back into the Bible.

Study Exercise

'Yahweh is king forever and ever' — Psalm 10:16
Look for the link between 'Lordship' (and 'Sovereignty') and the idea of the God who IS, who always exists, in the following passages:

* Psalm 90 (note especially v.2)
* Psalm 139:7
* Matthew 28:18-20
* 1 Timothy 1:17

2C The Trinity

So far in this section, we have seen how the idea of Jesus being Lord involves him making a claim that was understood by the Jews of his time as blasphemy (i.e. he made himself equal with God). This has led us close to the doctrine of the Trinity, and we conclude this section with a brief look at this idea.

The Bible never makes an explicit statement about the Trinity, but it says enough to have led the church, down through the centuries, to adopt the idea that while there is only one God, and that God is one, there are at the same time three *persons* within the Godhead: the Father, Jesus the Son, and the Holy Spirit.

We should add immediately that while this idea is simple on one level, Christians have always found it easier to say what the Trinity is not rather than what it is. Thus: we are **not** saying that there are three Gods, and we are **not** saying that there is one God who appears at different times as Father, or Son, or Spirit, and, in fact, we are **not** even saying that these three *persons* are *people* in the way we usually understand that term.

Biblical Pointers

- First, the old King James Version text of 1 John 5:7 must be disregarded. It is almost certain that this was included only in the Middle Ages in an attempt to fill in what the Bible conspicuously did not say: a straightforward version of the doctrine of the Trinity. All modern translations omit this verse.
- Other passages do point towards the idea. One of the clearest 'Trinitarian' verses is Matthew 28:19.
- But the most helpful way of understanding the biblical witness to the idea of the Trinity is to see how both Jesus and the Spirit are described in terms which are only really applicable to God. We saw this in John 8 above. Another important passage is John 14:8-31 where Jesus promises that the Father will send the Holy Spirit.

Is Jesus God?

A similar approach can be taken to the question of whether Jesus is God, since many modern people (both Christians and non-Christians) feel that they would find things simpler if the Bible had a clear statement like 'Jesus is God'. But we would not really expect to find first century Jews calling Jesus of Nazareth 'God', since the idea of God being a human being went against all of Jewish tradition. What is more significant in the New Testament, on this view, is that Jesus is described in ways which are in fact descriptions of deity, as we saw in John 8. (Note: Romans 9:5 may be a more obvious description, but the translation and punctuation of this verse is disputed.)

 A clear example of this, at least in Jesus' self-understanding, is his view that he can forgive sins. See Mark 2:1-12. What do the Jews think that he is claiming here? (See verse 7).

This is another example of where we need to let the Bible speak on its own terms, and in its own, powerful way, rather than wishing that it spoke as we do ourselves. If we let it speak on its own terms then it will be clear enough.

For Further Study

We do not have space to go further into this area, although some suggestions are made in the appendix for further reading. Much of early church history was taken up with clarifying an understanding of the nature of God: we should not expect to be able to cover that ground in this short section!

Three Persons, One God. . . ?

The phrase 'three persons' has confused many people. It is an attempt to translate the old Latin word *personae* which was used in some of the great doctrinal debates of church history. In fact, it is the wrong way round to argue that we know what a person is, and the Trinity has three of them. Rather, we see what the Trinity is, from the biblical witness, and we then draw some conclusions about what it means to be a person. (We will actually do this in the next unit, on 'Understanding Ourselves'.) Many people say that they do not mean 'three Gods' when they say 'three persons', but it is often not clear what they think the difference is.

For those who do wish to go further, it is worth looking at the difference between, on the one hand, the deity of the Father, the Son and the Spirit, and on the other hand the fact that *what they each do* is different. (It is therefore simplistic to argue about whether they are all equally God, since on one level the answer is yes, and on another it is no.)

What functions do the three persons of the Godhead have according to the Bible? (Use reference books if you wish to pursue this example.)

3 The Compassionate and Gracious God, Slow to Anger

3A Studying the Attributes of God

Yahweh's self-revelation in Exodus 34:6–7 moves on after the opening phrase to describe some of his different characteristics. These are often called 'the attributes of God', and through the rest of this unit we will be looking at knowing God through the framework of these attributes as described in this Exodus passage. In this section of the unit, we focus on the next part of v.6: 'The compassionate and gracious God, slow to anger'.

Our aim throughout these sections is not just to acquire knowledge of some things we can say about God. Our aim is to let these truths about God penetrate into our thinking and help change us as people. So again, we need to listen carefully to the biblical text and make sure that we hear what it is saying. It is easy to be over-familiar with religious sounding language, or to bring inappropriate understandings to some of the words used. Much of the rest of this unit, therefore, will be concerned with variations on word studies as we look at different attributes of God. (You may find it useful at this point to review briefly our discussion of word studies in Unit 2).

3B The Compassionate God

One of the biblical ideas of compassion is a deep, inward feeling of tenderness especially towards babies, children and other helpless people. It is especially characteristic of the love parents have for their children, but the particular significance of the idea in the Old Testament is the way it is applied to God's love for human beings.

> Two verses which make this explicit comparison are Isaiah 49:15 and Psalm 103:13. Write in your own words the point these two verses are making. (Check also the context of these verses)

The phrase used in Hebrew to indicate that compassion or mercy came from deep within the person was 'bowels of mercy (or compassion)'. Some older translations put this literally, while newer translations tend to convey the sense of the phrase, as a comparison may reveal:

Genesis 43:30
'Joseph made haste, for his bowels did yearn upon his brother' (KJV)
'Deeply moved at the sight of his brother, Joseph hurried out' (NIV)

1 Kings 3:26, describing the woman whose child Solomon has ordered to be cut in two:
'her bowels yearned upon her son' (KJV)
'filled with compassion for her son' (NIV)

Both of these verses suggest a deeply personal care for someone who is greatly loved. We might say that when God is described as compassionate we can see him looking upon us with the tenderest affection.

Study Exercises

Read **Jonah** chapters 3 and 4. How would you compare Jonah's attitude to the people of Nineveh with God's attitude? Does this suggest ways that God's compassion goes deeper than our own? Can you relate to Jonah's feelings in any way?

In what ways is Jonah 4:2 significant in understanding God's actions?

Another passage which fills out the idea of compassion is the story of the Lost Son, in **Luke 15:11–32**. Write in your own words one or two sentences which describe God's character as shown in this story.

For Personal Reflection

• Do I believe God has ever forgotten to be compassionate? (Psalm 77:9)
• When has God ever forgotten me? (Isaiah 49:15)
• Where do I go when I am in distress? (1 Chronicles 21:13)
• What attitude do I display to those without God? (Luke 7:13)
• Can I accept that God looks on me with feelings of deep compassionate love? (Matthew 23:37)

3C The Gracious God

To be gracious is to feel sympathy and compassion, but carries especially the idea of showing it by granting a favour. A gracious act is undeserved, and perhaps meets a need which could not have been met otherwise. There is thus an overlap of meaning between 'compassionate' and 'gracious', but we can have some feeling for the idea of the word 'gracious' by looking at how it is used.

A key passage is Isaiah 30:15–21, where Yahweh, using the same word as in Exodus 34 (and 33:19), repeats his commitment to Israel even though they are acting in a way which does not invite God's grace. See especially vv.18–19. In what way does God's graciousness link with a human response in this passage?

The idea of God's grace being totally undeserved is captured well in Ephesians 1:3–14 (which is all one sentence in the Greek, as if Paul was so caught up in his praise of God that he just carried on and on . . .).

The description used in vv.7-8 is 'the riches of God's grace that he lavished on us with all wisdom and understanding . . . '.

 Look through Ephesians 1:3-14 and list some of the ways in which God has lavished the riches of his grace on us.

3D Slow to Anger

With the next phrase, 'slow to anger', we again meet a Hebrew phrase which is both picturesque and which needs recontextualising into our modern understanding. The KJV translated this phrase as 'longsuffering', which captures the idea of 'slow to anger', and also reflects the literal Hebrew more closely, where the words used indicated that God had a long nose (or long nostrils). This was a particular way the Jews had of saying that someone did not easily show their anger.

Does this fit with your image of God?

 Look at the following words and put a tick against the ones you think describe God:

angry	kind	patient	irritable	cross
firm	easy-going	distant	gentle	approachable
threatening	moody	accepting	annoyed	unpredictable

(Use a dictionary if any of these are unclear.)

'Slow to anger' describes someone who has a friendly, not an irritable character.

 Two Old Testament verses which reflect God's character are Jeremiah 9:24 and Micah 7:18. What do they tell us about God? (In both cases you can see what they say about God without having to know too much about the context, although of course knowing the context will help you better understand the significance of what is said each time.)

 Jesus takes another Old Testament theme, that of friendship with God, and applies it quite widely. Who does it apply to in the Old Testament, and who does Jesus reapply it to? See Exodus 33:11, 2 Chronicles 20:7 (see also Psalm 25:14, where some translations use the phrase 'the friendship of Yahweh'). See also John 15:13-15.

Now consider whether the following statements are true or false:

1. God is difficult to please
2. He gives unconditional love to all
3. He loves us, but only if we keep his commands
4. To be afraid of God is only right because he is holy
5. God gets angry when we fail
6. God is waiting to punish us
7. He is easy to live with

Some people feel awkward with God in the sense that they expect him to be pointing out their faults and to be angry with them over small things. We should note that the word *satan* is actually the Hebrew word for 'accuser', and when the term comes to represent a particular being (Satan) in the New Testament, he is described particularly as 'the accuser of our brothers' (Revelation 12:10). God, in contrast, is more usually shown as our defender.

 A particularly powerful image to describe this is used in the Psalms: e.g. 59 (vv.9,16,17), 62 (vv.2,6) and 94:22. See also Proverbs 14:26. What strength can you draw from this image?

God is slow to anger. He is patient and long-suffering, but more than staying patient with us, he looks for opportunity to show compassion and grace.

 At times he shows this through discipline, but we should be careful to distinguish experiencing God's discipline from his anger. A key passage here is Hebrews 12:1-11, which provides a good context for understanding this idea. What would you say are the major differences here between anger and discipline?

For Further Study

A good passage to study which brings together many of the ideas in this section is Nehemiah 9, where the Israelites have recently returned from exile. They respond to hearing the words of the Book of the Law with a long prayer which helps them to focus on who God is, as he has revealed himself down through history. If you study this passage look for the way that their understanding of how God has acted in the past helps them in the present.

4 Abounding in Steadfast Loving Kindness and Truth, Maintaining Love to Thousands

4A The God of Love

The next phrase in Exodus 34:6-7 describes God as 'abounding in love and faithfulness' (NIV), but we shall see that both of these terms communicate more than perhaps they do at first sight. Before studying them in detail, it is worth noting the word *abounding*.

We noted the way that Paul describes God *lavishing* his grace on us (see the discussion of grace in section 3C above). In the same way we have here the idea of God being full to overflowing of the qualities listed.

 What other ideas come to mind with the word 'abundant'?

What is *Love*?

Unfortunately the word *love* is so widely used today that it has often lost a great deal of its meaning. A verse like 1 John 4:8 ('God is love') is so frequently quoted as if it were the entire biblical teaching about God that in fact the idea can have very little content. And in this Exodus passage that we are studying, 'love' is perhaps not the most helpful translation of the Hebrew word *hesed*. Some translations use 'goodness' or 'steadfast love' for this word. As usual, we can best understand *hesed* by looking carefully at some of the contexts where it is used.

Hesed

The word *hesed* in the Old Testament is often joined to a variety of nouns to fill out the sense in which God is a God of love.*

---

* **Note**: this is not the same as saying that *hesed* means all these extra things. In fact, the way in which it is used suggests that it is quite a flexible word with not too much definite meaning, but that when used with other terms it helps us grasp the wide-ranging nature of God's love. Another way of putting this, with reference to Unit 2 ('Introduction to Hermeneutics'), is to say that we are more interested in a topical study than a word study here. The danger with a study of a word like *hesed* is that we confuse a general word which can be used in many ways with a word which has a special multiple-level meaning. Christians often make this mistake with the Greek word *agape*, as if it referred to a special kind of love just because it is used in many different ways in a wide variety of contexts. This is perhaps the classic example of the kind of word study mistake discussed in Unit 2.

Three particular nouns that combine with *hesed* are as follows:

hesed + *emeth*	(32 times)	'loyal love', 'faithful love', 'true love'
hesed + *rachum*	(15 times)	'tender (true) love', 'tender (loyal) love'
hesed + *berit*	(7 times)	'covenantal love'

From this we can see that to say that God is love invites us to go on and say much more about what that love is really like. One way the Old Testament invites us to do this is through the examples of loving human relationships, as in the following passages:

> God's love is like the love evidenced between Ruth and Naomi, and between Ruth and Boaz. (Ruth 1:15-18, 2:11-12, 3:10) In what ways is Boaz's care for Ruth a picture of God's love for us?

> This love is also evidenced between Jonathan and David (1 Samuel 18:1-4, 20:6; 2 Samuel 1:26). See also David's treatment of Jonathan's family (2 Samuel 9:1-13). What words would you use to describe the love between David and Jonathan? Are they helpful for understanding God's love?

> Consider the ways in which you think of the word love. How should your understanding be altered to fit the biblical picture shown here? (You may find it helpful to approach this exercise using the word-web approach of section 2A).

The use of the phrase 'covenant of love' in the Old Testament is helpful for bringing out the kind of context in which love was understood then. (See Deuteronomy 7:9,12; 1 Kings 8:23; 2 Chronicles 6:14; Nehemiah 1:5, 9:32; Daniel 9:4.) As we see the word *hesed* being used so often in the sense of a serious love that will endure, we are perhaps justified in translating it a bit more strongly than 'love', and some kind of phrase like 'steadfast love' may be a helpful translation. This may be particularly useful in a world where 'love' is a cheap word reduced to sentences like 'I love chocolate'. Something more than this is in mind in the Old Testament!

> God's steadfast love is the kind of love celebrated in Psalm 136. If you are not familiar with this Psalm then look at it now. It is called 'antiphonal' since it invites a kind of call and response, with the refrain 'His love (*hesed*) endures forever'. God's love is eternal. Using ideas and events from your own life, as well as more general reflection,

write your own Psalm in the same format as Psalm 136. Note what kind of things the Psalmist says which allow him to affirm that God's love will last forever.

4B Truth and Faithfulness

The word 'truth' occurs in several different contexts in the Bible. One feature of the Hebrew language is that the word *emeth* can be translated as either 'truth' or 'faithfulness'. Of course this does not mean that in any particular case it means both of those things, but it suggests that the two concepts were not entirely unrelated.

It also explains why some translations describe Yahweh as 'abounding in truth' and others as 'abounding in faithfulness' in Exodus 34:6.

✍ What comes to mind with the word 'truth' for you?

Jesus uses this word in John 14:6, but although this verse is often quoted and frequently defended against various forms of religious pluralism, it is not perhaps immediately obvious what it means to describe someone as 'the truth'.

We need to be careful about our word study, but the following list of different uses of the word 'truth' in the Bible may be helpful for giving us an overview. Look up a representative number of the verses in each case.

'Truth' may refer to. . .
(1) A description which corresponds with the facts of the matter (as in a report of what has happened). See e.g. Genesis 42:6, Proverbs 12:19, John 10:41, Ephesians 4:25
(2) Faithfulness, honesty or reliability (this is especially a possibility when the word used is the Hebrew *emeth*). See e.g. 2 Kings 22:7, Psalm 25:10, 2 Corinthians 6:4-7
(3) The gospel of Christ (as opposed to some other gospel). See e.g. Galatians 2:5, 2 Corinthians 11:4
(4) God, as the God who is 'true' i.e. 'real'. See e.g. John 1:9, 4:23-24, 6:32, 15:1
(5) What is exposed or revealed (i.e. not hidden). See e.g. the idea of the Spirit of truth in John 14:17, 15:26, 16:13
(6) Some combination of these, where the context seems to suggest it.
Source: Summarised from A.C. Thiselton, *The Two Horizons* (Grand Rapids: Eerdmans, 1980), pp.411-415.

The context of John 14:6 suggests that it falls into the last category above, and that different aspects of 'truth' may be in mind in this verse.

✍ How would you explain the meaning of 'truth' in John 14:6?

If we now return to Exodus 34:6, we can see that 'Yahweh is abounding in *emeth*. . . ' suggests 'faithfulness' as much as 'truth' given that it is a character description.

For Further Study

📖 Study Psalm 89, which is full of references in various ways to God's faithfulness. Make a list of the ways in which God shows faithfulness. (Note especially v.28)

4C Maintaining Love for Thousands

Again various translations can help us get a feel for the meaning of this phrase, which also uses the word *hesed* (see above), and is sometimes translated as 'keeping love (*or* steadfast love) for thousands.'

Perhaps the key thing to note here is that having just stated that he is *abounding in love*, Yahweh now emphasises this by saying that this love will be *maintained*. He not only begins, but sees through and completes a relationship.

One of the great unsolved questions of our knowledge of the Hebrew language concerns the word 'thousand'. This often complicates our understanding of large numbers in the Old Testament, but here allows some translations (such as the NRSV) to translate this as 'keeping steadfast love for the *thousandth generation*'. This may or may not be accurate, but it does draw out even further the immense commitment of Yahweh to his people which this verse is showing.

In the New Testament we read that God is able to do more than we ask or imagine (Ephesians 3:20), and this characteristic is a recurring theme throughout the Bible. We could describe it as God's 'largeheartedness'.

✍ What for instance is the extent of God's plan when he calls Abram? How far ahead is He looking? (See Genesis 12:2-3)

> Although throughout Genesis Abram and others give God plenty of reason not to persevere with them, He always does. See especially Genesis 22:16-18 and 24:60 for re-emphases of God's promise.

The blessing to all nations envisaged by this covenant is taken into the New Testament focused on Jesus as the Messiah (which also, of course, was signalled in advance by God, see Isaiah 9:7). This can give us confidence that God will even now maintain his love throughout all generations until his purposes are fulfilled.

For Further Study

> The theme of expectancy about God fulfilling his purposes and maintaining his love is clear in many New Testament passages. You could study either Colossians 1:15-20 or Ephesians chapter 1 as examples.

> Note also how God's love for his people worked out in evangelism, which in itself is a way in which his purposes are worked out. (See for example Matthew 9:36)

5 Forgiving Wickedness, Rebellion and Sin and by no means Clearing the Guilty

5A Sin and Its Consequences

To understand the significance of Yahweh forgiving wickedness, rebellion and sin, all good 'religious' words, we really need to work first at understanding what sin is and what it means. The following Old Testament words give us a start:

avon	from a verb meaning 'to make crooked' and signifying moral and spiritual perversion
pesha	rebellion, revolt or lawlessness
hata'ah	sin; 'missing the mark', anything less than wholeness

The first of these words suggests a helpful way of looking at the concept of sin: the perverting of something which might have been good, but which is put to a wrong use. The greatest wickedness, in these terms, is to pervert the character of God, e.g. in spiritual manipulation (which is the background to the 'unforgivable sin' of blasphemy in the Holy Spirit in Mark 3:23-29 and parallel passages).

This perversion of what God requires is at the heart of the story of the fall (Genesis 3), which leaves us as humans unable, by our own efforts, to be perfect.

 Isaiah 53:6 is a prophecy of how Yahweh will lay on his servant the iniquity (*avon*) of us all. This idea draws on an image used in Leviticus 16:22. What is that image and what is the context of it (i.e. the particular Jewish celebration being described)?

The Old Testament Sacrificial System

This last observation leads us on to a brief look at the system established by God in the Old Testament to deal with sin. In particular the opening chapters of Leviticus describe five different types of offering set up both to maintain and restore a right relationship with God. (Leviticus 1-5 details these sacrifices, with 6-7 giving additional conditions for them).

Exercise

Complete the following chart of these offerings:

	type of offering	*purpose*	*what was offered*
Lev 1	burnt offering	to gain divine favour	perfect male animal
Lev 2	——	thanksgiving	——
Lev 3 (+22)	peace offering	——	——
Lev 4:1-5:13	——	——	depended on who offered it
Lev 5:14-19	——	——	a perfect ram

The major focus of the sacrificial system was the Day of Atonement, described in Leviticus 16. See especially vv.21-22 and v.30. We have already noted the link between v.22 and later descriptions of the Messiah. One other point is to note the difference between this repeated sacrifice and the sacrifice offered by Jesus.

See Hebrews 10, and especially vv.11-14. What is significant here about Jesus' sacrifice, in this context?

Thus we can see that the God who is described in Exodus 34 as forgiving wickedness, who has just been described as maintaining love to thousands, is the same God who is revealing himself through Jesus in the New Testament.

Forgiveness

The above study should help us to understand the terrible seriousness of sin. To use our earlier language, in forgiving us God makes straight our crookedness. Forgiveness takes sin seriously, just as the Old Testament sacrificial system did. God does not pretend that our sin did not matter after all, but rather accepts the consequences of it and still goes ahead and forgives us.

 What *emotions* are involved in forgiveness? Do a spider diagram around the word: FORGIVENESS

5B By no means Clearing the Guilty

The danger with grasping the forgiveness of God, as described in the above section, is that it then becomes possible to take it for granted and fail to appreciate it. Perhaps for this reason the statement of forgiveness in Exodus 34:7 is immediately followed by a contrast which, when properly understood, actually emphasises what we have just been considering, rather than contradicting it. The NIV communicates the contrast by inserting the word 'Yet': 'Yet he does not leave the guilty unpunished . . . '.

It is not that God is an angry God who is occasionally satisfied or occasionally happy with us. Rather, in the context of this Exodus 34 passage, God is a compassionate and loving God who nevertheless will not be mocked, and if ultimately people refuse to accept his forgiveness and compassion then he must punish sin.

Resolution

A helpful way of looking at this is to see the sacrificial system, and its fulfilment in Christ, as offering *reconciliation* between humans and God. It restores a broken relationship. But if the brokenness is not resolved in that (positive) way, then it must ultimately be resolved in another way, through a punishment which is, in fact, fully deserved.

This understanding of God is also what is meant when we use the term **holy**. To call God holy is to remind ourselves that he is totally 'set apart' from us, and in particular that he cannot tolerate sin. If our sin is not dealt with through atonement (resolution), then it will be dealt with through the inevitable punishment which comes when the holy comes into contact with the unholy (or sinful).

 This is the background to such difficult passages as the death of Uzzah in 2 Samuel 6:1-7. Here we see unholiness confronting holiness in the shape of the ark of God. Write in your own words the reason for Uzzah's death.

This perspective would perhaps be too much to bear if we had not first been assured by Yahweh of his compassion and steadfast love. Our God of love is not some weak-willed 'teddy bear' or 'grand-daddy' in the sky who loves everyone regardless. He is a holy God who cannot accept sin, who will not pretend that the guilty are innocent, but who still offers his unending compassion and his gracious forgiveness to us.

Exercise

Reflect on how you approach God for forgiveness. Think of some particular sin for which you have asked forgiveness. What are your thoughts *now* about that sin and are they in line with this teaching on resolution and reconciliation?

Are there any practical steps you need to take now, perhaps in prayer? Take time to reflect on this.

The Third and Fourth Generation

We must look briefly at the final phrase of this revelation. Perhaps the best way to understand it is to draw a distinction between whether God still counts our guilt against us and the different idea of whether we live with the consequences of our sin. This distinction to some extent holds even when we are forgiven: we may be forgiven for instance for illegally wasting money, but the money is still gone. The consequences of a sin may just have to be lived with.

The point being made here is that our sin affects not just us but those around us.

 Ezekiel 18 is a passage which further suggests this line of thought. What does Ezekiel argue here about who is punished for sin? But who suffers from the kinds of sin described in this passage?

5C Summary

When Yahweh has finished speaking, we go on to read in Exodus 34:8 'Moses bowed to the ground at once and worshipped.' Our aim in this unit has been not just to know about God, but to grow in the process of knowing God. As we have seen God reveal his character so, hopefully, we have been able to open ourselves up more and more to him. We are, astonishingly, welcome in his presence.

Like Moses, we too should respond in worship. We finish with some words from Hebrews 10:22-23:

'Let us draw near to God with a sincere heart in full assurance of faith, having our hearts sprinkled to cleanse us from a guilty conscience and having our bodies washed with pure water. Let us hold unswervingly to the hope we profess, for he who promised is faithful.'

Memory Verses

Exodus 34:6-7
Hebrews 10:22-23

Unit Four
Understanding Ourselves

Outline and Notes

This unit builds on our understanding of God in Unit 3. In an age when self-analysis and counselling are becoming more popular, where does the Christian stand in terms of an appropriate self-image for a child of God?

Aims

The Global Action training program goals include the aims that at the end of their Global Action training the student will:

- be able to communicate appreciation for his/her position, identity and acceptance in Christ
- take responsibility for his/her choices and actions
- handle money and possessions with integrity
- have recognised and begun exercising his/her spiritual gifts in the body of Christ

Study Objectives

As well as laying the foundation for the above training goals, this unit will enable you to:

- say what a person is
- describe an objective basis for our self-image
- assess steps which may need to be taken in changing behaviour

Unit Outline

1 Personhood

 1A Introduction
 1B You and Your 'Self'
 1C A Biblical View of a Person
   The Image of God
   Created for Relationship
   What are we made of?
 1D Definition
   Summary

2 Self-image

 2A The Importance of a Good Self-image
   Jesus: Our Model?
 2B Where Does Our Self-image Come From?
 2C Refocusing Your Self-image

3 Needs and Boundaries

 3A Introduction
 3B Our Needs
   When Needs are Not Met
 3C A Model for Changing Behaviour
 3D Responding to Life's Hurts
 3E Boundaries

4 Using the Will

 4A The Will
   God's Will
 4B Guidance
   But God told me..

5 Spiritual Gifts and Personality

 5A What are Spiritual Gifts?
 5B How can you discover your Spiritual Gifts?
   Spiritual Gift Questionnaires

1 Personhood

1A Introduction

What is a person?

This apparently abstract question lies behind many practical issues which we shall be considering in this unit, and indeed throughout our lives.

It is especially important to address it because we live in a self-obsessed age. Not only does the world around us spend enormous amounts of time and money discovering its 'true self', but many Christian bookshops around the world have their shelves packed with books on how to help yourself be a better person; how to develop this or that skill; how to have a better self-image, etc.

Linked with this is the common belief that we are all innocent victims of other people's mistakes and errors. We are told that nothing is really our fault anymore. We can blame everything on someone else, or some circumstances which affected us badly, or the problems we had in childhood, or perhaps on some evil spiritual enemy. Very few people today talk about *sin* as the root of our problems.

We will come back to some of these points, but first we need to find the right balance. And to do that we need to spend time looking at God's perspective on who we are, and developing a biblical view of humanity.

1B You and Your 'Self'

There is some confusion amongst Christians over the idea of 'self'. On the one hand we often hear people say 'I need to discover myself: to find out who I really am', which sounds fine. But on the other hand we hear others say 'No, we must lose ourselves in Christ, and not concentrate on who we are at all'. That also sounds worthwhile. Why this confusion?

Probably one of the reasons for this kind of confusion is the word 'self'. It is being used differently at different times. Some people find it helpful to distinguish between two different ideas connected with the word 'self' in the Bible:

(1)   the self which is your **identity**

        and

(2)   the self which we will call the **sin principle**

Another way of getting at this distinction is to look at the difference between who God has created you to be (identity) and your experience of battling with sin in your daily life (the 'sin-principle').

 The Greek word *sarx* has been a constant problem for translators. One of its basic meanings is 'flesh', which is not a positive or negative idea: e.g. 'A man will be united to his wife, and the two will become one flesh (*sarx*)' (Mark 10:7-8). But another meaning corresponds to our idea of 'sin principle', and the NIV often translates it as 'sinful nature' when it is used this way. Look up Romans 7:5-25 for a passage where this principle is described clearly (the word *sarx* occurs in vv.5, 18 and 25). Notice also the contrast in Galatians 5 between verses 19 and 22. Do you think that 'sinful nature' is a good way of understanding 'self' when it is used in this way?

Because *sarx* has sometimes been translated 'flesh' even when it is being used in this second way, some people have developed the view that *who we are* is determined by this negative idea.

It is important to keep these two different uses of the word 'self' in view through our study. In the remainder of section 1 we look at *identity*. Section 2 will build on this with a study of *self-image*, where again there can be confusion if we are not clear about what we mean by 'self'.

1C A Biblical View of a Person

We don't have to read very far in the Bible to get the key insight into our humanity:

 Read Genesis 1:27 and 2:7. What are the basic truths taught here?

But this does not solve our problems, because what does it mean to be made in the image of God? You may not be too sure about this. Spend a moment writing down your own answer to this question.

The Image of God

This phrase is mainly used in the New Testament to refer to Jesus.

 Look up 2 Corinthians 4:4, Philippians 2:6 and Colossians 1:15 (NB: many translations do not always use the phrase 'image of God' to translate the different Greek phrases, which use words like *eikon* or *morphe*, or, in Hebrews 1:3, *character*).

In Hebrews 1:3 we can see quite clearly why the phrase refers particularly to Jesus: God who is unseen is *represented* by Jesus, who is such an exact representation that he is the radiance of God's glory.

But we get a fuller picture as far as humanity is concerned from the Old Testament, particularly Genesis.

 Look up Genesis 1:26-27; 5:1; 5:3; 9:6.

The key idea, especially in the first and last of these references is this: God creates humankind and leaves them to rule the earth *in his place*. Genesis 1:26 can best be translated 'Let us make man to be our image'. In Genesis 9:6 the point is not (primarily) that murder is forbidden, but that where God would be the one to bring about justice on those who murder, he gives this responsibility to human beings in his place. We are thus representatives of God. Our task on earth, as creatures, is to do the will of our creator, who has put us on earth for this purpose.

We can see then that the NT use of *image of God* to refer to Jesus fits exactly with this idea (and so does the other NT use of the phrase in James 3:9). Clearly there is some sense in which the phrase refers to *the way we are* (how we are made) but we must say that none of the biblical verses fill out this idea in any particular way. So we must focus instead on what they do make clear: that **image of God** is primarily a description of us from the point of view of how we are to live.

(Some of the points made here are also made, with further references, in D.J.A. Clines, 'Image of God' in G.F. Hawthorne, R.P. Martin and D.G. Reid (eds.), *Dictionary of Paul and his Letters* (Downers Grove, Ill: IVP, 1993), pp. 426-428.)

How would you express in your own words the idea that 'image of God' refers to how we should live? Can you think of examples of how we should live given that we are made in the image of God?

Created for Relationship

One significant point which comes out of the creation story in Genesis 1-2 is that we are made *to be in relationship*. In Genesis 1:26 we read God saying 'Let us make humankind in our image; according to our likeness'. The 'us' here has always been difficult to understand, with some arguing that it refers to the Trinity, although we must accept that the author of Genesis is unlikely to have been thinking this. Others see some kind of angelic reference. But whatever it means exactly, one point is clear: God is already *in relationship* at this point of creating humans.

The other way to approach this issue is from the other creation account, in Genesis 2. After all the things which have been found 'good' in creation, the first exception is given in 2:18.

 What is 'not good'? What is God's response?

Thus we see that, even in the perfect, pre-Fall world, *relationship* was essential to being fully human. We should also note that among the first consequences of sin as recorded in Genesis 3 are hiding from God (v.8) and blame-shifting (v.12): both of which are breakdowns in relationships.

Finally, even if the Trinity is not in view in Genesis 1, we can see that the God who is Trinity, three persons in perfect relationship, still offers a model of what it means to be a *person* in this relationship sense. To use the terms of our 'image of God' discussion again, this is looking at humans from the point of view of *how we are to live* rather than *what we actually are*, which we must briefly consider below.

 In what ways do we see the effects of individualism and relationship breakdown in the world around us as part of human rebellion against God?

What are we made of?

Another feature of the biblical view of a person, which we do not have time to go into, is that we do not come divided up into several parts. People sometimes appeal to 1 Thessalonians 5:23 to say that we can be divided into spirit, soul and body, but this idea runs against all that Paul teaches, and in this verse itself he is probably saying that these different aspects of us are inseparable. (Note: he is asking God to sanctify us through and through, i.e. in every way, such as spiritually, bodily . . . etc. These are different ways of looking at us as humans, not different parts of us). This idea of seeing separate parts of us goes back to Greek thought and not to the Bible.

The main reason for mentioning this is to help us avoid trying to separate out our spiritual life from our life in general. We do not have a spiritual part of us which needs to be given a certain amount of time each day. Rather, we are completely spiritual beings, who also have physical needs, and relationship needs, etc. We will return to this later.

Application . . . ?

What causes stress: Workload? Spiritual warfare? Poor eyesight? Loneliness? It could be any of these things. This is why our study is not just an academic exercise about 'personhood'. If we are thinking biblically about ourselves, then we can see that our stresses could be from any area of our life. Do not tell everyone you are 'really under attack' if the actual problem is that you need to get more sleep. Or if you are often tired perhaps you need to spend less time working at your desk and more time exercising. You may be able to think of other applications to your own situation.

1D Definition

With all this in mind we can attempt a definition of the word 'self':

Your *self* is *person* in essentially the same way as God is person. Being in the *image of God* means that you do what God would do if he was in your place. 'Self' is not a negative word (as in selfish) and does not primarily refer to your *flesh* (which in some Bible translations is your *sinful nature*).

 In *The Universe Next Door* (Downers Grove: IVP, 2nd edition, 1988) James Sire describes a person as having two main characteristics (see especially pp.30-39):

(1)   Self-reflection = the ability to reflect on who we are and what we do

(2)   Self-determination = the ability to make choices which affect who we are and what we do

Do you think these two points cover the main things which make us different from other animals? Is there anything else? Would our study of the image of God make you want to add something to this list? What would you add?

Summary

What key things come out of our study?

- we are created to be God's representatives on earth. This has many moral and ethical implications.
- we are created to be in relationship with God and his creation
- we are whole people, or at least created to be whole people. We cannot be divided up into different sections.

Perhaps it is no coincidence that in societies where people experience a lot of loneliness and isolation, many have tried to look inside the person for solutions (e.g. in counselling or psychotherapy), and while this can be a help, it misses one of the roots of the problem: the loss of a sense of relationship and human worth that comes from being part of a wider society. This in turn is a loss which comes from our society's loss of belief in God: since our relationship with God is a part of who we are.

2 Self-image

2A The Importance of a Good Self-image

Continuing to think of our 'self' as our identity, we come now to the question of self-image. Here in particular we find confusion, and sometimes a great deal of so-called 'psychobabble'. What is the role, if any, of a positive or healthy self-image?

Jesus: Our Model?

Jesus' own view of himself may be a good place to start. (We say it *may* be because the situation is complicated by a long debate about how much Jesus was aware of his own divinity, and the observation that Jesus is unlike us anyway in being more than just human. However, he was fully human too, and so some good points may be made.)

Read John 13:1-5 and consider the following questions:

- What is the context? (What is Jesus about to say and do?)
- What is 'the time' which 'had come'? (see John 12:23-33 also)
- What does Jesus now show his disciples? (v.1)
- The phrase 'to the end' is sometimes translated as 'the full extent' or sometimes as 'to the end of his life/time on earth'. What difference does this make?
- In v.3 what kind of self-understanding does Jesus have?
- What does Jesus do in the light of his self-understanding?

> "From the platform of this personal integrity, he stepped down to serve the disciples."
> Is this is a good summary of what we can learn here?

One of the most familiar, and important, passages from the Bible is very clear:

> 'Love the Lord your God with all your heart and with all your soul and with all your mind. This is the first and greatest commandment. And the second is like it: Love your neighbour as yourself.'
>
> Jesus, in Matthew 22:37-38
>
> (See also Leviticus 19:18; Matthew 19:19)

But is this an implied order to love ourselves? Does this passage mean, as is often argued, that we should be loving ourselves so that we can then love others?

John Stott has argued that it does *not* mean that. Here is an outline of part of his argument:

> This command is not to love both yourself and your neighbour, but rather 'to love my neighbour as much as, in fact, I love myself. That is, self-love is not a virtue that Scripture commends, but one of the facts of our humanity that it recognises and tells us to use as a standard.' We already know how we want to be treated, hence Matthew 7:12 (the 'golden rule').
>
> But this does not mean that the concept of *self-acceptance* is wrong, just that: 'the ultimate basis for our positive self-image must be God's acceptance of us in Christ.' Stott summarises by saying: 'We need to learn to affirm all the good within us, which is due to God's creating and recreating grace, and ruthlessly to deny (i.e. repudiate) all the evil within us, which is due to our fallenness . . . True self-denial leads to true self-discovery.'
>
> Summarised from John R.W. Stott, 'Must I Really Love Myself?' *Christianity Today*, May 5, 1978.

> What do you think of Stott's argument?
> • Does he understand Matthew 22:38 correctly?
> • If not, how would you defend a different understanding?
> • Is he talking about our identity with self or the sin-principle which we discussed earlier? (or both? or neither?)

Note: Ultimately, the issue is not how we understand Matthew 22:38, since we can be sure that Jesus did not have our modern idea of 'self' in mind when he was speaking. You could thus, for instance, agree with Stott's summary without agreeing that he has understood Matthew 22:38 correctly.

2B Where Does Our Self-image Come From?

Although using a slightly different term than 'self-image', Joanna and Alister McGrath sum up very helpfully the basic idea:

> Self-esteem consists of a global evaluation or judgement about personal acceptability and worthiness to be loved, which carries with it pleasant or unpleasant feelings. It is strongly related to the perceived views of the person by important others in his life.

Joanna and Alister McGrath, *The Dilemma of Self-Esteem*, p.29

Different people working through this unit will be at different stages in assessing themselves. The following exercise may help you to evaluate where your own self-image comes from:

Exercise

| | Describe yourself. | How do you feel about these descriptions? | Why? |

1. Physically
2. Emotionally
3. Intellectually
4. Morally
5. Strengths
6. Weaknesses

Analysis

Now try to describe the basis on which you came to the above conclusions

e.g. 'My description of my intellect is based on the marks that I received at school'

1. My description of my physical build is based on . . .
2. My description of my emotional make-up is based on . . .
3. My description of my intellect is based on . . .
4. My description of my morality is based on . . .
5. My description of my strengths is based on . . .
6. My description of my weaknesses is based on . . .
7. My description of my special skills is based on . . .

Remembering our study of what makes a human being in section 1, we can see that it is all these different factors added together which make up our self-image. We are constantly receiving messages about how well or badly we fit in with other people, and with the world around us. If you are doing these exercises with others who know you, you may be receiving very different messages from what you are used to. Why might that be?

Alternative Exercise

Another way in which you can develop your understanding of yourself is to describe two people whom you like and with whom you get on well, and then to ask yourself what qualities you have in common with them. Do they reflect something of yourself which you like?

Then describe two people with whom you do not get on. What qualities do you have in common with them? Do they reflect any aspect of yourself with which you are dissatisfied? In which areas are you in competition with them?

2C Refocusing Your Self-image

We should not stop at this point, which gives the impression that there is no fixed point to relate to and that we are all stuck with the way we have grown up, and the inputs we have received along the way.

We need to remember first that **everyone has value** because everyone has been created by God. All created men and women have the same image, and we need to affirm the value of every man and woman in God's eyes. But at the same time this does not mean that sin is not important, or doesn't matter. The question is then: how can we be realistic in the face of our sinfulness?

As Christians we can be realistic because God has dealt with sin in a way which both overcomes it and also accepts its seriousness: through the death of Jesus on the cross. We could say that our worth comes from our creation, compromised by our fallenness, but that it is emphasised, and refocused, in our **redemption**.

Thus on one level we are still a mess. We have every reason to have a low self-image! We are still sinners who are failing daily in our attempts to serve God. On another level God looks on us and sees the perfect righteousness of Christ (see, for instance, 2 Corinthians 5:21). We will examine this tension further in Unit 5 (on Justification and Sanctification).

Therefore the question — Should I have a good or a bad self-image? — is a bad question. It is asking you to state in one way what needs to be stated differently on different levels. Popular psychology often makes this mistake when it comes up with one formula for how we should feel about ourselves. (More serious psychology recognises at once that life is never this simple.)

 The gospels are full of stories of people whose self-image was transformed by a meeting with Jesus, but the reason for this is always more objective than 'feeling good'; it is due to their ability to see themselves as Jesus sees them. In other words, they go from one way of looking at themselves to the other. Examples include Mary in John 12:1-8, the woman with bleeding in Mark 5:25-34, and, perhaps, Peter in John 21:15-23. There are many others. In what ways can you relate to them?

Refocusing does not just happen, it takes an effort of the will. Our ability and/or our desire to make an effort of will in this area will be discussed below in section 4. First we turn to some of the ways in which our lives actually work out the implications of being anchored to Christ while still suffering from tremendous negative influences, as well as struggling with sin.

3 Needs and Boundaries

3A Introduction

Refocusing on Christ does not mean that we have no more problems. We continue to experience life as a mixture of good and bad. Sometimes problems run very deep inside us, going to the heart of our character. We need to accept here the limitations of a self-study (or group-study) course like this one. Some issues are best worked out between you and a more experienced person who can get to know you and provide help, or counsel. It would be out of place to discuss counselling here, although some suggestions for reading in this area are given in the Appendix. And in any case our aim in this unit is not so much to look at problems, but more to achieve a constructive view of how we can understand ourselves in a helpful way. Most importantly we have to learn what kind of responses and responsibilities are *appropriate* in different situations.

3B Our Needs

The basic personal need of each personal being is to regard himself as a worthwhile human being . . . Basic personality functions all depend upon meeting the central need to regard oneself as worthwhile.

Larry Crabb

There are several Christian myths about this subject:

- it is wrong to have needs
- all my needs are met in Jesus
- real Spirit-filled Christians don't have needs
- we should deny ourselves our needs: it's more spiritual . . .

God has appointed appropriate ways of expressing our needs and meeting our needs. This is not saying that all wants and desires are legitimate, so we will have to lay a careful biblical foundation on this subject before discussing how needs may be met. In this section we are referring to legitimate needs.

Study Exercise

A key passage on this subject is Genesis 2, and it is particularly helpful since it looks at Adam in his pre-fall state, so none of the needs here are a result of sinfulness.

Read through the passage and ask yourself to what extent you see needs in the following categories:

- Dignity, Worth, Value
- Meaning, Purpose, Significance
- Intimacy, Belonging, Affirmation

If humans have needs in all these areas, what exactly went wrong in Genesis 3, in these terms? Was there a wrong approach to need fulfilment, or would you rather say that Adam failed to see a clear line between what he needed and what he wanted? In which of the above categories did he go wrong?

 What light does Jeremiah 2:13 shed on human needs in terms of our relationship with God?

When Needs are Not Met

When people's needs are unmet then they often make excessive demands on those around them. A loss of dignity, or of meaning, or of valuable relationships will lead to pain and hurt, and that hurt is real. Nobody can survive for long without their dignity, or some understanding of their significance, or a relationship network around them.

Working as a missionary often produces great strain in precisely these areas. All the usual ways in which you measure your purpose, or social position, or network of friends, are thrown up in the air and it can be a painful process to re-position yourself in a new environment.

If you are suffering from stress or hurt in these areas then that may be quite normal. But what can you do about it?

Take the example above of emotional needs for intimacy, belonging and affirmation. If God has made us this way then God will have a way of meeting our needs, even if it is not the way we might choose ourselves. One of the classic behaviour patterns which people can fall into here is of bottling up frustration in these areas, and then trying to meet their needs illegitimately, perhaps through immoral behaviour (such as a sexual affair, or the use of pornography). This is then followed by remorse and guilt, which forces the person away from the immoral behaviour until the pressure becomes too great and they turn again to immorality. The resulting behaviour is a cycle of addiction and anxiety. How can this cycle be broken?

> Romans 12:1-2 suggests that one key is the renewing of our . . . .? What is the difference between what Paul says here and advice to simply try harder?

Unmet needs may work themselves out in different types of problem in someone's life. **A need cannot be healed!** It must be met: either through being fulfilled or somehow dealt with realistically. What is most important is that you are able, in your own life, to think clearly and biblically about your life, and understand that *God as Lord of your life desires that you will not try and meet your needs without involving him in every way, and he wants this for you because that is best for you*. In the long run, God is not trying to make your life difficult, even if in the short term some major surgery is required.

A Private Exercise

Spend some time considering what your needs are and how they are met. Do you need to reorientate your life in any way? Are you thinking correctly about God? Perhaps more Bible study would be at the heart of your response to this study. Do you believe that obedience to God is for your own benefit as much as anything else?

3C A Model for Changing Behaviour

Larry Crabb has developed a helpful model which allows us to put into practice some ways of dealing with these issues in daily living (see his *Effective Biblical Counselling* (London: Marshall Pickering, 1977), ch.9, pp.139–153.) The following is a modified version of his model.

(1) If our **behaviour** is a problem then, perhaps through exhortation from others, we may be able to develop a more biblical plan of action and carry it out. *But behaviour is often influenced by our feelings and emotions, so if step (1) does not work:*

(2) If our **emotions and feelings** are a problem then, perhaps through encouragement from others, we may be able to address our feelings and develop biblical, spirit-controlled feelings. *But feelings are often influenced by our inner beliefs, so if step (2) does not work:*

(3) If our **deep inner beliefs** are a problem then we need to change our way of thinking, and this is best done through biblical teaching and Bible study.

3D Responding to Life's Hurts

Being wounded and being sinful are not the same things. Jesus was severely sinned against, but he never responded sinfully.

How did Jesus respond? (Some indications of Jesus' attitude are given in 1 Peter 2:23; Hebrews 2:10, 4:14, 5:7-8, 12:3)

We, on the other hand, find self-protecting ways of dealing with life's hurts (Jeremiah 2:13, Isaiah 30:15-16; Psalm 81:10-16). What kind of ways are these?

When we respond like this, we are failing to take hold of the truth about God's care for us (see the above section). Instead we open ourselves up to reap what we sow, to use Paul's image.

Look up Galatians 6:7-10. In the light of this passage how should we respond to life's hurts? (e.g. when we are insulted, or ridiculed, or ignored, or left out . . .)

One clear example of all this is in the area of **judgement**. In Matthew 7:1-5 Jesus gives a serious warning about judging. What other biblical warnings are there? (Romans 2:13; Romans 14:4; James 2:12-13; Hebrews 12:15) Do you think this means that it is always wrong to judge, or that judgement carries certain serious responsibilities?

This study of judgement leads us on to a broader consideration of what is our own responsibility and what is not. Some burdens are not ours to carry.

3E Boundaries

Genesis 1:28: we are made in the image of God, and we were created to take responsibility for certain tasks. It is important to know what we are responsible for and what we are not. Confusion in this area creates problems. The term **boundaries** is simply a way of making the point that we have to draw a line somewhere in terms of what is in and what is out of our area of responsibility.

 Look at the Good Samaritan in Luke 10:30–35. In what way does he draw boundaries between what he will do and will not do for the suffering man? Does he place upon himself an impossible burden?

In a Christian setting such as your church, or in mission work, for example you may experience the need to draw boundaries in many different areas. Wrong boundary setting can lead to the following:

- taking on another's responsibility
- over-work and workaholism
- misplaced and wrong priorities
- difficult co-workers
- critical attitudes
- conflicts with authority
- too high expectations from work or co-workers
- work-related stress into family life and personal life
- wrong gifting and placement

 Do you find yourself with problems in any of the above areas? If so, here are some questions to ask:

- what are the symptoms of the problem?
- what are the roots?
- what is the boundary conflict?
- who needs to take ownership?
- what is it that you need in the situation?

This topic is more complex than space will allow us to go into here. You should consult the book *Boundaries* by Henry Cloud and John

Townsend (Grand Rapids: Zondervan: 1992) for further thinking in this area. This section is a very brief summary of one or two of the main ideas developed by Cloud and Townsend, who also provide several helpful examples of how this approach works out in practice.

In particular their book allows you to examine the difficult issues of how boundary setting relates to our rights as Christians. It is sad that we need to consider this, but it is often true that people abuse the concept of authority and accountability and use it to have a negative influence on other Christians. In cases like these you may need to be thinking about how drawing boundaries between what is and is not acceptable could be a practical step to resolving difficulties.

4 Using the Will

4A The Will

What do we mean by 'will'? Remembering our earlier discussions of what it means to be human, we mean here the way in which we make decisions: to talk of our will is one way of talking about us, by focusing on our decision-making abilities and on how we manage or take control of our desires.

The will is one of the distinctives of being human. It is one of the capacities which distinguishes us from the rest of creation. It is because we have a will that we may make choices, that we can be obedient, and that we have to live with the consequences of our decisions. (This is at the heart of Genesis 2:16-17). All forms of slavery, whether physical, emotional or spiritual, violate this freedom and dignity.

The exercise of our will is part of our dignity and self-respect, as well as our responsibility as humans. Being God's people does not mean that we stop thinking carefully and then expect to be 'led' in all our decisions.

One example of the relationship between God's will for us and our own will is provided by Revelation 3:20. This verse is often taken out of context (though not perhaps very seriously) as applying to non-believers evangelistically. Jesus actually says it to believers. How do you see here the link between our own responsibility and God's will?

God's Will

Having a will is one of the ways in which we fulfil being made in the image of God, which as we saw was largely a question of acting in the way that God would want us to, and particularly making decisions which reflect the character of God.

How, then, has God revealed his will? It is one thing to say we must follow it, but how do we know what it is?

(1) **Through the Bible**. God has revealed moral and ethical principles in the Bible, as well as examples of specific guidance in certain situations. Particular ways in which God has done this through the Bible are:

(2) **Through history**. What God has done in human lives down through centuries stands as part of his self-revelation

(3) **Through Jesus**. God reveals himself most fully through Jesus, who then shows us certain aspects of God's will

(4) **Through the Holy Spirit**. In John 14:26 we read of how the Spirit will come after Jesus (see also John 16:7) and will teach us, reminding us of the teachings of Jesus.

> What is one of the biblical keys to determining the will of God? (Romans 12:2)

The above list makes it all sound very simple, but in fact the whole subject of knowing God's will is complicated and controversial, mainly because of the immense practical implications it has for living the Christian life.

4B Guidance

There are two opposite opinions about the subject of guidance which are both quite popular today:

(1) God has a particular will for your life which you must follow in all your decisions

(2) God sets boundaries and within those limits you must work it all out for yourself, and God doesn't mind which decisions you take.

Probably both of these statements are simplifications of the views involved, but they give us a start on the issues we have to consider.

View (1) draws on passages like Proverbs 3:5-6, Romans 12:1-2 and Colossians 1:9 for its general understanding. What do these passages teach about the will of God in your life?

All of these passages are open to being interpreted more generally: e.g. you could say that the application of all of these is more about learning general principles from the Bible so that we can live faithful lives.

View (2) takes this approach, and for those interested the work of Garry Friesen and J. Robin Maxson, *Decision Making and the Will of God* presents a thorough analysis of all the passages traditionally used to support view (1) and argues that all of them can be understood in line with view (2). On a general level their case is very strong.

Where both views have most difficulty is in dealing with biblical passages where God quite clearly made specific requests or commands, and intervened directly in leading someone in a specific situation. There are many examples of this:

- in choosing a marriage partner: Abraham's servant seeking a partner for Isaac (Genesis 24)
- in being 'called' into mission: Paul and Barnabas are set aside by the Holy Spirit (Acts 13)
- in changing ministry plans: Paul's vision to go to Macedonia (Acts 16:6-10)
- in looking after a child: Jesus' parents (Matthew 2:13-15)
- in the lives of the prophets (throughout the OT)

Look up these passages if you are not familiar with them

Both sides try and prove too much from this. View (1) argues that these examples are models for us always to follow. View (2) argues that they are unrepeatable historical events which are not models for us, and sometimes this view goes further and says that God never works that way any more.

You have another source to draw from in evaluating this subject: your own experience.

 If you have recently moved, or changed job (or both) then reflect on the way in which you made your decisions. How did you feel God was involved in them (if at all)? Are you prepared to have to make changes to some decisions depending on how things work out? Why or why not? In what way could you see God having a hand in that?

Both views can be taken to extreme. As a practical step you can consider the advice of wise believers when thinking through issues of guidance. There is more than a practical reason for doing this; there is a theological reason. The community of believers who make up the body of Christ is the place where the Holy Spirit is at work in transforming minds. You should expect other believers to be able to provide confirmation of God's will much of the time. Take the views of others seriously, even while remembering that they are not infallible.

 How would you express this idea, that there is an important role in the Christian community (e.g. your local church) for the Holy Spirit to guide other people to affirm or disagree with your sense of guidance?

But God told me . . .

If we ignore this sense of the Spirit-filled community of believers providing a way of checking what you think, then we are open to the worst possible form of bad 'guidance'. This typically involves someone saying 'God told me to . . . '. The result is often disastrous: 'God told me to marry you . . . '.

 What is wrong with speaking in this way?

You could refer back to Unit 1 for some of the reasons why humility is always appropriate in assessing God's word to us today. This approach certainly lacks humility. It is also very individualistic, which reflects a misunderstanding of how God works in people. The biblical emphasis is to see ourselves as part of the body of Christ. As a basic rule: be very cautious when someone talks this way; especially if they cannot show that other believers have some sympathy with what is being said. It might also be reasonable to expect God to confirm the message if it is true, in a way that convinces other people.

5 Spiritual Gifts and Personality

5A What are Spiritual Gifts?

Spiritual gifts are qualities or abilities or, sometimes, jobs and tasks, which are God-given and which allow the recipient to play a role alongside other believers in the body of Christ. Here are some exploratory questions to get you thinking about these gifts, and their relationship to your personality in general:

- do you have to have the gift of leadership to be a leader?
- are gifts natural talents that God uses?
- is it possible to serve God efficiently without knowing what your gifts are?
- is a spiritual gift something that other Christians recognise in you?
- if a Christian works as a school-teacher should they have the gift of teaching?
- can you ever criticise someone who is using a spiritual gift which you do not have?
- are all the gifts of the Holy Spirit found listed in the Bible?
- is the main purpose of spiritual gifts to help strengthen the body of Christ?

What do you think?

One linguistic observation is worth making: the Greek word for gift in most of the relevant biblical passages is *charisma*, but this in itself is not a spiritual word, as we can see from Romans 1:11 where Paul writes of *spiritual charisma*. In Paul's writing the *charismata* are indeed often spiritual, but they do not have to be. This might suggest that many so-called natural abilities or talents could be considered as *charismata*, and useful for building up the body of Christ.

The 'lists of gifts' which we have in the Bible seem always to be related to some specific purpose on the author's mind, or are even just examples of the kind of thing being discussed. We should therefore be careful about saying that the only gifts are those listed. As in our previous section, the ultimate issue is the role of the individual in the wider body of believers.

 The five main passages in the NT which are referred to for an understanding of spiritual gifts are Ephesians 4:11, 1 Corinthians 12:8-10, 1 Corinthians 12:28-30, Romans 12:6-8 and 1 Peter 4:11. Draw up a chart of these passages listing which gifts are noted where.

Study Exercise

Look at 1 Corinthians 12 as a whole to discover some of the biblical teaching on the wider purpose and nature of gifts.

5B How can you discover your Spiritual Gifts?

Your list is only a first step towards understanding spiritual gifts, since it is not immediately obvious what some of them are. Is the gift of being an apostle (Ephesians 4:11 and 1 Corinthians 12:28-30) for instance still valid today or did it refer only to the original apostles? What did Paul mean by it? This is a matter of some debate.

With 'gifts' being such a general word we need to be careful about putting too much weight on lists of gifts and their definitions and then making major decisions about our own lives and ministries based on them. The best approach is to see any 'analysis' of your gifts as a way of looking at general areas that you are good at or desire to grow in. The overall aim is this: try to avoid being stuck in jobs or tasks that you are not good at. This will lead only to frustration and will not build up the body of Christ. Put like this, of course, the whole topic places as much importance on your personality as your gifts.

 Do you think this is the best way to look at the subject? If not, how would you defend a different understanding?

Spiritual Gift Questionnaires

Spiritual gift questionnaires are simple tests designed to ask you certain questions which allow you to work out what your gifts are. We have not included one in this unit but they are easy to obtain. For instance, many books on spiritual gifts or on the Holy Spirit include one.

You need to be careful with these questionnaires. A quick review of the process of how you would compile one should illustrate the danger.

Suppose compiler A believes that your spiritual gift is something you are good at, then he will ask questions which basically all say 'Are you good at x, y, z . . . ?'. You will then score highly in areas you are good at, and look up your score in the chart at the end and conclude that this is your spiritual gift. Of course, all you have done is discover what compiler A thinks *you are good at*. If compiler B put together a test based on what you would like to do, then you will score highly on that instead, and perhaps come up with a different conclusion on what your gift is.

It is best to see these questionnaires as simply a way of focusing your thinking about areas you should explore more. In general, they work best when you have considerable experience to reflect upon in answering the questions.

Optional Exercise

Bearing in mind what has just been said, you may wish to do this exercise now or leave it until later. If you would like to, search for and work through a spiritual gifts questionnaire. Discuss your findings with someone who knows you.

Memory Verses

Matthew 22:37–38
Romans 12:1–2

Unit Five

Discipleship

Outline and Notes

This unit brings together in a practical way some of the implications of our understanding of God and of ourselves for the way we live and work together, and grow as Christians.

Aims

The Global Action training program goals include the aims that at the end of their Global Action training the student will:

- be progressing in demonstrating the fruit of the Spirit in daily living
- have a meaningful devotional life based on God's word, personal prayer and worship
- have participated in regular worship and fellowship with other believers
- be learning to exercise faith in God as a way of life and in response to challenges
- demonstrate progress in living a balanced and disciplined lifestyle
- be able to apply biblical teaching on repentance, confession and forgiveness in their relationships
- be seen to put into practice biblical teaching on loving, caring, esteeming and encouraging others
- be seen to put into practice the basic principles for handling interpersonal conflicts
- be learning to serve others willingly, sacrificially and unselfishly
- be learning to share cheerfully from his/her resources

Study Objectives

As well as laying the foundation for the above training goals, this unit will enable you to:

• take truths about discipleship and make them a part of your experience
• play a part in leading prayer meetings
• worship in a way that reflects biblical worship
• assess the appropriateness of your lifestyle for the ministry you are involved in
• explain how different aspects of your life fit into your understanding of discipleship

Recommended Reading

Part of the work for this unit is to read a book on discipleship. Some titles are recommended in the Appendix.

Unit Outline

1 What is a Christian?

1A   Introduction
1B   About You
1C   Justification and Sanctification
1D   Discipleship
       Two Exercises

2 Prayer

2A   Introduction: An Old Problem
2B   Biblical Examples of Prayer
       Prayer is Dependence on God
       The Lord's Prayer
2C   Prayer and Intercession
2D   Prayer Meetings

3 Worship

3A   Worship in the Bible
3B   'I Don't Feel Like Singing'

4 Lifestyle

4A   Introduction
4B   The Simple Lifestyle
4C   Being 'Worldly'
4D   Stewards of Creation
4E   Your Work

5 Relationships

5A   Introduction
5B   Unity
       Unity in Ephesians – A Study
5C   Implications
5D   Practical Unity

1 What is a Christian?

1A Introduction

The world should not be the way it is.

More than one writer has taken this as a starting point for an understanding of our topic in this unit: discipleship. Discipleship is the process of living a life in this world which will help the world become a different world. It is not just what you do, but what you think and feel and say and believe and want to become, too. It is, in this broad sense, 'following', which is where the word comes from (a 'disciple' was a 'follower'). It is, perhaps, everything you are, as you are in Christ.

 To help you consider what you already think, try answering this before going on to the question below: How would you define 'discipleship'?

A question: what makes someone a Christian?

- Is it something they believe?
- Something they do?
- A particular set of words which they say?
- Is it the presence of the Holy Spirit in their lives?
- Is it baptism?
- Is it knowing who Jesus was and is? If so, how much do they have to know?
- Perhaps it is knowing who Jesus was and is, and believing it?
- Is that what we mean by 'having a personal relationship with Jesus'?
- Is it the desire to do what Jesus did? Like preaching the gospel, healing the sick and raising the dead? Or just any one out of three?
- Do alternatives like casting out demons count?
- Or is that not enough: a Christian is someone who does even greater works than Jesus (John 14:12)?
- Or let's try again: is it someone who believes the Bible?
- All of the Bible? Or just some bits of it?
- What if you haven't read all of the Bible yet: how can you believe it?
- Is it someone who joins a mission and does "full-time Christian work"?
- Is it possible to be a Christian and not be a missionary? Isn't that disobedience?

- Is a Christian someone who believes the gospel and can explain it?
- Is it someone who goes to church?
- Is it someone who speaks in tongues?
- Someone who has been baptised as an adult? As an infant?
- Is the kingdom only open to little children? Or at least only to people who are like little children?
- Can someone be a Christian without knowing what sin is?
- What is sin, actually?

It is agreed that we do not have to agree on non-essentials. But you might feel that knowing what a Christian is, is perhaps an essential. So think through the above list of questions, and if possible discuss it with friends, and see if you do in fact agree on any or all of these definitions.

We have seen in Units 3 and 4 that who you are (and what you believe) affects your view of God. It will certainly affect your view of the Christian life.

 One major Bible college changed the title of one of its classes from 'Discipleship' to 'Spirituality' to give it a slightly different emphasis. What emphasis?

How would it affect your view of this unit if it had been called 'Spirituality'? Do you think the two words are interchangeable?

1B About You

Complete the following sentences:

 I am a Christian because . . .

Three activities which I do because I am a Christian are . . .

What I find most appealing about Jesus is . . .

Think about these, and write what is true of you, not what you think should be a good answer. Remember, this unit is for your benefit, not to prove to someone else that you know all about discipleship.

Let's focus in briefly on the second of those questions: three things you do. Consider two Christians, Andy and Zohar. Suppose Andy answered 'Going to church, reading the Bible and praying' and Zohar put 'helping at an inner-city playgroup for street children; playing tennis every Tuesday night and joining local political marches against government policy'.

Which of the four following judgements would you then want to agree with:

1.   Andy is more spiritual than Zohar

2.   Zohar is more spiritual than Andy

3.   They are both spiritual people

4.   Neither of them are spiritual people

If possible, discuss your view with someone else who has a different opinion. If this is not possible, write out 100 words in defence of your position, and then try and write out 100 words against it. Do you end up changing your mind?!

If you chose position 1 then this unit is for you, but if you chose option 2, then this unit is still for you! In fact, whatever option you chose this unit is for you. Remember this: spirituality may or may not be definable, and you may or may not have a good definition of discipleship; but the real issue is *how are you living?*

 Do you agree that how you live is more important than how well you can explain the way you live? Why or why not?

Some have put it this way: God sent his Son and not a doctrinal statement. Although this is a clever way of putting it, you may have to think about how far you actually agree with it.

1C Justification and Sanctification

These two words look quite imposing, and it would be great if we could get through this whole unit without them. But they do bring out two different concepts which we will find helpful as we go through the unit, so let's spend a moment looking at them in more detail. Here is the issue:

• You want to do what God wants. Perhaps you resolve to make an extra effort to be good in all areas of life and be the kind of person who is acceptable to God.

• On the one hand, this is clearly a good thing. On the other hand, it appears to be a denial of the gospel. Does the gospel not centre on the fact that we cannot be good enough to do what God wants?

- Perhaps the solution lies in the role of the Holy Spirit to empower us to do God's will. Is that true? Do you find that it works? Always? Sometimes?

What is going on here, and is probably a familiar experience to you, is that you are struggling to live out in practice what is true in theory. People use different metaphors to try and communicate this point. One of them is a *legal metaphor*: when Christ died on the cross he secured, in a way which we cannot fully understand from our human perspective, the forgiveness of our sins. It is sometimes explained by saying that *it is like a court-room situation where our crimes are no longer counted against us*. Note that this is a metaphor because God is not literally a judge trying us for certain crimes, and we are not really in a courtroom.

But the consequences of our sin are all around us: the world remains a fallen place and we live with the results of what we have done, just as the criminal, even if he is allowed to go free, lives with the consequences of his crimes, e.g. if he has murdered someone. The word theologians use to describe this is **justification**: God justifies the sinner, who is thus considered to be a righteous human being, even though life goes on and the person finds themselves far from perfect.

The word used to describe the process of living out that justification is **sanctification**. This comes from 'sanctify', which has a root meaning 'to set apart' or 'make holy'. It thus refers to the way in which we become Christ-like, on that day-to-day level. It is a life-long process.

This is very important in the Christian life. Many Christians are sure that they have been *justified*, and equally certain that when they die they will be *glorified*. But they are puzzled about what is going on in between. Such puzzlement certainly makes evangelism a confusing activity. 'Become a Christian' will be heard as 'become like me': and who wants to join a group of confused and directionless people?

But the problem is that even though you may realise this, that doesn't make it easy to do anything about it. Jesus' solution was perhaps best expressed in these words from John's gospel: 'I am the vine; you are the branches. If a man remains in me and I in him, he will bear much fruit; apart from me you can do nothing.' (John 15:5, and see v.8 especially in this context).

But what does 'remain in me' mean? You may need to look up some different views on this. It is an important question. Spend some time on it.

Are you justified? In what sense? In what way were you guilty? In what way are you no longer guilty? (Key passages for the concept of justification are Romans 3:21–4:25; 8:30, 33 and Galatians 2:15–3:29.)

Exercise

'Sanctification is the work of the Spirit, not us.' Try to discuss this statement with a friend or in a group, perhaps with one person giving a short speech agreeing with it, and a second person giving a speech disagreeing with it, and then each person commenting on the two presentations. Also discuss: what are the implications of your view of this statement for discipleship?

1D Discipleship

A disciple is a follower.

 Think of the disciples in the New Testament. Did they know where they were going? (e.g. in Mark you could look at 1:16–18; 2:14; 3:14–15; 4:10; 4:38; 5:31; 6:7–13; 6:37; 6:48–52; 7:17–18; 8:4; 8:14–21; 8:27–29. This is just in the first half of Mark, but is plenty to get a picture).

(Do you think there is a simple yes or no answer here?)

 What are the advantages and disadvantages of this definition: "A Christian is someone engaged on the path of discipleship"?

Personal Task

 Write a short piece (approx. 200 words) about your own experience as a Christian, and include some thoughts about how you would like to see yourself change over the next year, and over the next 10 years. Your 'experience' does **not** mean your 'testimony', but how you find living as a Christian works out in practice.

There is a lot to be said for keeping things simple in our understanding of discipleship. If you make prayer, or worship, or evangelism, or the simple lifestyle, or even Bible study the main thing in your life, then you are probably committing what the Old Testament calls idolatry. This is a simple idea but a difficult balance to hold: for a Christian, Jesus should be at the centre of everything.

Personal Reflection

What are the implications of each of the following statements:

> The Bible is at the centre of all we do
> Prayer is at the centre of all we do
> Worship is at the centre of all we do
> Jesus is at the centre of all we do.

Would you be happy for your church to adopt any or all of them?
For reflection, ask yourself:
Who or what **motivates** my life? And how is it working out at the moment?

Two Exercises

(1) Read a good book on discipleship. Choose one that will challenge you. Some recommendations are made in the Appendix. Write 200 words summarising the main things that the book taught you.

(2) For the next seven days (excluding Sunday, if you wish), keep a spiritual journal. Write for no more than an hour every day, and preferably write at the end of a period of quiet where you have been able to think about God and your life; or have been able to do a Bible study. The aim is to encourage you to reflect on your life with God. Sometimes having to write something down helps you to clarify it a little. You do not have to show what you write to anybody, so write in your own language, and be very honest.

2 Prayer

2A Introduction: An Old Problem

What could be simpler than prayer? Prayer is talking to God. It is obviously an important part of discipleship. But ask any Christian about it in depth, and we soon uncover familiar questions and realise that what is simple to do may not be easy to understand (or vice versa).

This section is not designed to confuse you, and it is good to point out now that you are probably already praying to God and if there are things we do not understand at all about prayer this hasn't stopped you so far, and it shouldn't stop you in the future!

The following story could be multiplied hundreds of times, but it does show the issues clearly.

Not long after Dallas Seminary was founded in 1924, bankruptcy knocked at its doors. By noon on one particular day, every creditor threatened foreclosure. That morning, the founders of the Seminary met to pray in president Lewis Sperry Chafer's office. They asked God to provide the needed funds. Harry Ironside was part of that prayer meeting. When it was his turn to pray, he prayed in his characteristically pointed manner: 'Lord, we know that the cattle on a thousand hills are thine. Please sell some of them and send us the money.'

Meanwhile, as these men were praying, into the seminary's business office came a tall Texan. Addressing a secretary, he said, 'I just sold two carloads of cattle in Forth Worth. I've been trying to make a business deal go through and it won't work, and I feel that God is compelling me to give this money to the seminary. I don't know if you need it or not, but here's the check.

Well aware of the seriousness of the seminary's financial situation, and knowing that it was for that purpose the founders were gathered in prayer, the secretary took the check to the door of the president's office and timidly knocked. When she finally got a response, Chafer took the check out of her hand and stared at it with amazement. The amount matched the exact size of the seminary's debt. Looking at the signature on the check, he recognised the name of the cattle rancher. Turning to Harry Ironside, he said, 'Harry, God sold the cattle!'

What a story! It demonstrates the reality that God is active in our everyday world. But for some this story may raise questions. Was God planning to allow the seminary to go under, but changed his mind when so many godly men gathered to persuade him otherwise? Would that Texan have come to the seminary with money even if these men weren't praying? Just what can we expect of prayer?

Lance Hartman, 'Does Prayer Change God's Mind?', *Discipleship Journal*, March/April 1994, Issue 80, pp.36–38.

These days we have no shortage of things to pray *for*, but we lack an understanding of *how* to pray, and we frequently reduce 'prayer' to 'intercession'. The solution to both of these problems is the same: a greater focus on what the Bible actually shows us about prayer. This is where we turn next.

2B Biblical Examples of Prayer

This subject is worth a book in itself (see the Further Reading suggestions for some examples of just such a book). Many of the Psalms are prayers, and we can learn much from them about the wide biblical understanding of prayer. Much of Paul's most profound theology occurs in his prayers. It has rightly been said that when someone prays, you get to find out what they really believe. And on two occasions we have the privilege of listening to the words of Jesus as he prays, in the famous Lord's prayer (Matthew 6:9-13 and Luke 11:2-4), and in what is often called his 'high-priestly prayer' (John 17).

Prayer is Dependence on God

Most biblical prayers come about as part of a person struggling with their situation, and wrestling with the questions of what to do and how to do it. It is often in response to an understanding of who God is.

- Clear examples are Nehemiah 1:5-11 and Daniel 9:1-19. What is it Daniel is doing (v.2) when he turns to prayer (v.3)?
- In Psalm 51 David is struggling with his own sin. Look through this Psalm and ask: what kinds of things does David ask in it? And who can do those things?
- John 17:1-5 is even clearer. Here we see Jesus submitting himself to his Father, knowing that only the Father can be in control of events.

The same is true of Paul. Paul almost always begins his letters with thanksgiving and prayer. Consider these two examples: how he prays for the Philippians (1:3-6) and for the Colossians (1:3-14). In both cases, he prays with confidence because it is God who will act (Philippians 1:6).

 In particular, note the order of Paul's prayer in Colossians 1:9-10 concerning God filling them with knowledge, and the Colossians living a life worthy of the Lord. We do *not* read 'We pray that you may live a life worthy of the Lord', but instead Paul sees this as a result of his first prayer, which is what? Does this teach us anything about biblical priorities in prayer?

We can pray with confidence when we are asking God to do something which he has promised to do. There is less cause to be confident when our prayer reflects our own priorities and desires.

The Lord's Prayer

This prayer is unusual in the Bible because it does not arise out of any particular situation of struggle or difficulty, but is simply given to the disciples as some kind of model of how to pray. What kind of model?

 What aspects of this prayer could be a model for us? Study Matthew 6:9–13 and see whether you find in it elements of praise, thanksgiving, intercession, petition (asking for something); and look at who is the subject of each part of it: the one praying? someone else? God? other believers? the whole world?

Note: part of the exercise for this unit will be to study in depth one or two biblical prayers to see what emphases they have. You may wish to make the Lord's prayer one of them and start now with such a study, in depth.

2C Prayer and Intercession

The discussion above of biblical prayer leads naturally to the following conclusion: there is a lot more to prayer than intercession. The danger exists in mission work, that we turn prayer into *something we do*. This would be a fatal mistake, and experience shows that it is all too easy to be attending regular prayer meetings and spending plenty of time interceding for all kinds of situations, and actually to be spiritually dried up inside and have little sense of personal contact with God.

Prayer in the Bible is usually some kind of response to who God is, and then sometimes, secondarily, a request for God to do something. Does this emphasis link up at all with section 1 of this unit and our thoughts there on the Christian life?

 What is your reaction to the following two statements:

- If we do have spiritual depth in our relationship with God then we will naturally want to be knowing him more and responding to who he is, and then intercession will flow at times quite naturally out of our regular prayer life.
- Most Christians know this anyway, but are too busy to do anything about it.

Incidentally, if these statements are true, then they may go some way toward dealing with the difficult questions we raised at the beginning of this prayer section. Those questions, on reflection, were entirely about intercession. If our main focus in prayer is actually God, then we might say that 'answers to prayer' are those times when we manage to see things God's way.

We should note that sometimes people talk of an 'answer to prayer' which is just a kind of 'it turned out OK for *me*' statement. A very clear example of this is the following:

 Alan Wilkinson tells of one lady during wartime who prayed 'I heard a bomb coming and I prayed to God as hard as I could to push it a bit further down the street and he did' (in *Dissent or Conform?*, London: SCM Press, 1986, pp.277f.) What kind of understanding of God does this prayer indicate?

Two-Part Exercise

Assess your own relationship with God. Write out one paragraph after doing this, perhaps in the form of a prayer to God, about how you see your relationship now, and whether you feel the need to make changes in your priorities and refocus your prayer life in any way.

Secondly, and much more difficult, stop 'studying' now and turn to God and be with him in a time of stillness and peace.

Note: It is true that God is with you at all times. But even those in the Bible who knew and believed that still set aside time to be with God, with Jesus being the most obvious example (e.g. Mark 1:35). We all tend to have a lot of 'noise' in our minds: perhaps songs in our thoughts, conversations being re-run over and over again, worries about some difficult situation we are in, reminders of 100 things we need to be doing, etc. It is difficult to slow down and really be quiet. You may need to go for a walk, or change where you are sitting, or do something which will enable you to set aside all the background noise in your head. But you won't clear out that noise by focusing on quietness: what you need to do is focus on God, or on Jesus. This could be by meditating on a Bible passage, for instance. Whatever you do, it will most likely take time. But it is a valuable and important time in which you can stop and make contact with God. So take a break now, and do it.

2D Prayer Meetings

We finish this section of the unit with a few thoughts about how all this can relate to holding prayer meetings. The obvious point to make is that worship and Bible reading should be part of our prayer meetings: in this way we will be having the necessary contact with God which allows us to go on and pray.

Also, it may be a good thing in prayer meetings to allow more time to be spent in prayer which is not particularly intercession.

When using prayer letters and reports, some simple guidelines may help:

• use maps to show where you are praying for
• write prayer requests on a board or an OHP to give people a visual reminder of what you have said
• do not talk for so long that people forget what they are praying for

We also note that praying *biblically* may involve reflecting in depth about how precisely to ask God to be at work in someone's life. This may take time. You may often find that prayer meetings vary between activity and periods of quiet.

Finally, hold the prayer meeting at a convenient time. Breakfast prayer meetings are OK, but for many it is best to hold it in the evening. This allows extended time together, is often likely to be free from interruptions, and can easily be combined with a shared meal which helps to build up the fellowship of those praying together.

The strength and enduring benefits of much Christian activity can probably be traced back to a habit of regular prayer together. It is sad to note how frequently prayer meetings are relegated to a secondary role in some churches or Christian organisations.

Exercise for This Section

Study two of the biblical prayers to see what they can teach you about prayer. Think through how far the subjects raised in this section of the unit apply.

You could choose:

Psalm 51 (or many other Psalms)   Daniel 2
Nehemiah 1   1 Samuel 1–2 (Hannah)
Luke 1:46–55 (Mary)   Matthew 6:9–13
John 17   Colossians 1:1–13
  or many other passages.

3 Worship

Few topics are as widely discussed, as controversial, and as frequently misunderstood in the modern Christian world as worship.

Here are just some of the things that we will **not** be considering in this section:

- What kind of songs does God prefer: hymns or choruses or singing in the Spirit?
- Should we lift our hands in worship? If so, how far?
- Is the organ more spiritual or less spiritual than the guitar for Christian music?
- How should Sunday morning's 'Worship' section in the church service be organised?

The reason we will not be considering them is that they reflect a misunderstanding of what worship really is.

3A Worship in the Bible

Fundamentally . . . worship in the New Testament means believing the gospel and responding with one's whole life and being to the person and work of God's Son, in the power of the Holy Spirit.

David Peterson, *Engaging with God - A Biblical Theology of Worship* (Leicester: Apollos, 1992, p.286).

One of the original meanings of the word 'worship' was **'worth-ship'**: i.e. reflecting the worth of the thing or person worshipped. So we could say, if you think that money is the most important thing in your life and has greater worth than anything else for you, that you worship money. In the same way, people can worship Elvis Presley, or Coca-Cola.

What or who do you worship?

If you value something or someone then what you do is designed around it: e.g. to earn more money; or to please the person you value. Thus, another important angle on 'worship' is to see it as **'service'**: what you do in response to the worth of your thing or person.

These two ideas are inseparable. (In fact, some translations of Psalm 100:2 begin 'Worship the Lord with gladness', while others begin 'Serve the Lord with gladness': the Hebrew can be translated either way because both ideas are present in the word).

Why worship God?

Write out Romans 12:1-2 in your own words. What is the key point about worship in these verses?

Perhaps your first response is: 'Because he is God'. You are stating it very simply, but you are basically right. As our study in Unit 3 showed, who God is requires a response of worship from us. But we can be a bit more specific:

We worship God for two reasons:

(1)   Because of who God is;

(2)   Because of what God does:
- in history: his great acts in the past
- in your personal history: key things in your life that God has done
- in the world around us today
- in the future: things which we are promised he will do.

Biblical examples of this kind of worship include Psalm 136 (which looks at several different kinds of God's activity); the various songs of praise in Luke 1; or the scene of heavenly praise in Revelation 4-5.

 Write your own Psalm, focusing on these different aspects of worship. Take time to do this: do not rush it! You may even find that you have more questions than things to praise God for, and you might want to incorporate some of these questions into your Psalm, as did some of the biblical Psalmists. Perhaps you can strike the same balance between questioning and asserting God's goodness that they did.

3B 'I Don't Feel Like Singing'

Having said that we will not be focusing on the practicalities of worship, there are some things which we should consider. What we have said above is true of worship in general. We now look specifically at worship as a public activity rather than a private one.

Worship and singing are not the same. If you find singing an embarrassing or puzzling part of your Christian experience then perhaps you are discovering that singing is certainly not always worship. There is no problem with thinking about 'a time of worship' as a time set aside for songs and prayers when Christians meet together, whether in church or on a team. But you need to remember that much of the rest of your life is worship too.

Two common misunderstandings about worship are revealed by these two statements:

(1) Singing something doesn't make it true.

(2) Worship does not depend on how you feel.

As we observed in the Bible unit, music is very powerful in the way it allows us to experience emotionally things which we already perhaps understood, but needed to understand more. But if anything this should make us even more careful about *what* we sing. However, if you spend your singing time analysing words then you have certainly missed the point. You need to think through what you sing in general, not just at the moment you are singing it.

Exercise

Think of the two or three most frequently sung choruses or hymns in your church. Spend some time going through the words which you sing: in what way is it worship? Is it addressed to God? To each other? To Jesus, or the Spirit? Is it asking, celebrating, proclaiming, confessing . . . ? Are all these acceptable? Do they simply require different attitudes as you sing? If you discover that some of your favourite songs are actually mysterious to you, then try and discuss them with other people and see if that helps.

If worship is a *response* to God, then you can come to him however you feel. Most of the historic liturgies of the church (e.g. the creeds, or prayers for coming to God) are designed in part to lead you towards God from wherever you are. As you affirm great truths about God so you are drawn to him. It is an effort of will to focus on God, not a question of feelings.

The gospel teaches us that we are only made ready because of God taking the initiative: we will never have the strength within us to be worthy to come before God.

For Reflection

How do you focus on God as you come to a time of worship? What is your usual pattern before or at the start of a church service or a time of worship? Is it a helpful pattern? List two or three things which you feel you should work on to help you in the process of worshipping God.

4 Lifestyle

4A Introduction

How can we determine whether our view of discipleship is based primarily on what is culturally acceptable or on the actual teaching of the Bible? Cultural standards change. Was 1960's radicalism 'more Christian' than today's way of life? What are today's issues?

In fact the Bible is difficult to pin down on some basic lifestyle issues.

 How much do you have to give away to become a Christian? Is it everything? (Luke 18:22) Or is the cut-price admission fee of 'half of everything I possess' which Zaccheus had (Luke 19:8) acceptable today?

When you go out on evangelism is it better to take nothing with you (Luke 10:4) or has that suggestion been replaced by the later words of Jesus (Luke 22:35-36)?

When you pray is it better to pray all night with great persistence (Luke 18:1), or quietly and simply, since your Father in heaven knows what you need anyway (Matthew 6:6-8)?

And that's almost all in Luke!

4B The Simple Lifestyle

The fact that the rich young ruler and Zaccheus, in the first of the above questions, were confronted in different ways about their possessions and wealth suggests immediately one thing: wealth is not the central issue in Jesus' conversations with them. It is clearly an issue, but he felt able to deal with them differently. The key thing was *attitude*.

Different lifestyles are appropriate for different situations. If you are working on a mission field, for example, then there may be some limitations forced on you which have nothing to do with biblical teaching but are practical considerations necessary for functioning as a member of the mission.

Exercise

Spend some time thinking about your present lifestyle. Which features of it would you say are determined by biblical standards? Which features are required by the kind of work you do? Which features, on reflection, do you think are unacceptable? The following sentences are examples to help get you thinking:

- I have little money at the moment becauseI am a student
- I give 10% of what money I have to my church because that is a biblical requirement
- I have a boyfriend/girlfriend but our relationship is not sexual because the Bible lays down clear moral guidelines forbidding sex outside marriage
- I have a computer because I need it for my work
- I never criticise mychurch leaders even though I think they are wrong. Why . . . ?

Other subjects: time spent in prayer; leisure activities; vacations; church commitments; clothing and dress styles/fashions; eating habits . . .

(Note: you do not have to agree with the above examples. If you don't, why not?)

What or who sets the agenda for your present lifestyle?

It would be easy to try and reduce the Christian life to a set of rules and regulations at this point, but we are not going to do so. Rules are useful for a time, but in the long – term they do not promote holiness and godly living, at least according to the apostle Paul (Colossians 2:20-23).

Having discussed all this we should note also that if the simple lifestyle ever becomes the main issue for you, then your focus is in the wrong place. Think back to section 1 of this unit. What should your focus be?

4C Being 'Worldly'

Is the 'world' a positive or negative idea in the Bible?

This, of course, is an unfair question. It depends on where you look. A lot of people see life in two compartments: spiritual and worldly. The 'worldly', on this view, is negative: it is often characterised by some verses from 1 John: 'the cravings of sinful man, the lust of his eyes and the boasting of what he has and does' (1 John 2:16).

But we need to remember the cautions about word studies and taking verses out of context from Units 2 and 3. The word 'world' is clearly being used in different ways at different times in the Bible. How John is using the word in 1 John 2:15 is shown by the passage that follows; but how it is being used in John 3:16 is different, and is shown by that passage.

 Look up both these passages. What are the contexts, and what therefore does 'world' mean in each case?

One practical implication of all this will be explored in the next section, on stewardship.

You only have to look at changing attitudes down through history to see how much our idea of what is 'worldly' has been conditioned by the **social attitudes** of the times, or cultural attitudes. People have described drinking alcohol, smoking, going to the cinema, dancing, eating ice cream on Sunday, listening to popular music, wearing jeans (or even women wearing socks!), using modern translations of the Bible, gossiping, being nationalistic or proud, and swearing all as worldly behaviour. Probably you have different attitudes to different items on this list.

It is good to ask yourself how much your presentation of the gospel might rely on these kinds of lifestyle issues rather than the central truths of the Christian faith. And it is important to be willing to let your lifestyle assumptions be challenged. Many of these issues will resurface in later units looking at mission and cross-cultural communication.

Exercise

Imagine that you are leading a youth group which has persistent problems with smoking. Some even seem to be addicted. Write out a short talk you might give to them which encourages them away from smoking but does not resort to legalism. Is this even possible? If not why not? What implications does this have, if any, for your understanding of Christian discipleship?

4D Stewards of Creation

If, as we saw above, the 'world' may be either positive or negative, depending on our attitude, then this gives us an important clue about our understanding of ecology, or the subject of looking after the world around us.

The book of Genesis has been appealed to as evidence both for and against the idea that Christianity is concerned about its environment. While it clearly has a view of the universe as a good thing created by God, it also includes God's giving of permission to humans to 'Be fruitful and increase in number; fill the earth and subdue it' and to rule over all the animals and use nature for food (Genesis 1:28-30).

 What is your own conclusion from Genesis on this issue?

Are there any ways you are currently able to look after your environment, or make a difference in your area in the use of natural resources?

It is sometimes argued that this issue is irrelevant compared to the moral urgency of spreading the gospel. Do you think it is possible to separate out issues in this way?

4E Your Work

If you are devoted full-time to Christian work in one way or another, it becomes tempting to think of this as somehow more 'spiritual' than the work being done by others who are not in Christian organisations. But if the important thing in our lifestyle is that we are focused on Jesus, and want to worship him in all we do, then *what* we do is perhaps less important than *how* we do it. In fact, even the desire to be an evangelist can often be better served in a job in a non–Christian organisation than a Christian one.

Working in the World

 List five ways in which being in a non–Christian organisation offers you more of a chance to develop an evangelistic ministry.

Furthermore, your *work* is not necessarily the same as your *paid employment*. Many people who have plenty of work are not part of any business and receive no pay. Think of those whose main task is in the home bringing up children, for example.

5 Relationships

5A Introduction

You will already have seen in the first parts of this unit how much the issues of discipleship involve corporate activity: our lifestyle automatically involves other people. We live out the Christian life in church communities. Our relationships with each other in the body of Christ are an important part of our Christian experience.

You already have a grasp of the way in which you love yourself. You probably did this naturally: you didn't have to teach yourself how to be loving towards yourself. Perhaps one way of thinking of your goal in this relationships study is to learn how to relate to others in a way that is automatically loving.

We looked in Unit 4 at how being created in God's image had implications for our relationships. And in Unit 2 we looked in depth at 1 Corinthians 13. You may like to review both of these studies briefly at this point.

5B Unity

The apostle Peter did not state that correct beliefs, or missionary zeal, cover over a multitude of sins, but he wrote that love covers over a multitude of sins (1 Peter 4:8).

One of the major problems in the early church was the division between Jews and Gentiles (non-Jews). This is understandable: the Jews had been following God for centuries and were perhaps not surprisingly unclear about exactly how their traditions fitted with the new Christian communities that were developing. Did you have to be circumcised? How did the law and the temple fit into the new system? The tensions between the two communities were frequently bitter and divisive.

Probably few divisions today are any more difficult or aggressive than this one was, and so it is instructive to see how Paul deals with this issue in the letter to the Ephesians, one of the most powerful New Testament letters.

Unity in Ephesians – A Study

If you are not familiar with the book of Ephesians, spend some time looking through it. If there is a **key verse**, it is probably 1:9-10. The Greek word translated 'to bring all things together' is a difficult word with a variety of possible meanings, but it probably includes the sense of 'putting everything back into its rightful order': in other words the universe is suffering from the effects of sin, but Christ is in charge of the healing process, and one day will present a renewed creation to his father.

Is there any sign that this renewed creation is underway? Paul's answer is YES. It has been a mystery in the past ('mystery' here has the straightforward meaning of something which was formerly hidden but is now clear; it is sometimes described as an 'open secret'), but the wisdom of God is now made known, to whoever is watching.

 How is this made known? (Eph. 3:10)

In what way does the church make this known? (Eph. 3:6)

Jews and Gentiles being in the same church is here seen as a powerful statement about what God is doing in the world. We could paraphrase Paul's argument like this: if even Jews and Gentiles can form one new united body then this is surely evidence that God is breaking down all the walls of hostility which separate people.

Eph. 2:11-22 describes how Christ has won this new unity at the cross, and in vv.19-22 Paul gives a picture of how we (Christians) fit together with Jesus, the Spirit, and the Father, into God's new creation.

 Study this passage in detail. In the light of this teaching, what kind of divisions do you think would be acceptable for Christians to have, whether divisions in teaching, attitudes, organisations, churches, etc.?

It should now be no surprise that Paul himself draws some **conclusions** about unity in the later chapters of Ephesians. See especially Eph. 4:2-6.

What different reasons for unity does Paul give here?

4:25-32 gives further examples of the kind of behaviour which Paul thinks is an appropriate response to his teaching about Jews and Gentiles, in terms of the relationships between each other in the body of Christ. Chapters 5 and 6 include more detailed sections about how these renewed relationships work out in certain kinds of relationships.

 What kinds of relationships?

It is important to note the order of Paul's reasoning: he does not say 'You should be as one – that's the most important thing to think about', but rather: 'You should **focus on Jesus**, and you should therefore see that unity is important'. This is a point we have encountered throughout this unit. Note, for example, that his prayer for the Ephesians in 3:14-21 is a prayer that 'Christ may dwell in your hearts'. The implication is: if this happens then God's wider purposes will advance too.

5C Implications

These exercises follow on from the above study. They may not be easy, but they are important.

Now think of your own situation. Are there divisions or difficulties between you and others, e.g. in your church? Go through Ephesians again and see whether anything that Paul says speaks to your own situation.

 Jesus prays about unity for all believers. Read John 17:20-26.

Why is unity seen as important here?

Is your own life part of the fulfilment of this prayer? Set aside some quiet time now to pray and ask God to deal with problem situations you are facing.

The Bible does not leave us unclear about what to do in situations when unity is threatened. 'Do not let the sun go down while you are still angry' (Eph. 4:26). Even more startling is Matthew 5:21–26. Here Jesus says that if someone is angry with you, then it is your responsibility to do something about it. Does he really say this?

If so, spend time now considering practical action you should take as a result of this teaching.

Do not let the opportunity for obedience slip away. This is more important than whatever else you were planning to do next.

Note: the biblical principles are clear. But you will need cultural sensitivity in applying them. This will become clearer when discussed in Unit 6 on mission (see particularly the section on ethics) and Unit 8 on communication (especially cross-cultural communication).

5D Practical Unity

We conclude with a few practical questions about relationships which you should take the time to work through on whatever level is appropriate to you.

Exercise

- We have focused on **love** and **unity** as two of the key concepts in relationships. Using these two concepts immediately brings in others, such as communication with each other, dealing with anger, serving one another, etc., as we have seen. What other concepts do you think are important issues for relationships?

- In what ways, if any, does the biblical teaching on unity differ if one of the people involved is a **leader**?

- How does **sin** affect unity? (You might like to study Matthew 18:15–20 in connection with this question.)

- What is the balance on your team between having guidelines for team living and having the **grace** that comes from the gospel at work in your relationships? In what ways could you contribute to gracious relationships? Are love and unity key concepts in your team relationships?

- How would you distinguish between unity and **uniformity**? Does 'being one in heart and mind' (Acts 4:32) require everyone to think or act in the same way? If so, in what areas?

Memory Verses

John 15:5,8
Ephesians 4:1–3

SECTION III:
CHRISTIAN MISSION

Unit Six
World Mission

Outline and Notes

Mission: God's work or ours? A job for 'full-time Christian workers' or part of Christian discipleship? Too much Christian thinking on mission lacks a solid biblical foundation, and has focused on approaches which have a lot of managerial thinking about how to perform tasks, but not much theological thinking about what task should actually be performed. This unit tries to encourage some biblical reflection on this huge topic.

Aims

The Global Action training program goals include the aims that at the end of their Global Action training the student will:

- have been given opportunities to develop a concern for the lost
- be able to communicate a vision and concern for the challenge of world mission
- show an attitude of respect to local church leadership
- persevere in the face of difficulties and trials
- apply biblical criteria when making moral decisions
- respond with love and wisdom to evidence of economic disparity
- be able to adapt the presentation of the gospel to various situations
- have made regular use of materials such as *Operation World*, prayer letters, etc., to help pray for the world
- have developed a practice of praying both corporately and individually for local and global needs of the world
- have engaged in a balanced and biblical understanding of spiritual warfare

153

Study Objectives

As well as laying the foundation for the above training goals, this unit will enable you to:

- demonstrate biblical understanding in your use of the word 'mission'
- evaluate different ways of approaching non-Christians and make decisions about what is best in your own situations
- explain the moral and ethical factors involved in Christian mission
- offer a biblically based critique of some current missionary practices (both positive and negative)

Recommended Reading:

See the introductory note in the manual on recommended reading for this unit, drawing especially on John Stott's *Christian Mission in the Modern World*.

Unit Outline

1 A Biblical Theology of Mission

1A   Introduction
1B   What is Mission?
        Mission and Evangelism
1C   Do We Care?
1D   Study Exercise – The Basics of a Biblical Theology of Mission
        (1)   The Old Testament
        (2)   The New Testament

2 Christianity in Today's World

2A   The Uniqueness of Christ and of Christianity?
        The Biblical Record
2B   What of those who have never heard?
        The Debate

3 Methods for Mission

3A   The Human Condition
3B   Different Approaches
        Dialogue
        Proclamation
        Social Action
3C   The History of Mission

4 Ethics and Mission – Living as God's People

4A   Introduction
        Us and Them: The Changing Face of Mission
4B   The Basis of our Ethical Standards
        Ethical Dilemmas
4C   Mission and Ethical Integrity
4D   Case Studies

5 Current Issues in Mission

5A   Introduction
5B   Contextualisation
5C   Indigenisation
5D   Church Growth, People Groups,
        Unreached Peoples and the 10/40 Window
5E   Global Intercession
        Spiritual Warfare
5F   Church Planting

1 A Biblical Theology of Mission

1A Introduction

'Mission is the mother of all theology'

Martin Kahler

Mission is exciting! It is a tremendous privilege to be involved in God's plan for his creation; to play a part as his co-workers in doing his work. Sometimes that excitement gets the better of us and we reduce mission to a set of formulae, techniques and salesmanship as we try and 'recruit' people for our 'religion'. But when we take a step back and look at God's great work from Genesis to Revelation and on into today's world we become aware of the world-changing nature of Christian mission. Mission is exciting.

Few evangelicals would want to say that mission is all about obedience to the Great Commission, but that is sometimes the way it has come across. In fact, the whole Bible is a missionary book. We have a much greater mission mandate than the closing verses of Matthew's gospel. Sometimes when we talk of a 'biblical basis for mission' what we mean in practice is the selection of a few texts which prove a point, while all the texts which have other implications are left out. When we talk of a biblical *theology* of mission we attempt to avoid this problem by learning how to *think biblically* about mission.

That means reading the whole of Matthew's gospel for its insight into the nature of Christian mission, and not just its last five verses. It means wrestling with how Paul viewed the nature of mission to the Jews and the Gentiles in Romans 9-11 as well as how he expressed his view of sinfulness in Romans 3:23. It means understanding the ethical implications of Israel's existence throughout the Old Testament as well as the few explicit words God spoke to Abraham in Genesis 12. God's interaction with his humanity stands at the heart of the biblical story, and provokes our deepest reflection and thinking. Truly, mission is the mother of all theology.

What is Mission?

Probably few words have been as badly misunderstood or as frequently abused in Christian thinking as 'mission' and so the first thing to do is to think what we mean by the word.

What do you mean when you use the word 'mission'? Write down your preliminary thoughts before going on to the rest of this section.

One cause of confusion is that although the word *mission* comes from the Latin root *misse* 'to send', it is not necessarily the case that when we use the word *mission* today we mean 'sending'. Even so, a good place to *start* is to ask: who is doing the sending and who or what is being sent in the Bible?

 In John 20:21, which appears to be John's version of the 'great commission' (see below), what link does Jesus draw between different kinds of sending? Write in your own words how this idea is part of Christian mission.

The phrase *missio Dei* (literally: God's mission) is often used to underline this point: the church's mission is in fact the mission of God. It is God who sends the church into the world, to play a role in fulfilling his purposes. Andrew Kirk has provided one way of drawing together the biblical material into a list of five aspects of the church's mission (in no particular order):

1. Stewarding the resources of *creation*
2. Serving *human beings* in all circumstances
3. Bearing witness to *truth* (specifically the truth found in Jesus Ephesians 4:21)
4. Engaged in seeing God's *justice* done in society
5. Showing what it means to be *a reconciled and liberated community* in a despairing world.

(Source: 'Missiology' in S.B. Ferguson and D.F. Wright (eds.), *New Dictionary of Theology* *(Leicester: IVP, 1988), 434-36.)*

Therefore, if you are to be a 'missionary', you will have to understand God's purposes. This is easier said than done, of course, but it is at least the right way round. It is a mistake to think of yourself, as a missionary, being the one who takes God to the people. In fact, God is taking you to the people.

Mission and Evangelism

One other introductory topic needs to be cleared up. Mission and evangelism are not the same things! As we have already seen, *mission* refers to a wide range of activities, *including* evangelism, but not limited to it.

There is a very unhelpful practice in some countries and cultures of calling *evangelistic outreaches* by the name of *missions*. (Why do you think this practice started?) But it would be difficult to defend biblically the idea that what God is sending us to do is run evangelistic outreaches, except as part of a much wider role.

Evangelism will be the subject of our next unit, and so we will postpone further discussion of it to then. And as a result, this unit will look unbalanced. We want to affirm here that evangelism *is* part of our missionary work, but in this unit we will be focusing on some of the many other characteristics of God's mission.

1C Do We Care?

This might seem an odd section to have in a study of a biblical theology of mission. But it is important to get our thinking straight at this point: we will be facing a lot of difficult questions in this unit, and at times the study will seem abstract. But behind all the ideas, verses and concepts are real people. It is sadly all too easy, when you are engaged in Christian work, to start thinking in terms of projects, tasks and goals, but we need to be letting God work in our hearts too.

This goes deeper than just 'caring for the lost' (in fact, we will have to look at what we mean by 'lost' later in the unit). It involves caring about the lives being lived all around us: about injustice, poverty, oppression, spiritual darkness, pain and suffering. The challenge of world mission is to respond to life as it is experienced, without just treating people as 'potential converts'. The Christian life is so much more than being a name ticked off on a list of 'converted and going to church': and likewise mission must also be a matter of compassion and concern *for individuals*.

Stop and Pray

We will return to different aspects of this point throughout the unit. Now may be an appropriate time for you to pray about this very issue. If we do not care for and love people, then all of our understanding and activity will be worth very little.

1D Study Exercise – The Basics of a Biblical Theology of Mission

(1) The Old Testament

- Why is humanity on earth? (Genesis 1:28; 2:15)
- What can you conclude about our role in life from Genesis 1:27 and 2:18 concerning relationships?
- When God sends out Abraham in Genesis 12, what is his ultimate purpose? (see especially verses 2–3)
- In what ways is Israel unique and therefore intended to play a role among the nations? (Deuteronomy 4:32–40)
- How is this uniqueness described in Exodus 19:6? What is the significance of this for Israel's mission?
- How does Israel's God relate to other nations? (Isaiah 43:9–12) (Note: this is a complex question, and much of the book of Isaiah deals with it from various angles. You might like to study Isaiah 2, 60 and 66 as examples of some of the perspectives the book has on how other nations relate to Yahweh, Israel's God).

(2) The New Testament

The Great Commission (Matthew 28:16–20, and parallel passages) and the words of Jesus in Acts 1 just before his ascension are now often taken by evangelicals as foundational to the work of mission. But it was not always this way.

In fact the majority of the reformers (leading figures from the time of the Reformation, in the sixteenth century and later) believed that to interpret Matthew 28:16–20 correctly was to see here Jesus sending out his immediate disciples on a particular errand. Many explicitly stated that the command no longer applied. (e.g. Calvin in his *Institutes* and also his commentary on 1 Corinthians 12:28 drew a line between temporary gifts/offices which helped establish the church, and permanent ones which enabled the continuing government of the church. Luther's comment on Mark 16:15 was that after the apostles obeyed it, 'no one again received such a general apostolic command, but every bishop or pastor has his own particular parish.' (Luther's works, vol.31, pp.210–11).)

- What evidence could help you to evaluate the reformers' claim about this? Were they right or wrong?
- What might be the significance of Matthew 28:16–20 in today's church?

(Some of the material in this section is discussed at length in R.E. Davies, 'The Great Commission from Calvin to Carey', *Evangel* 14.2 (1996) pp.44–49)

- Why does the New Testament itself make no reference to the Great Commission as the actual reason why any of the activity in Acts takes place? What is seen in Acts (and also in Paul's letters) as the main **motivation for mission**?

In answering this question perhaps you remembered the brief look at Acts in Unit 1, where we considered that the book might be called 'the Acts of the Holy Spirit'. Consider these words from Asian theologian Ken Gnanakan:

'[A] closer look at the biblical account of the life and witness of the early church surprisingly reveals a total absence of any reference to this commission . . . the commission derives its meaning and power wholly and exclusively from the Pentecost event . . . One wonders whether the over-emphasis on [neatly packaged] mission has resulted in the mammoth multinational strategies which lack sensitivity to what the Spirit impels us to become in our individual contexts . . . Our modern lack of stress on an inner compulsion and on the spontaneity of the work of God who is far beyond human comprehension, is glaring'
Ken Gnanakan, *Kingdom Concerns* (Leicester: IVP, 1993), pp.176, 179, 182, 183.

In saying this, Gnanakan stands in a long line of people who have tried to remind us that there is much more to mission than obedience to a command. To say that the Holy Spirit inspires people to mission still leaves room for a variety of ways that this actually happens in practice. If we consider the record of the book of Acts, what different ways can you find in the following passages?:

- Acts 8:1   How does the Spirit get believers out of Jerusalem?
- Acts 8:26ff How does the Spirit get Philip where he wants him? (Note: how far through the whole process does he Spirit guide him explicitly? Does Philip take over at some point?)

- Acts 13:1-3   In what context does the Spirit call individuals into mission?
- Acts 15:28   What is the (complex) process through which agreement is reached concerning some of the difficult ethical decisions which mission raised?
- Acts 16:7-10   How does the Spirit get Paul over to Macedonia?
- Acts 18:5   What methods does Paul use to spread the gospel in Corinth?
- Acts 18:9   What keeps Paul going in the face of opposition in Corinth?

These are just some of the relevant passages.

If there is a simple conclusion to our search for a biblical theology of mission, it should be this: the entire Bible is a missionary document, and the more we understand it the more we are compelled to live out the gospel wherever we are. All that we do as the people of God is a response to God and his mission to the world, and there are no limits to what God will use to carry his mission along.

The rest of this unit examines areas which arise out of this so-called holistic understanding of mission as the living out of God's kingdom on earth.

2 Christianity in Today's World

Christianity is a faith caught between the times: between the first and second comings of Jesus. We see signs of the kingdom all around us, and yet we also see evidence of the old order: sin, disease, suffering and death are all common. Mission requires us to hold in balance our understanding of the reality which is passing away and the reality which is taking its place. Where does Christianity stand in this confused world?

2A The Uniqueness of Christ and of Christianity?

Almost all religions have a sacred book, major figures in their past whose views and teachings are especially respected, and stories and traditions which are passed down by believers. Many religious groups would feel able to talk about the special sense of belonging to their own group: positive experiences they can recall, and valuable friendships. Probably most religions would also have their own stories (or 'testimonies') of people joining them (and also of people leaving them). What, if anything, makes Christianity more than just another religion?

Christianity stands out not just because of the teaching and example of Jesus Christ, but because of who Jesus himself was.

The Biblical Record

The record we have in the gospels is selective, but it draws from actual first-hand experience of what Jesus did.

 How is this expressed in Luke 1:1-4, John 20:30-31 and also Acts 1:1?

Jesus' own understanding of his uniqueness is expressed most radically in John's gospel in these words (John 14:6): 'I am the way and the truth and the life. No one comes to the Father except through me.'

Equally comprehensive is the New Testament development of Jesus' theology, particularly in Romans, where Paul argues that sin is a universal problem for mankind and that the required solution was the death of a perfect man, Jesus. This whole way of understanding life rules out other possibilities for salvation. Furthermore, where we do find powerful summaries of the gospel, such as in 2 Corinthians 5:16-21, we always find them expressed in Christ-centred terms.

 Which verse in 2 Corinthians 5:16-21 particularly focuses on Christ, and in what way?

The earliest Christian preaching saw this as a straightforward matter:

 What does Acts 4:12 say about this? (Do you think it is legitimate to appeal to this verse given its context?)

When we discuss the 'uniqueness of Christ' we therefore have two things in view: the unique way of salvation which is *through* Christ; and also the uniqueness of who Christ was. Unlike any other teacher Christ did not just point the way to God, he was a unique person since *the fulness of the Deity lived in bodily form* in him (Colossians 2:9). (Refer back to Unit 3, section 2C for further discussion of this.) This is not true of any other teacher or great figure, and indeed no other teacher has ever even claimed it.

2B What of those who have never heard?

A problem with the position defended above is that it can be easier to state it in theory than to defend it in practice. Many missionaries, starting from this position of the uniqueness of Christ, have had doubts when confronted with people in other cultures and other religions, who perhaps appear to be living a life characterised by many of the qualities of a Christian life. The position is further complicated when such people, on hearing the gospel of Christ, respond to it positively almost as if it is (for them) a better way of expressing what they have believed all along.

The issues this raises are focused in the following question:

Is it true that those who have never heard either the gospel, or even the name of Jesus Christ, will be judged as guilty of failing to call upon Jesus?

This difficult question has been debated passionately for many centuries. Before looking at the debate, we should underline carefully something on which we may all agree as evangelicals.

When people are saved they are saved through the unique work of Jesus Christ on the cross and in the resurrection. This is not, at least in our discussion, a matter for debate (although of course there are those who effectively deny the authority of the Bible by denying this too). The issue here is rather: how much does someone need to be aware of in order to be saved?

Could we say that someone may be saved through the death and resurrection of Jesus, but that they may not be aware of that, if, for instance, they have never heard of Jesus Christ. Such people obviously do not profess to be Christians. (In fact, in some versions of this theory, they may profess to be Muslims or Hindus or anything). But we may think of them *as saved as if they were* Christians. (Some people would call them 'anonymous Christians'.)

The Debate

In a recent book edited by John Sanders, called *What About Those Who Have Never Heard?* (Downers Grove: IVP, 1995), several different views are discussed which all agree that Jesus is the only saviour, but which nevertheless see that worked out in different ways. The following list defines some of the major views, and gives key references used in defending them.

Sanders' book discusses the 1st, 3rd and 4th of these options in detail. In practice, most evangelicals see the biblical evidence as pointing to

> **Restrictivism** God does not provide salvation to those who fail to hear of Jesus and come to faith in him before they die (John 14:6, Acts 4:12, 1 John 5:11-12)
>
> **Universal Opportunity Before Death** All people are given opportunity to be saved by God's sending the gospel (even by angels or dreams) or at the moment of death or by 'middle knowledge' (Daniel 2, Acts 8)
>
> **Inclusivism** The unevangelised may be saved if they respond in faith to God based on the revelation they have (John 12:32, Acts 10:43, 1 Timothy 4:10)
>
> **Divine Perseverance (or Post-mortem Evangelism)** The unevangelised receive an opportunity to believe in Jesus after death (John 3:18, 1 Peter 3:18-4:6)
>
> **Universalism** All people will in fact be saved by Jesus. No one is damned forever. (Romans 5:18, 1 Corinthians 15:22-28, 1 John 2:2)
>
> Source: Sanders (ed.) *What About Those Who Have Never Heard?*,

either **restrictivism** or **inclusivism**. You will need to study the biblical passages carefully to come to any conclusion on this issue.

We should probably say that, at first sight, there are strengths in both approaches. Can you think of any?

Inclusivism

- It accepts what *appears* to be true: that some have a faith in Christ without knowing it.
- It holds to the belief that if anyone is saved, it is through Christ.
- It honours peoples' sincerity in their own expression of faith.
- It tries to do justice to a certain strand of biblical thinking, namely that Christ is the true light who has come to every human being (see John 1:9, and the whole context of John 1:1-18)

Restrictivism

- It accepts the real nature of spiritual conflict in different religions, and the power of worshipping false gods.
- Being a good person is not the same as being a Christian. Can we really call someone a Christian if they do not profess Christ?
- It would actually be an insult to someone in another faith to tell them that they are really a Christian but just don't realise it. It doesn't honour them at all.

- It tries to do justice to a certain strand of biblical thinking, namely that mission is an essential part of taking Christ to those who are lost without him (e.g. Romans 10:14–15).

Keep in mind the following thoughts as you tackle this issue:

(1) Whatever the answer to this question, it does not affect the fact that **God is calling people into mission**. If it is *possible* for people to be forgiven their sins without hearing of Jesus we are given no reason at all to suppose that it is *easy* or that *it happens very much*. The debated New Testament examples in any case are few and far between. It is undoubtedly God's desire that people should hear the gospel where possible.

(2) **If anyone is saved, it is through Christ**. The nearest we might imagine to any other way of salvation was a law–abiding Jew in Israel. But no, says Paul, even that was never the point: Abraham himself was saved by faith (Romans 4) and is thus the true father of all who believe. And Gentiles could, by their own good conscience, have had the same understanding that judgement depends on what you do (Romans 2:12–15), and, like the Jews, have realised that only by God's gracious gift could forgiveness be attained. And the nature of that gift has now been revealed: it is through Christ. The real issue here would be: *how much do you have to understand of that?* (e.g. obviously Abraham did not call on the name of Jesus.)

(3) Those who do respond to the gospel want to say that **it is God who does the work of justifying**, by the power of his Spirit. Is God able to do that work in places where the gospel is not yet known?

(4) Many passages are relevant to this topic. As well as the references given in the above list, you may like to consider:

Individuals in the OT	Genesis 14 on Melchizedek
	Exodus 18 on Jethro
	2 Kings 5 on Naaman
Individuals in the NT:	Acts 10 on Cornelius (e.g. vv. 1–2, 34–35)
	Acts 19 on 'disciples' who have not fully understood?
General:	Hebrews 11:6

It should be noted that sincere Bible reading Christians disagree on this issue (and on many of these passages), but you should still try to think through your own position clearly.

Exercise

Write out your own view in 100 words, defending it briefly. Give scriptural references which have helped persuade you, but beware of taking verses out of context.
If possible, discuss this with someone else who has also thought through the issue.

To think about:

Perhaps one of the issues underlying the debates of this section is the question of what exactly is 'lostness'. What does it mean to be in need of salvation? This is the question of the human condition. We will touch on it briefly in the next section. Spend some time thinking first about what you believe.

How does this discussion affect your missionary practice? Are you trying to confront people and tell them they are wrong, or are you trying to draw out of them more fully ideas which they may already be developing? This leads us on to a discussion of methods we can use in mission, in the next section.

3 Methods for Mission

3A The Human Condition

Francis Schaeffer used to say that if he had an hour to explain to someone the gospel of Christ he would spend 50 minutes of that hour showing the person how 'lost' they were. For Martin Luther, the whole purpose of the law was to demonstrate the impossibility of pleasing God except in response to his grace. These views on the 'human condition' reflect an important biblical truth, put very clearly by Paul when he reminds the Ephesian Christians of what they used to be:

> Read Ephesians 2:11-13. How would you describe the 'human condition' of these Ephesians before they were Christians?

One of the reasons for such debate about mission questions as we saw in the last section is a failure to take seriously what this 'lostness' is, and therefore to understand what 'salvation' really is. Carl Braaten put it as follows:

> 'Christian theologians are debating the question whether or not there is salvation in other religions, and taking sides on the issue, without first making clear the model of salvation they have in mind . . . What is the salvation that theologians expect to find or not to find in other religions? Most of the debate so far has taken us nowhere, because vastly different things are meant by salvation. If salvation is whatever you call it, there is no reason for a Christian to deny that there is salvation in other religions . . .'
>
> Carl Braaten, 'The Uniqueness and Universality of Jesus Christ', quoted by Chris Wright in *The Unique Christ in our Pluralist World* (ed. Bruce Nicholls, WEF, 1994), pp. 39–40.

We may find certain aspects of lifestyle, such as *moral behaviour*, in any religion (or even in atheism), but is this the same as saying that the Christian concept of salvation can be found in other religions?

> Read John Stott's *Christian Mission in the Modern World*, chapter 4, on 'Salvation'. Summarise what he is saying about what salvation is, in just a few sentences.

3B Different Approaches

Our conclusions about 'lostness' will affect our conclusions about mission.

Dialogue

> Read John Stott, *Christian Mission in the Modern World*, chapter 3, 'Dialogue'.

Dialogue may be defined as 'a conversation in which each party is serious in their approach both to the subject and to the other person, and desires to listen and learn as well as to speak and instruct' (see Stott, pp.60–61).

Some questions:

• Do you think that dialogue involves a willingness to be argued or persuaded out of your own position? Is it appropriate to be that open to the other person?

- If dialogue involves both listening as well as speaking, does this make it a good thing?
- The Greek word *dialegomai* is often used to describe Paul's activity in Acts, see especially Acts 17:1-4 for a particularly clear example where Luke uses several different words which all have similar meanings to describe Paul's approach. Do we see here positive reasons for following Paul's example?
- Does a commitment to dialogue involve denying the certainty of our faith?
- Can dialogue be part of a wider approach to mission?

Proclamation

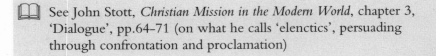

See John Stott, *Christian Mission in the Modern World*, chapter 3, 'Dialogue', pp.64-71 (on what he calls 'elenctics', persuading through confrontation and proclamation)

Another approach we find in Acts as much as anywhere is that of 'proclamation': presenting the truth about Christ to those who have not heard it, or perhaps have not been persuaded by it. Peter's sermon in Acts 2 is a good example of proclamation (see especially vv.36-41 for how Peter concluded this talk, and the response it got).

- The idea of proclamation involves speaking with authority. In a world where authority is often not respected, is this still a good way for Christians to be presenting their position?

Social Action

Read John Stott, *Christian Mission in the Modern World*, chapter 1, 'Mission'.

This topic takes us right back to our original list of five different aspects of mission. It has been hotly debated in the last century by Christians with different convictions. The separation of faith from political and social issues has been a disastrous development in so-called 'modern' cultures (where *believing* something in faith is a personal matter to be contrasted with being *reasonable* about issues affecting the wider public, which has not been a distinction made in most human societies). The following quote puts it very clearly:

> When people say that politics and religion do not mix, I wonder which Bible they have been reading.
>
> Archbishop Desmond Tutu

On the other hand, it is hardly ever the case that one political party or system represents the 'Christian' option, and sometimes the error has been made of compromising the gospel by over emphasising the agenda of one political party.

Exercise

Is it possible for you, where you are, to be involved in the work of relief organisations, or supporting the work of groups like Amnesty International? Discuss with those around you the possibilities and relevance of some kind of ministry to those who are, in the terms of Luke's gospel, the poor, the prisoners, the blind and the oppressed, for whom Jesus was himself anointed (Luke 4:18-19).

- Many times Christians deal with this passage in Luke 4 by taking the references to the poor and blind, etc., in spiritual terms. Do you think this is justified? Is it an appealing interpretation? Why or why not?

3C The History of Mission

It is not possible in this unit to cover all that we would like to cover, and the history of Christian mission is one subject that we cannot do justice to. But it is worth pointing out briefly that the different approaches to mission we have been discussing, and the theological debates about what mission really is, are all questions which have been around for a long time.

In 1792 William Carey, the shoemaker's apprentice from England, wrote a booklet called *An Enquiry into the Obligations of Christians to Use Means for the Conversion of the Heathens*. He went further than seeing a need for missionaries, and actually went out and did something about it, travelling to India in 1793 where he lived for forty years. In a famous meeting before he left he presented his desire to go, and was informed by a local minister: 'Young man, sit down. When God pleases to convert the heathen, He will do it without your aid or mine'. (Do you think this minister had a point at all?)

Mission history since Carey has been full of great successes and advances mixed with human sinfulness and serious failings. No study of mission history can avoid the difficult questions this raises, and we find time and again the view of Carey's minister friend being re-expressed down through the years: Christians should stop shouting about their faith and let God do whatever he wants. In recent years there have been some who have called for an end to the sending of missionaries at all, but this has been an over-reaction against the way that mission itself has frequently been misunderstood and even misused (hence the importance of studying it, as in this unit).

If you have time, you will benefit immensely from becoming familiar with this history. Of course, mission goes back much further than Carey, and some of the different emphases we are looking at in this unit have been better represented at different times. See the Appendix for some suggestions for further reading.

4 Ethics and Mission – Living as God's People

4A Introduction

Why look at ethics in a study of mission?

Perhaps this question has already occurred to you. If so, then you are in good company. But it is strange that as evangelicals, and therefore of all people the most committed in theory to living out a life of ethical integrity, ethics has a very low profile. Have you noticed how many Christian organisations, including missions, manage to agree on a statement of basic beliefs (or basis of faith) which includes reference to many different theological points, but which has no ethical component at all. Why do you think this is?

Us and Them: The Changing Face of Mission

There has been a massive shift in mission over the last few decades. Once it was possible, even if undesirable, to think in terms of a world map divided into 'us' and 'them': the great Christianised sending countries, and the needy, often 'backward', unreached lands full of people who needed to hear the gospel. Such a view reached its height at the beginning of the twentieth century in a mood of optimism amongst the Western nations that increased effort was all that was needed to finish the work of global mission.

Many factors changed, not least of which was the outbreak of the first World War in 1914, to destroy the mood of optimism. Equally, as the twentieth century progressed it became obvious that Western countries, while often called 'developed', were frequently morally and spiritually bankrupt when compared to other nations. As the century draws to a close, the Church seems to be growing and strengthening in every continent except Europe, and to be nowhere more struggling and disillusioned than in the West. The 'third world' of old has become the 'two-thirds world' which, in missionary terms, is now as much a sending area as a receiving area.

This phenomenon can be called the 'globalisation' of Christianity. Its relevance here is that it exposes, more clearly than at any time in the Church's history, how much we read the Bible, and see God, through our own cultural experience. To simplify: if the Church used to find ethics relatively simple, it was probably because it assumed that Western ethical standards were God's standards. Today the Church can no longer make that assumption. Thus ethics has become a cross-cultural subject.

Do you think this is a good thing?

4B The Basis of our Ethical Standards

Christians have taken different positions on this. Some of the main ones are listed here:

(1) Biblical ethical principles and commands apply directly and literally at all times
This is the basis for so-called 'restorationist' or 'theonomic' ethics, which often focuses on restoring the full Old Testament social and legal system to modern society.

(2) Biblical examples bear witness to principles which always apply
In this view, the Bible has ethical authority, but not because of what it says but because of the principles it demonstrates. These are sometimes called 'intermediate principles' because they try to bridge between then and now.

(3) Biblical examples of ethical teaching are specific to their original contexts and no longer apply today
This view takes the original context of passages seriously and concludes (often with regret) that we are therefore left with little direct ethical guidance.

Several writers argue for positions which fall in between these three views. The issues frequently come down to questions of interpretation, and interpretation always involves assessing the cultural influence on the interpreter.

Ethical Dilemmas

You are hiding a Jew in Nazi-occupied Europe in 1940 and a Nazi official knocks at your door to ask you whether you know of the location of this Jew. What do you say? What does this say about the absoluteness of the command to tell the truth? This very example is close to a biblical one:

> ✍ What did Rahab do in Joshua 2 (see vv. 4-6)? How is this act described in Hebrews 11:31?

Is polygamy wrong? That is: should a person never have more than one husband or wife? Some missionaries, convinced that polygamy is wrong, have arrived in polygamous cultures and enforced divorce. Of course, the question of divorce raises all kinds of ethical issues itself. In fact, polygamy is not forbidden in the Bible, even though kings are advised to have only one wife (Deuteronomy 17:17), and Israel's history shows what happened when Solomon, for instance, was led to idolatry because of his wives' religious beliefs. David, on the other hand, is not criticised for having more than one wife. So . . . is monogamy an ideal which the Bible was pointing towards but never legislated about? And as for divorce, is it true to say that the point of Jesus' teaching was to attack no-fault divorces as they were frequently practised, and not to condemn divorce outright? (The fact that this subject is debated is at least partly due to the differing passages on the subject in the gospels: compare Matthew 19 and Mark 10).

In some countries it may be an accepted part of the system that officials are underpaid and receive 'voluntary payments' from clients when requested to perform an official task. Do you call this bribery or do you view it as a way of helping a hard-working official to earn enough to feed their family for the week?

Case Study

You are crossing a border on a bus and an official comes on to invite all travellers to make a donation towards the cost of a new portrait of the local mayor. Those who decline to donate will receive the statutory medical injections for foreigners entering the country, but exceptions may be made in the case of those who feel inclined to contribute to this worthy cause. You suspect that there are no medical facilities nearby and that any needles used would not be clean. What do you do?

Mission and Ethical Integrity

Israel was called to be ethically distinct from the nations around it (this is the constant theme of Deuteronomy, see e.g. 7:1-6, 8:19-20, 12:4ff. etc.) Christians are equally called to be ethically distinct from those around them (a constant theme in the New Testament).

Perhaps few aspects of Christian mission are more complex than this: living as people of integrity in a crooked world. But equally, few are as important as this. Everything we do in response to God's mission involves ethical judgements. And ethical integrity is foundational to being ambassadors for Christ.

Specifically as this relates to mission, it should remind us of how easy it is to be blind to the very real ethical issues which we confront day after day in different cultural situations. Ethics is a part of our message and lifestyle, as the following story demonstrates:

> In a course on cross-cultural ethics one of my students was a conservative missionary who had spent many years in Africa. She was an independent thinker and refused to be swayed by my emphasis on social justice. Throughout the course she aggressively argued that verbal evangelism was primary. Social ethics was not an integral part of the gospel, she said, but an optional byproduct. I thought her ideas were simplistic, but as the course progressed I admired her more and more.
>
> She had spent her whole life living with the poor and working for their welfare. For many years she had lived in a grass hut with a mud floor. She gave away her possessions, helped the people obtain clean water, organised them to resist government attempts to take their land, taught them to read and affirmed their pride in traditional culture. She had not gone to Africa to do these things, but she loved the people. The Christian social project was part of who she was, irrespective of her theology. Her location among poor people made her actions possible and necessary.
>
> A Christian Marxist was on the same course. He was passionately concerned for justice. He had a comfortable apartment in a prosperous community and worked for the bank of America. He was still young, so it is impossible to judge the trajectory of his life. But it is safe to guess that unless he changes his social location, his rhetoric will fade into a mere self-justifying ideology.
>
> . . . The first step for anyone concerned about social justice may be to move house.
>
> Bernard T. Adeney, *Strange Virtues: Ethics in a Multicultural World* (Leicester: Apollos, 1995), p.226.

Case Studies

It is often helpful to think in terms of actual situations rather than abstract principles where cross-cultural ethics are concerned. An excellent resource to help you do this is Paul and Frances Hiebert's *Case Studies in Missions* (Grand Rapids: Baker Book House, 1987) which contains many such thought-provoking exercises. If you have access to this book discuss one or two of the case studies on your team. (Part 5 of the book, on 'Finances and Bribery' is particularly thought-provoking, see pp.133-48).

Exercise

If you do not have access to the Hieberts' book, then consider some of the ethical issues of your own work or of missionaries that you know. A familiar issue faced by mission teams is what to say about their work and identity in countries where it is illegal to be a missionary. Many have felt a terrible tension between the need for secrecy and the belief that one should always tell the truth. What do you think?

5 Current Issues in Mission

5A Introduction

In this final section we look briefly at some issues which arise in modern mission practice. Many of these would need fuller discussion in specific contexts, and it is often difficult to generalise about these topics. Some are more relevant to certain types of ministry. The fact that we have gathered them together at the end of the unit does not imply that they are not important, but that they are usually better dealt with in specific situations.

5B Contextualisation

This word is used loosely to refer to the way in which the task of Christian mission is adapted to the specific situation encountered by the missionary. This can be a reformulation of the gospel message in new words or concepts, the structuring of a local church in a new way, the understanding of ethical standards in a new light, or any part of Christian mission which allows the **context** of the local situation to play a role in deciding what is done. This does not mean accepting a culture uncritically, but being open to see how a culture functions, and which particular aspects of it may actually allow the gospel to be expressed in an appropriate way.

Thus on one level 'contextualisation' is a concept which simply accepts that Christian faith is always a *lived out* faith, and does not exist as an abstract philosophical system. While most people today would accept that this is a valid thing to do, the word itself ('contextualisation') only goes back to the beginning of the 1970's, and that shows how often the local context was in practice ignored in mission work. The sight of British missionaries exporting the concept of 'afternoon tea', for instance, has gone down in mission history as a classic example of a failure to appreciate local culture.

But the issue here goes much deeper, even to the point of affecting the *whole presentation of the gospel*. Some people would call the things discussed above 'cultural adaptation', and would reserve the term *contextualisation* for the process of reformulating the actual gospel message. For instance, some cultures might respond well to the logical and compact arguments of Romans, while others would be unmoved by them and might respond instead to Old Testament narratives which they see as picturing the gospel truths. Certainly different cultures will prioritise different themes.

Examples and Exercises

What does it mean to call God a 'king'? Is it worth changing this to use a term which communicates now what the word 'king' used to communicate in Bible times? What is gained and what is lost by describing God as 'the boss' or 'the president'? If the king of a country is a figure of ridicule or of ceremonial or nominal value, then what would it mean to call God 'king'?

Another example which you could think about is what to do with the peaceful rural imagery of Psalm 23 in an urban inner-city setting. Do you want to communicate that the Lord is best met out in the country? Can you *recontextualise* any of the phrases of Psalm 23?

A more abstract example is the New Testament language of the 'powers'. Did Paul, for instance, in Romans 8:38, Ephesians 6:12, Colossians 1:16 and 2:15 have in mind actual beings or entities called 'powers', or was this a way of describing what we today might call 'economic/social/political forces'? How are the two linked? When we talk today of Christ reconciling *all things* to himself (Colossians 1:20), which in Paul's list clearly included the powers he had created, does this include a divine influence over political and economic power? Or was it some kind of personal force of spiritual darkness?

This is a complicated example, and to be fair there is not much agreement on how best to approach it, but it shows up clearly the heart of the issue of contextualisation. Perhaps you can see why critics of the idea see it as a dangerous compromise with whatever is fashionable in cultural thought, and supporters of the idea defend it as part of making the gospel message relevant today.

5C Indigenisation

This term is related to 'contextualisation' above. **Indigenisation** refers specifically to the process of developing a church which fits culturally without compromising its beliefs. It is a particularly valuable concept where there has been a tendency to recreate church life from the sending culture without asking questions about how appropriate it is.

For example, in Africa it is a cultural habit for men and women to sit on different sides of the church. Missionaries who have tried to 'teach' that married couples should sit together have in fact discovered that they are trying to force an unsuitable foreign way of doing things on to a group of people who are happy with the way things are, and where the gospel would not seem to say much either way.

More serious examples can be thought of in terms of church leadership structure, or even the bizarre sight of a national church starting itself up in a foreign country, so that, even in countries where nobody was ever concerned with the original disputes, we find separate Lutheran, Anglican and Southern Baptist congregations!

Example and Exercise

A classic example of the problems involved in these questions is the one of church music. In the West many great hymns were adapted from drinking songs, along the lines of taking captive to Christ what was already popular in culture. Such tunes today, associated with famous hymns, somehow 'feel' religious, but that is simply a cultural assumption. When you are working in a different culture, what kind of music is appropriate for worship?

Some have argued that Western rock music is inherently evil and that 'Christian rock' is unacceptable. Likewise some African music is linked to calling up dead spirits: can its melodies be used for Christian words? In some cultures people do not sing anymore, except in church. Does this make music an unnecessary barrier to people who would like to come to church but don't like singing? Discuss these issues with people in the culture around you.

5D Church Growth, People Groups, Unreached Peoples and the 10/40 Window

A more recent development in mission has been a focus on statistics and research with a view to charting the progress of the gospel across the world. When such statistics are simply used for clarity in understanding a situation this may be helpful, although sometimes people seem to attach spiritual significance to numbers. For example, it may be significant that a church has got bigger or smaller, but perhaps this tells us nothing about things like spiritual depth, personal commitment, mature discipleship, or even ethical integrity. Maybe a church becomes smaller because all the hypocrites who never believed the gospel anyway have been thrown out?

Church growth is the name given to statistical analysis and research when it is used in this way to analyse trends in church attendance and size. In its better writings it avoids these simplistic judgements (see the suggestions for further reading). Even so, it is always worth bearing in mind that aspects of mission such as working for social justice and alleviating pain and suffering are very difficult to quantify.

A related but different use of research and statistics is involved in the concept of a **people group**, which is a way of considering groups of people in terms of their ethnic background or characteristics. A 'people group' is held together in some way, perhaps by speaking the same language, living in the same place, having the same kind of job, or class, or ethnic background. The most frequent use of the term is to describe an 'ethno–linguistic' group (although this is sometimes distinguished as a **people**). Some have linked this concept to the Greek word for nations (*ethne*) which is used in the Great Commission. Generally, the term 'people' refers to a broader set of people than a 'people group'. This concept has proved more useful in dealing with remote rural groups ('tribes') and tends to break down in more complex settings like large scale urban contexts.

Where such groups have not been exposed to the gospel, or where there is little if any local church presence, they are sometimes called **unreached peoples**. This term has some practical use, but is better when used in a relative rather than an absolute way. In absolute terms different people define a nation or group or people as 'reached' in different ways. But when used comparatively it can be helpful to say, for instance, that the people of France are less reached with the gospel than the people of Zambia.

One other popular concept is the **10/40 Window**: a shorthand way of referring to the area of the world between the latitudes of 10° and 40° north of the equator stretching from North Africa to South Asia. The vast majority of the world's least evangelised and poorest countries and cities are to be found here, which has been an inspiration for many to concentrate their missionary efforts in this region.

Exercise

Some of these concepts are quite widely discussed, and the finer points of definitions are debated. A more practical concern for you may be: how far can these ideas help you and your mission team or church in the ministry God has given you where you are?

Obviously some people in some areas of the world will find certain ideas more relevant than others.

5E Global Intercession

As we saw in Unit 5, prayer is easier to practise than understand, and we need to remember constantly the fact that in prayer we are encountering the living God, rather than presenting a list of requests to him.

This provides an appropriate context for focusing on **global intercession**. This is most simply defined as *praying for the world*, and on a practical level you can do this through e.g. a weekly prayer meeting, access to prayer letters from missionaries around the world, or using Patrick Johnstone's prayer resource *Operation World*. This book, last updated in 1993 and published by Operation Mobilisation, gives a vast amount of information about different areas and countries of the world, and includes specific prayer requests for each place. You can, if you wish, use it on a daily basis since it is set out in that way, although you should avoid falling into the trap of setting an impossible daily target for yourself and then spending most of the year feeling guilty by being unable to keep up with it. It is a tool which can help you, and you should not let it control your spiritual life!

Spiritual Warfare

Such global intercession, as we saw in Unit 5, is only one aspect of prayer, but as part of prayer it does play a role in the actual task of world mission. Although you may be at home or in your office you can be part of what God is doing world-wide through prayer. Sometimes this aspect of prayer is separated out and given the name **spiritual warfare**, to refer more narrowly to active participation in the spiritual battle referred to by Paul in Ephesians 6.

 Study Ephesians 6:10-20. What are the different roles of prayer, bible study, faith, etc., in being part of the spiritual battle?

5F Church Planting

Church planting is the whole process of evangelising, disciplining, training, and organising a group of believers to a level of development which allows them to function as a local church, so that the church planters themselves can leave and let the local believers carry on the life of the church. This term, again not itself a biblical one, is an attempt to describe what seems to be happening in New Testament times.

 See for example 1 Corinthians 3:6. Do you think this verse is relevant? Why or why not?

Methods for church planting differ widely, and all we can do here is underline its significance as part of a mission's longer-term strategy. For effective church planting there is a great need for people willing to commit themselves to a longer time period in mission if they wish to see things happen. In very few situations is church planting a short-term option.

One other word of caution: we should be slow to read back into the book of Acts our modern concept of 'church planter'. Paul would probably not have seen himself in that way, even if we feel comfortable using the term to describe what he did. The actual term 'church planting', like contextualisation, is not very old.

Church planting as part of mission really focuses on the evangelistic side of mission, and so it is appropriate that we move on in the next unit to look at evangelism itself.

Memory Verses

Luke 4:18–19 (note that these are Jesus' words)
John 20:21

Unit Seven

Evangelism

Outline and Notes

Evangelism is concerned with the spreading of the *evangel*, the gospel. What does this mean in theory and practice?

Aims

The Global Action training program goals include the aims that at the end of their Global Action training the student will:

- be able to share his/her personal testimony
- be able to lead someone to faith in Christ
- have actively pursued friendships with non-Christians
- understand the significance of and be able to do initial follow-up and ongoing discipleship

Study Objectives

As well as laying the foundation for the above training goals, this unit will enable you to:

- give a definition of evangelism
- explain the content of a gospel presentation
- explain the difference between proclaiming the truth and seeing conversion
- explain the importance of defending your faith
- analyse the situation where you are and begin to adapt your evangelism to it

Unit Outline

1 What is Evangelism?

1A   Definitions

1B   Can Evangelism be Measured?
         The Process of Becoming a Christian

1C   The Goal of Evangelism
         Evangelism in the Bible

2 The Gospel

2A   What is the Gospel?
         The Gospel is a Man, Not a Plan

2B   A Gospel Presentation
         The Bridge to Life
         Notes on the Bridge to Life
         Verses for an Expanded *Bridge to Life* Illustration
         Additional Note: An Alternative *Bridge to Life* Illustration

2C   Optional Section: Apologetics

3 Becoming a Christian

3A   Telling Your Story

3B   Leading Someone to Faith in Christ
         Confession
         Repentance
         Thanksgiving
         Follow-Up

4 Practical Issues

4A   Introduction: Big and Little Stories

4B   Conversations, evangelistic events, friendship, preaching the
         gospel in church

4C   Researching your Area
         In what situations do people become Christians?

5 Follow-Up

5A   Conversion and Discipleship

5B   The Local Church

1 What is Evangelism?

1A Definitions

C.H. Spurgeon said that evangelism is one beggar telling another beggar where to find bread.

In this unit we draw on much of our understanding of previous units, including our discussion of what makes a Christian (in Unit 5), and in particular how evangelism relates to mission in general. As we said in Unit 6, evangelism is best seen as one element of mission, but here we choose to focus on it in more depth.

Why bother with definitions?

In some countries *being committed* is fashionable. 'Are you devoted to what you do?' becomes a main question. In other countries it is very unfashionable, and everyone wants to have an easy life. But either way, there is a particular problem for Christians concerning commitment. It becomes easy to define our commitment to Christ as a matter of *doing* something for him: the mark of being a real disciple is seen as our activity. This is either because that's just the way the culture is, or because Christians are reacting to the way that the culture is not interested in commitment at all.

It then becomes too easy to hear lots of encouragement to 'get out and do it' when it comes to evangelism. Catchy phrases like 'let's not talk about it but let's get on with it'; or 'we are aiming to evangelise the world in our generation' are common.

But there is a problem. *What is the **it**? Or: what does **evangelising** the world actually mean?*

If we are not careful then we will find ourselves committed to doing the wrong thing, or perhaps not understanding what evangelism really is, or why it is important. We may end up burning out from constant activity which in fact was never what God wanted in the first place.

In defining 'evangelism', some of the possibilities are:

* telling people what the gospel is
* asking people to make a commitment to Christ
* seeing people become Christians
* preaching the gospel whether or not anyone listens
* distributing tracts and literature
* setting up new churches filled with new believers
* leading people to Christ and following up their commitment until they are part of a local church

> ✍ Write out your own understanding of what evangelism is. (This is to help you think about what you already believe before studying the ideas of others.)

Here is William Temple's definition:

> 'To evangelise is so to present Jesus Christ in the power of the Holy Spirit, that men shall come to put their trust in God through him, to accept him as their Saviour, and serve him as their King in the fellowship of his church.'

Is this what you are committed to when you talk about evangelism?

1B Can Evangelism be Measured?

Although Temple's definition is very helpful, and reminds us of some of the priorities we need to have in evangelism, such as the cost of Christian service and the role of the local church, it does raise another difficult issue:

- Can we define evangelism in terms of how people respond to it, or must we limit our definition to what is said and done by the evangelist?

Think about it

You might ask: does it matter? Perhaps not. Consider this: you have spent the day preaching the gospel on a street corner and talking with people individually about it. No one seemed either interested or thankful at the end of the day. Would you say that you have been involved in evangelism or not?

The Process of Becoming a Christian

How long does it take to become a Christian

Some say it takes an instant. Once you were in darkness but now you are in light. The old self is gone and the new is come. Others say it is a process: that you grow as a disciple but it is only the final arrival in heaven that demonstrates that you were saved. This unit is not going to tell you what to think about this issue, although we should point out that the topic of evangelism raises several difficult questions like this about the Christian life. Look out for others as you go through the unit.

However, one option which the Bible really does not allow is to say that once you have 'made a commitment' to Jesus it does not matter if you never follow it up with any kind of lifestyle changes or commitments.

 When Paul encounters back-sliding among the Galatians he is quite blunt about it: Look up Galatians 5:7 and 5:13 (and indeed the whole letter of Galatians). What does he say?

This raises a vital question about evangelism: is it your responsibility to introduce people to Jesus and see them make a commitment but not to go any further? We deal with these questions more fully at the end of the unit.

But this should warn us to be careful in thinking that we can measure evangelism very well. God is probably not particularly interested in how many commitments are made or whether people say they agree with you. What matters is that lives are changed in the long run, and that people become disciples of Jesus.

We must keep an important balance in our evangelism: our 'gospel message' is important but equally important is the friendship within which we share it, as well as the witness of our lifestyle. When we present the gospel we will almost certainly leave things out and fail to communicate clearly all we want to say. But if we have a friendship where we can help someone deal with the ongoing issues of living a transformed life then we are much more likely to make an impact for God's kingdom.

1C The Goal of Evangelism

We can now attempt to say what the goal of evangelism is. On one level it is to see people become Christians. Of course this is something only God can do, which can make evangelism a bit frustrating at times (and perhaps explains why Christians sometimes do all kinds of other things, things where they *are* in control of the goal, instead of evangelism; such as paperwork, or holding meetings, or developing missionary policies . . .). On the other hand it can be a big encouragement, since the miracle of new life is in God's hands and not ours, which takes an impossible weight off our shoulders.

What do you think of this statement:
Our goal in evangelism is to communicate the gospel faithfully and appropriately, so that it is heard and understood.
Can you think of advantages and disadvantages with stating the goal this way?

Many good things which we are doing are not evangelism. For instance, we believe that our evangelistic activity should take place in the context of friendships. Friendships take time and cannot be 'programmed' to achieve certain goals. It is very important to take time with people that we care about. But this is not evangelism.

We will explore the issues this raises concerning *communication* in general in Unit 8. For this unit, we look at the nature of the gospel, and some suggestions for how to share it appropriately.

Study Activity: Evangelism in the Bible

The word 'evangelism' comes from the Greek *evangelion*, meaning literally the good news, or the gospel. This word occurs 72 times in the New Testament: look up at least the following:
Mark 1:1, Acts 20:24, 1 Corinthians 15:1-8 and Romans 1:16.

The word 'evangelist' (*evangelistes*) is used three times:
Acts 21:8, Ephesians 4:11, 2 Timothy 4:5.

- Note here how an 'evangelist' may be someone with the gift of evangelism, but equally someone with some other gift who nevertheless must work as an evangelist. Which of these verses tell you this?
- To evangelise (*evangelizo*) is usually translated as 'to preach the good news' or 'preach the gospel' in modern translations: *Luke 4:18, and frequently through Acts: e.g. 8:4, 12, 25, 35, 40.*
- What does Paul preach (*evangelizo*) in Acts 17:18?

Note that in Acts 8, and in general in translation, the word 'evangelising' is not used. It would be easy to overlook how much actual evangelism is recorded in the pages of the New Testament.

2 The Gospel

2A What is the Gospel?

'God loves you and has a wonderful plan for your life.' These familiar words are the opening sentence from a famous evangelistic presentation which has been printed as a tract many thousands of times. While God has clearly used such presentations greatly, we can observe that he has chosen not to include one in his inspired Bible. Why not?

There is sometimes a tension when you present a non-Christian friend with a Bible but prefer them to read a tract first (with some title like 'How God can be your friend' or 'Life Now Free!' etc.). Some Bibles deal with this by printing a gospel outline inside the front or back cover. But why then did God not provide an inspired version?

(Some people answer this question by saying that the book of Romans is God's inspired gospel-presentation. But although it has often been read as an account of how an individual can obtain salvation we should note that it is actually about how God has been at work among Jews and among Gentiles down through history, as *groups* of people. Romans, like all the New Testament letters, needs to be understood in its original context, as we discussed in Unit 1. So while there is a lot in it that we can use in presenting the gospel, it is not actually a gospel presentation.)

We could put it this way: God has provided everything that we need to know. But it is our desire to present Christianity as a simple set of points which he chose not to make a part of his revelation. In fact, Christianity stands out among the world's religions because although its teachings are important, it concentrates on the teacher more than his teachings. The person of Jesus Christ is at the centre of Christianity in a way that no other major religious figure is at the centre of any other religion.

The Gospel is a Man, Not a Plan

 What did Paul write to the Corinthians in 1 Corinthians 2:2? (We can assume from the general context of the letter that by 'crucified' Paul is referring to both the death and resurrection of Christ here.)

We should not see a false contrast here between knowing Christ and knowing the Bible. How would you express the relationship between these two kinds of knowledge?

If our message is focused on Jesus then we shall never lose our balance.

- In your evangelism are you trying to get people to agree with a worldview or a personal philosophy or a set of doctrines or with the person who was God in human flesh?

Many of Jesus' sayings are uncomfortable, and most of us find ways of almost explaining them away as we grow as Christians (which says a lot about our idea of 'growth' perhaps). But it has almost always been true that people find Jesus a lot more appealing than they find Christians or the church (or missionaries, or . . .). Let people deal with Jesus and come to their own conclusions with him. As an evangelist, you should be seeking to take a back seat.

Questions for Reflection

- If the gospel is a person, then how would you introduce someone to the gospel?
- How would you introduce someone to a friend of yours?
- Wouldn't you want them to meet your friend themselves and hear what your friend has to say?
- Is it a good idea to say that your aim in evangelism is to let people hear Jesus speak?

This may provide a helpful suggestion for how to run an evangelistic Bible study: study a gospel and let people meet Jesus through his own words and deeds, instead of your own particular package of 'things you need to know'. You will probably find that Jesus says all kinds of things which you find hard to explain, or even embarrassing, but that's OK. Better to let your friends deal with Jesus on Jesus' terms and start working out what it means to be a Christian for themselves than turn them into a copy of yourself. Jesus has strong words for those who do that (see Matthew 23:15).

 One way of looking at who Jesus is, is to study the 'I AM' sayings of John's gospel:

Look up these references and for each one summarise in one sentence what it says about Jesus, and how it shows that *the gospel is more about a person than a set of truths*:

John 6:35; 8:12; 10:9; 10:11; 11:25; 14:6; 15:5.

(You may remember also from Unit 3 our study of John 8:58 in its context as a specific claim which Jesus was making about himself.) Use reference tools to help you with these verses if they are not clear.

2B A Gospel Presentation

We have learned that Jesus is our focus. Our practical aim here is to develop a *gospel message which allows others to focus on Jesus.*

Most evangelism, at heart, takes place one-to-one; with individuals. Jesus' own ministry is a good illustration of this. Although the gospels give details of only around 50 days in his life, they show him talking to at least 19 individuals (who?). This is true even in situations where we are told that he spoke to a large crowd.

Opportunities to share the gospel are common, and the biggest obstacle most people have in taking them is not lack of opportunity, but being unsure about what to say. There are, of course, as many ways of sharing the gospel as there are people to talk to, but sometimes people use this variety as an excuse for failing to master *any* method of presenting the gospel. As we observed in section 1 of this unit, evangelism takes place when the gospel is presented. What follows, then, is one model you can use in doing this. It is a very simple model, and you are free to spend time mastering some other presentation if it suits your situation better. However, nobody should find this one too difficult.

The Bridge to Life

This well known illustration has 4 advantages:

(1) It is **biblical**: it can be done using many verses, but the method shown here uses and explains only one verse, Romans 6:23.

(2) It is **visual**: the diagram is easy to draw and easy to understand.

(3) It is **adaptable**: it can be done quickly with those who are familiar with the Gospel message, *and* more thoroughly with those who need a more complete explanation. It can also be used with people coming from different religious backgrounds.

(4) It is **memorable**: if you encourage someone to read through the verse several times as you are using the illustration then many will find that they have memorised Romans 6:23 by the time you have finished.

Brief guidelines for using the 'Bridge to Life' Illustration:

- When the time is right, ask your friend: *'Can I take a couple of minutes to share with you a little diagram that has helped many people come to know God in a personal way?'*

- Turn in your Bible to Romans 6:23 and ask your friend to read it for you. (Or perhaps to read it twice, since it is so short.)

- Write it out on a piece of paper (or any convenient place, such as a serviette) a word at a time, asking questions like:
    What is a WAGE?
    What is SIN?
    Whose SIN is God talking about here?
    What is DEATH? Do you know the difference between spiritual, physical and eternal DEATH?
    What's the difference between a WAGE and a GIFT?
    Who is the GIFT for?
    Who wants to give you this GIFT?
    Who is GOD and what is he like?
    What is ETERNAL LIFE?
    Who paid for the GIFT?
    Why did JESUS CHRIST have to suffer DEATH?
    What does his resurrection prove?
    Where would you see YOURSELF in this diagram?
    What must you do to get from DEATH to LIFE?

    Notice that these aren't *yes* or *no* questions. This kind of question:
        . . . keeps the conversation from being a monologue
        . . . helps keep the other person involved (and awake!)
        . . . enables you to know where they are in their understanding
            and interest

- Sketch the diagram neatly and clearly, and leave it with them so that they can refer to it later. Start with the outline of two cliffs, add in each word as it comes up, and when you get to Christ add in the cross, and with the resurrection add in the heart.
- When you've finished, ask your friend if they can repeat the verse from memory.

The Bridge to Life Illustration

Build up the diagram as you go until it looks something like this at the end:

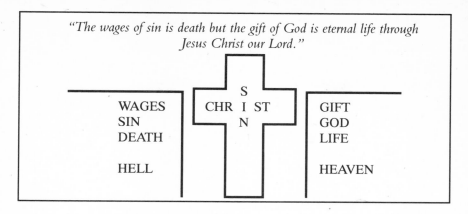

"The wages of sin is death but the gift of God is eternal life through Jesus Christ our Lord."

WAGES   CHR I ST   GIFT
SIN   N   GOD
DEATH   LIFE

HELL   HEAVEN

Notes on the Bridge to Life

Although you have now demonstrated some essentials of the gospel based on just one verse, you should see that the questions you asked, and perhaps the questions which your friend raised, involve going quite deeply into your faith. That is the way it should be. Do not think that here is a simple method which will save you having to face the deeper questions. Rather it is an opening into more conversation and discussion about our lifelong response to Jesus.

Like any other memorised presentation this is a *tool* and should not become your master. It may be that you will never use it quite as you have learned it. In fact you should always be looking to adapt it and develop it according to the people you meet (see the alternative presentation below, for example). As a tool, it is simply a way of enabling you to start somewhere.

Exercise

Memorise this *Bridge to Life* illustration. To demonstrate that you have memorised it share it with a Christian friend, perhaps someone in your church, who should play the role of a non-Christian.

If you already know just this basic one-verse presentation, then try the following longer version here, using different verses to illustrate your points.

You may have an altogether different presentation which you would like to memorise. As long as it is appropriate to your situation in your culture that's OK!

Verses for an Expanded *Bridge to Life* Illustration

MAN		GOD	
God's Image	- Genesis 1:27	Creation	- Genesis 1:1
Sinner	- Romans 3:23	Perfection	- 1 Peter 1:16
	- Exodus 20	Love	- 1 John 4:18
	- Mark 7:20-23	Abundant Life	- John 10:10
	- Romans 1:29-32	ETERNAL LIFE	- 1 John 5:11-13
Judgement	- Hebrews 9:27		
ETERNAL	- Romans 6:23		
DEATH			

But through the cross: (Romans 5:8; 1 Peter 3:18; John 5:24)
God offers the chance to:
- repent (Mark 1:15)
- believe (Acts 16:31)
- confess (Romans 10:9-10)

Obviously there are many different ways of using Bible verses to illustrate your points. This one, for instance, does not use John 3:16, but you could use it on its own as another one-verse Bridge illustration.

Even if you do not learn this expanded version, spend some time looking up these verses and making sure you understand them.

Additional Note: An Alternative *Bridge to Life* Illustration

Since not everybody starts from the same position, you may find the following presentation more useful with some 'religious people', i.e. where you are trying to get someone from what they already know of God to what they do not know, especially if at the same time they are trying to convert you . . .

The following diagram can be developed in 7 stages:

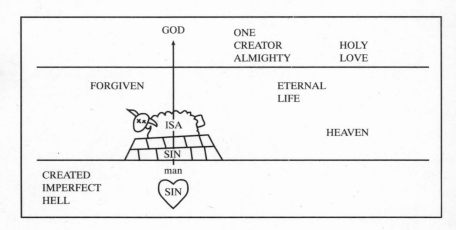

1) Tell me what almighty GOD is like; what do we know that is true about him . . . ? Of course there is ONE true and living God. He alone is the CREATOR of all things. He is certainly ALMIGHTY. Would you agree that he is HOLY, absolutely perfect? It is important to know as well that he is a God of LOVE. He loves YOU as we'll see in a moment.

2) Now what can you tell me about human beings . . . ? One thing is obvious, we are CREATED beings. Our talents display God's greatness! But we're also IMPERFECT, unholy. What imperfections do you see in the human race . . . ? In others you know . . . ? In your own HEART . . . thoughts, words, actions . . . ? God calls such things SIN and says it makes a separation between himself and mankind. Sin creates a barrier, a wall that prevents us from knowing God now, and will also result in HELL on the day of judgement!

3) The gap between us and GOD is serious, and only gets worse as our SIN and rebellion are uncared for. The question is, what can be done to remove this sin barrier?

4) Do you know the story of Abraham sacrificing his son? Can you tell it to me . . . ? In obedience to God Abraham raised the knife to slay him, when suddenly God told him to stop. A *RAM*, caught in the bushes, was put in the son's place and sacrificed instead. The son lived as the ram died in his place! This is a perfect picture of how God demonstrated His love

for you and me. When John the Baptist, known as the prophet Yah-Yah to Muslims, saw the Lord Jesus, ISA MESSIAH, he exclaimed, 'This is the Lamb of God who takes away the sin of the world!' . . . John 1:29.

5) This is something you must try to understand. ISA gave his life as a sacrifice, a substitute, to pay for the sin that separates us from God. Sin had to be paid for by a perfect blood sacrifice . . . Hebrews 9:22. Jesus was the only One able to make that sacrifice because He is the only One who has ever lived a life of absolute sinless perfection . . . 2 Corinthians 5:21. We all *know* that Jesus, or ISA, was born and lived his entire life without sin. His death was payment for your sin. You can be sure it's true because three days later he proved it when he miraculously rose from the dead! God's Word tells us that 'the blood of Jesus Christ cleanses us from all sin' . . . 1 John 1:7. Through him we can be FORGIVEN.

6) Everyone must come to God through a blood sacrifice just as Adam, Noah, Abraham, Moses, David and others did. Through the perfect and complete sacrifice of the Lord Jesus we can come to God . . . 1 Peter 3:18. We can have ETERNAL LIFE with God *now* . . . John 10:10. And we can look forward to being with him in HEAVEN forever . . . 1 John 5:11-13.

7) We all know that ISA is alive today . . . and will come again to receive all true believers to himself, as the Word of God tells us. Through what the Lord Jesus

has done for us, you can see just how great God's love is for you . . . Romans 5:8. All those who repent of their sin and surrender to Him as Saviour, as Lord and God of their lives, can be saved now and forever.

2C Optional Section: Apologetics

Apologetics is concerned with providing an *apology* for the Christian faith: in other words defending its reasonableness and providing some answers to difficult questions. Apologetics has been more or less fashionable at different times and in different cultures. It places a lot of emphasis on reason, and on argument. Consider these two views:

Andy: I think apologetics is an important subject. We must learn how to defend our faith and show that what we believe is logical. Otherwise people will think that being a Christian is irrational: a kind of crutch for people who can't face life's difficulties.

Zohar: I think you're wrong. I think apologetics is a big waste of time. It pretends that the reason we believe in Jesus is because we are logically convinced, but that is rarely true, except perhaps for university students who like staying up all night discussing abstract ideas.

Andy: But there is a place for proving that Jesus exists, that miracles are possible, and that the resurrection really happened.

Zohar: No, those things are just attempts to argue people into the kingdom. They have swallowed the idea of the Enlightenment: that things are only important when they are proved. It's just a more refined version of the old idea that you could prove God's existence by thinking logically enough.

Andy: Not at all. I believe that Christianity is the only rational approach to life. All other approaches can only survive by being inconsistent: e.g. you deny that there is a God and soon you can't explain what right and wrong really is, but you can't live with the consequences of that. You can't accept that some people should have the right to abuse others, for instance, so you have to say that they are wrong, but that word only means that most people don't like it. If you were being consistent in your approach you would have to just say that you don't like abusive behaviour but others are free to do it if they wish. Non-Christians only get anywhere by being inconsistent with their basic presuppositions.

Zohar: That sounds good, but it's not as if Christians are consistent with theirs either. You'll say that in principle it's different: that Christians at least believe in a universe where it is possible to be consistent, but I don't think this has anything really to do with whether people are in or outside the kingdom, with whether they submit to Jesus as their Lord, or whether they 'keep in step with the spirit', as Paul put it. What I see apologetics doing is turning Christians into legalists who are trying to believe all the right things. I'm not at all denying the importance of correct doctrine, I'm just saying that our ability to defend clear formulations of doctrine to unbelievers is neither here nor there when it comes to talking to people in the real world. Christians don't have any better answers to the problem of evil or suffering than non-Christians do: they just trust in a God who doesn't seem to be making sense of it all but will one day welcome them into heaven. That gives us hope, not reasons.

Andy: Well we clearly disagree. I just think that apologetics is an important part of demonstrating the reasonableness of the Christian faith.

Zohar: And I think that in the cross God calls us to him in utter foolishness: shaming the wisdom of this world. What's being reasonable got to do with it?

There we have to leave them. Although their views cover a wide range of opinions on apologetics from A to Z, you might feel there are ways of incorporating insights from both their positions.

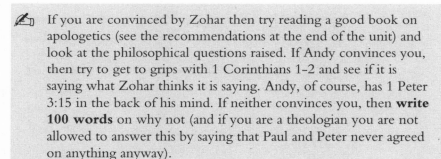

If you are convinced by Zohar then try reading a good book on apologetics (see the recommendations at the end of the unit) and look at the philosophical questions raised. If Andy convinces you, then try to get to grips with 1 Corinthians 1–2 and see if it is saying what Zohar thinks it is saying. Andy, of course, has 1 Peter 3:15 in the back of his mind. If neither convinces you, then **write 100 words** on why not (and if you are a theologian you are not allowed to answer this by saying that Paul and Peter never agreed on anything anyway).

3 Becoming a Christian

First review the sections in Unit 5 about what makes someone a Christian.

3A Telling Your Story

We should be interested both in the theory about how God changes people and is reconciling the world to himself, and also the actual evidence that he is doing it. And you have one case where the evidence is known to you in detail, and is known to you better than to anyone else: yourself. If you have an idea of what a Christian is and how to become one, then it should certainly be a view which includes your own personal history.

(For example, sometimes people say that you must understand certain facts before you can really accept Christ, but in their own case they themselves did not know all those things when they started out as a Christian. We sometimes make the mistake of thinking or behaving as if a new believer must understand all the things which it has taken us years to understand before we are willing to call them a Christian. God was not so strict with us!)

The essential exercise for this part of the course is for you to become confident about telling your own story (or 'giving your testimony', as it is often expressed in Christian jargon). Keep this in mind during the next few notes, before you turn to the practical task of going through your own story.

1. A story of your own experience is only of any use if it is genuine.

Resist the temptation to make your story more dramatic than it sounds, or to include things which you think ought to be in it but aren't really. Don't try and make correct theological points which in fact had nothing to do with what happened to you: e.g. *'I came to see that Jesus really is the Son of God . . .'* if in fact what happened was that you were impressed by his love for you.

2. Not everyone can point to a conversion experience, and not all conversion experiences are dramatic.

Paul talked about his 'Damascus Road' experience several times (we have records of two occasions when he did this: Acts 22 and Acts 26, and in each case we can compare these records with Luke's account of his conversion in Acts 9). He mentions bright lights and falling to the ground and hearing a voice. Few of us experience these things. Paul looks back explicitly to a time when he did not follow Jesus. Some of us cannot remember any such time. But *God has acted in your life in his own unique way* and that is what he has given you to share. You could say 'Trusting in Jesus has always been more important to me than trusting anyone or anything else . . .' and give reasons why you say this. Your own experience *is valuable.*

3. Your story is valuable because it is about God's work in your life, not because it is primarily about you.

Your aim is to point people to God and not to yourself. If you are describing some sin that was a problem before you were a Christian then do not make it a focus of what you say! Some people give the unintended impression that they used to live a really 'interesting' life but then they became a Christian and nothing much happens anymore . . .Focus on some way that God has changed you. Ask yourself: why in fact do I believe in God, or in Jesus?

4. You are not yet perfect. Be wise about how you present the Christian life.

'I used to have this problem but now that I have put my trust in Jesus and repented of my sins I am free from it and all my troubles are gone . . . ' is almost certainly an over-simplification.

5. Avoid jargon and be relevant.

This is especially important if you are communicating cross-culturally, but is relevant to everyone. Is the person you are talking to understanding the words you are using? You may know what you mean by 'Then I found Jesus . . . ' but what does it communicate. (Actually most people who use a phrase like this don't really know what they mean. What does 'find Jesus' actually mean?)

Related to this: you should be prepared to tell your story in different ways depending on who you are talking to. This does *not* mean being dishonest. But suppose two things in your life really stand out: the way that God comforted you through a time of suffering in your family when you were young, and the way that you found your intellectual questions dealt with by the Bible when you were a university student. You could see that you might tell these two stories at different times depending on the situation.

6. God treated you as an individual. Allow him to treat everyone else differently.

Some Christians seem to be confused about the point of telling someone of their own experience. If God has done something particular in your life (e.g. healed you or pulled you through financial difficulty) then what you are testifying to is *the greatness of the God who did that*. You are *not* saying that he will do it in your friend's life. He *might* but he might not. What you hope is that your friend will come to this great God who has done something which reveals who he is. How God will then deal with your friend is not up to you.

Above all: don't get confused by technique. You probably talked to people about your Christian experience most effectively when it was fresh and from the heart. You told people you had just become a Christian, for example. There was no manipulation or forced conversation: you just told them. If you 'rehearse' your story properly, then what you are doing is trying to recover the simplicity of that heart-felt thanksgiving.

A good preparation for this next exercise is to spend time giving thanks to God in prayer for your experience of him.

Exercise

Spend time writing out your own story. The purpose of writing it out is not to memorise it, but to make you think through points which perhaps you think you understand but cannot explain clearly. If you write 'then Jesus came into my heart' ask yourself *what does that communicate? what other ways of expressing it might be clearer?*

This sample structure is only a suggestion:

- *What I was like before I was a Christian* (if appropriate)
  - mention one problem or worry or area of sin in your life
- *How you came to put your trust/faith in Jesus:*
  - how did you become aware of who God is?
  - what was it about God/Jesus that really meant something to you?
  - did you, at some point, actually confess your sin to God and receive forgiveness?
- *What difference has it made in your life?*
  - perhaps refer back to the point you started with and talk about the change

Go through what you have written with one other person. (Perhaps do this exercise in pairs?). Consider especially the following *cultural* issues:

- Is anything you have said inappropriate in the culture where you now live?
- Are you assuming too much about how your own background will be understood?
- How would people in your current culture discuss the issues you are talking about?

Rewrite any parts that are unclear or full of jargon.

Further Study

Compare Acts 9 with Acts 22 and Acts 26. How do Paul's speeches, in their two different forms, illustrate the principles we have outlined above? (Or do they disagree with them?) What other points come out of his story which you think you could use in your own?

Note: we have not set this as the main exercise in this section because certain aspects of Paul's testimony should probably be regarded as unique. Very few have the kind of experience he did, and his calling as apostle to the Gentiles reflects a particular development of God's work in history. In fact, the situation is complicated still further because the first generation of Jews becoming Christians faced very different circumstances from anyone alive today: the question then was tied up with how the Gentiles related to Jews, and how followers of the Old Covenant could adapt to Jesus' redefinition of who God was. In some senses Paul was not 'converted' at all: he was still trying to follow the same God, but was shown that this required him to accept Jesus. The theological issues which this involves are worked out in Romans. This is a very good example of how mission and evangelism raise some of the deepest questions about life and God. If you want to avoid theology, don't be an evangelist!

3B Leading Someone to Faith in Christ

If you have mastered the basics of a gospel presentation, and truly understood how you yourself became a Christian, then leading someone to faith in Christ should not be a mysterious process. *But this does not mean that in practice it is easy.*

For one thing, some people have the gift of being an evangelist, but not everyone does. This must never be used as an excuse for not being a faithful witness to Christ. In fact, if you care about people then hopefully you will want them to come to Jesus anyway. But it is just to remind ourselves that while for some people it seems natural and even enjoyable to engage in evangelistic conversations, for others it can be hard work, perhaps frustrating or intimidating, and occasionally leave you more confused than when you started.

Even though we are looking at techniques and methods in this unit, we want to stress that *sensitivity towards the individual* is a key part of evangelism. Again: love is more important than strategy.

> In reality, the sudden conversions we find in the New Testament came about as the result of considerable preparation. The Ethiopian eunuch was returning from a religious pilgrimage and was reading the book of Isaiah when he first heard the gospel (Acts 8:26-39). The first Roman convert, Cornelius, was described as a devout, God-fearing man who gave to the poor and prayed to God regularly (Acts 10:1-2). The apostle Paul had, as his form of preparation, the heritage of sixteen centuries of biblical content and a powerful vision that struck him down and left him blind (Acts 9:1-9) . . . It is so true that we are 'God's fellow workers' (1 Corinthians 3:9). Where God has already made the preparations, we can and should proceed to reap.
> Jim Petersen, *Evangelism for Our Generation* (NavPress, 1985), 94-95.

There are many ways of expressing the essentials, and in some cultures certain points may need to be stressed more strongly than in others, but at least the following elements are important in leading someone to Christ.

First, the conversation. Before someone can make a commitment to follow Christ, they must have some understanding of what Christ is offering and asking. If you have presented the gospel as outlined above, and perhaps told them your own story, then there are certain attitudes you may encounter:

1. **Your friend is not interested**
   It is best here not to push matters, but perhaps change the subject, pray for them, and hope to come back to the gospel at a later stage.

2. **Your friend is interested but unwilling to make a decision**
   There could be several reasons for this, and you need sensitivity to determine what to do. Maybe they want to hear more, or to have time to reflect on what you've said, or they have problem questions they still want to think through. Perhaps they want to discuss it with someone else, or they feel the need to deal with some area of their life first. Maybe they just need to be asked whether they would like to become a Christian. There is, of course, no formula for determining how to proceed. Ask God to help you and give you wisdom. You may wish to arrange another time to talk further, or introduce them to a friend who could give a different angle (or who could deal with some questions which you don't know how to answer).

3. **Your friend would like to become a Christian**
   Praise God! If this is the case, then there are certain steps you should try to lead them through. It is good to think of these steps as responses to things they have learned: e.g. as they have understood about their sin they will need to respond by confessing it and repenting. As they understand about the cost of discipleship they will need to ask God to become Lord of their life, etc.

Confession

Conversion requires a realisation that you have done wrong. The concept of 'sin' is frequently not well understood today.

> ✍ How is sin defined in the Bible? Important biblical passages to look at would include Romans 1, 3 and 7. Consider also Jeremiah 17:9. A strong passage in which Jesus underlines the difference between the attitude of the heart and the outward appearance is Mark 7:1-23.

To become a Christian is, first, to admit, or confess, your sins. It is to agree with God's evaluation of you: that you are a human being who has value because you are created in the image of God, but that that image is distorted through sin and sinfulness. To 'confess your sins' is nothing mystical: it is to pray to God and ask for forgiveness with the knowledge that he will indeed forgive you.

Repentance

Repentance builds on confession by adding the commitment to change and go in a different direction. It is a decision to leave one way of life and begin another. Such a decision is only possible because of Christ's death on the cross: where he took on himself the punishment for sin, which is death. The repentant life is one which is lived by the power of the Holy Spirit. You could lead your friend in a prayer in which they ask Jesus to be their Lord; to fill them with the Holy Spirit, and thus to live a life of faithfulness and obedience in God's strength.

Thanksgiving

It is good to begin the Christian life as you mean to go on: with thanksgiving. One good reason for giving thanks is the certainty of God's faithfulness. The Bible records some of those promises which you could encourage your friend with at this point, for instance:

• God has removed our sins from us: Psalm 103:12
• God is always with us: Matthew 28:20
• God hears us when we pray: John 15:16
• We may *know* that we have eternal life: 1 John 5:13

Follow-Up

We set this aside for now, but it is part of the whole process. See section 5 of this unit.

 Take turns with a friend to role-play a situation where you lead someone to Christ. This is not a question of memorising certain words, or praying pretend prayers, but just to make sure that you know where you are heading as you deal with a friend's desire to become a Christian. Discuss your experience of this role play with each other and see in what ways you can improve what you would say.

4 Practical Issues

4A Introduction: Big and Little Stories

Before saying 'Jesus is the answer' you need to understand what the question is. Nicodemus came to Jesus and asked how he could be born again (John 3). The woman at the well asked Jesus why he wanted water from her, and then asked for the water he spoke of (John 4). Jesus treated them very differently. To one he gave a philosophical discussion about being born again. To the other he spoke of her five husbands and her immorality.

What, if anything, makes it better to talk of being 'born again' than to talk of immorality?

This is a particular example of what is increasingly being recognised as a key to understanding evangelism. There are lots of ways to describe it. 'Start from where the person is' is a common way of stating it. The point is this: God is more interested in people than formulas.

Another way of understanding it is to say that for the past 100 years or so most 'evangelistic techniques' have been developed in a very Western way. This relates to what was said about apologetics above. The mindset of the modern Western world is strong on techniques and methods. **Modernity** is the word used to describe this approach. Modernity tells *big stories*. It looks at the Bible and sees a grand story of creation and fall and redemption: of God's eternal plan in reconciling the world through Jesus to himself. In evangelism this tends to work itself out as providing a simple scheme of 'You are lost and you need Jesus to get back to God'.

There is a lot of truth in this. We would not want to throw out all that has come through modernity. But sometimes there is an undesirable side-effect: the individual situations in which people find themselves are undervalued. Surprised people are told what their problem is in terms which don't really communicate anything to them.

Post-modernity is a reaction to this which emphasises the personal nature of life: how life is experienced. It approaches the Bible willing to see in it lots of *little stories*. It doesn't try to work out why Jesus told different stories in John 3 and John 4; it just enjoys the fact that he does so. In evangelism this can have a big benefit: you relate to whatever the person is experiencing. Jesus meets them as an individual. This approach requires you to know a lot more about how Jesus related to individuals in the Bible.

In evangelism there is a **balance** to be struck between telling people where God stands and what their problem is (sin) and starting from where the individual is and seeing how God is going to work in their own life, in a way that may never have occurred to you. You are balancing the big story of the eternal God and his plan of redemption, and the little story of how your friend will encounter Jesus. This balance can never be worked out in theory: it is a matter of working it out in real life situations.

If you are living in a culture which has never been through modernity and post-modernity, then how does this 'big story/little story' balance show itself?

In fact, the traditional difference between classical and folk religion is a little like this. People may 'officially' believe something according to their religion, but in practice the belief is quite different. (This difference can also sometimes represent a combination of belief systems, which is called syncretism.) We find this with folk Islam, many forms of Christianity (especially Catholicism), and indeed with most religions.

 Is there a lesson to be learned from this about evangelism in certain cultures?

4B Conversations, evangelistic events, friendship, preaching the gospel in church

Following on from our introduction it is time for you to think about how all of this unit applies to your own situation where you are. By now you will see that evangelism is not a matter of having one sermon up your sleeve which you present on regular occasions. (After all, not even Paul, who stated his aim so clearly in that 1 Corinthians passage we mentioned earlier, preached the same sermon every time, as the book of Acts makes clear).

John Stott has developed the term 'double listening' to describe the process: listening to God through the Bible and also listening to the world around you (see his *The Contemporary Christian* (Leicester: IVP, 1991)). How does this work out where you are?

Practical Exercise

Think about recent **conversations** you have had with non-Christians. What has been your aim: to *dialogue* with them; to *tell them something*; to *listen* to what they want to tell you; to *convert* them? What do you think should be your attitude in such situations?

In what ways is it possible for you to develop **friendships** where you are now with non-Christians? What social contacts do you have? How do people where you are spend their time? Does your daily lifestyle allow you to be part of their world?

How does your church **preach the gospel**? How could you be involved?

(Perhaps the key to preaching the gospel both evangelistically and in general preaching is to observe that you cannot easily tell a group of people what their own individual situations are, but you can point them all to where Jesus is, since he stands above us all in every way. If you focus on Christ, and his expectations, then if people desire to come to him they will be able to spot the areas of their life which fall short and see what kind of action to take. This may involve subsequent one-on-one conversations. The point of preaching then is to *model* Jesus and encourage people to move towards him, not to attack people for their sinfulness and needs.)

What **evangelistic events** are you involved in now, and how do they relate to the possibility of interested people joining a church or group of local believers? What happens in your culture? Meals, sports events, public debates, computer clubs, groups for mothers with young children, local residents' groups, political societies, etc. may all provide platforms for holding events where the purpose is evangelistic. Think through the needs and habits of your local culture and ask yourself: what am I doing now and what could I be doing?

Write out for yourself your thoughts about how you could develop in all these areas, and spend time praying about your involvement.

4C Researching your Area

You cannot import your pre-packaged plan into an area you do not really know. What kind of questions should you ask about where you are living?

In his book *Planting Churches Cross-Culturally* (Grand Rapids: Baker Book House, 1980, pp.100–106) David Hesselgrave suggests that the following subjects need to be considered in understanding the place where you live:

- the kind of land in your area and what it is used for (e.g. farming, commercial, residential . . .)
- the size and rate of growth of the population
- economic factors for the community, including types of occupation and levels of income
- sociological and religious characteristics (including ethnic differences, age ranges, and religious affiliations).

What marks out your area may affect the kind of work you need to do to communicate the gospel meaningfully where you are.

This kind of information is often easily available through a local authority, or other groups in the area who have already done the basic research. You do not necessarily have to start by interviewing everyone to take advantage of this kind of data.

An Exercise for Another Time

Have you or your church been able to take advantage of the kind of survey just described? If not, then how could you go about organising one? What areas would it help you in?

You will certainly need some help in doing this. Hesselgrave's book mentioned above includes a sample survey. This will be a big project requiring careful organisation. But perhaps it is something you should seriously be considering.

In what situations do people become Christians?

Research suggests that in many parts of the world people do not become Christians the first time they hear the gospel. For many what is seen to be most important is the friendship of Christians who demonstrated love and compassion.

 Is this kind of research available for your area? If not, do a little questioning yourself:

- Are there people in your area who have just become Christians?
- What impressed them?
- How and to what extent did they hear the gospel?

This kind of thinking is all part of that 'double-listening': learning to see what kind of questions the world around you is asking.

One final comment: just because you have surveyed the area that does not mean that everyone you meet will be like your average local person. This is obvious, but sometimes people get carried away with their overall impressions. What you need above all is sensitivity to the individuals you meet.

5 Follow-Up

5A Conversion and Discipleship

When two people get divorced it is often the case that the root of their problem with each other goes right back to the early stages of the relationship. It has been said that the church's primary response to divorce should in fact be in the area of helping people prepare better for marriage.

Likewise: when someone 'loses their faith' or 'falls away from God', the problem may often be traced to the beginning of their Christian life. Perhaps they never heard the whole gospel. They were unprepared for suffering or persecution to be a part of the Christian life. They had thought that Christianity would be nothing but good feelings and blessing, and they found long-term discipleship too demanding. Their faith had grown in an atmosphere where other Christian friends sustained them and now they are alone and find no encouragement to keep going with God. (A good biblical example of later problems developing from an early misunderstanding is found in Acts 19:1-7, although Luke has not chosen to tell us here everything we might wish to know about this incident!)

 The focus in the New Testament is not on 'being converted'. This phrase is not used very often, and even when it is, it sometimes refers to converts to Judaism, not Christianity (compare Matthew 23:15, Acts 6:5 and 13:43 with Romans 16:5 and 1 Corinthians 16:15). What phrases are used instead? (See Acts 17:34 and 24:14, or Luke 14:27, or Matthew 20:26)

In these passages we see that the emphasis is on *being* a disciple: 'living by the Spirit' (or 'in' the Spirit), being 'in Christ', being a son (child) of God. How could these concepts be part of your own ministry of evangelism and follow-up?

If your hope in evangelism is to see people become disciples, then your 'job' does not end with the preaching of the gospel. Your hope is that your friend will join you on the path of discipleship. This is what the phrase **follow-up** is concerned with: the process of working with somebody who has said 'Yes' to a commitment to Jesus so that they can move on from there.

 If you are currently involved in evangelism, then what kind of provision have you made for 'follow-up'? Write out what areas you have covered in your preparation, before going on to the next section.

5B The Local Church

What should follow-up include?

If there is any one event which symbolises becoming a Christian, or entering into God's kingdom, it is **baptism**. The Bible may be less clear than we would like about how baptism is to be applied, but it is certainly clear on its importance. Baptism is a symbolic act representing God's welcoming of the new, 're-born' individual into his community, the body of Christ. It is not a biblical option to say that you can hear about Jesus and accept him but not be ready for baptism. In fact, one could argue very convincingly that if you are not ready for baptism then you have not understood the gospel.

Baptism is not into any one local church, but into the body of Christ, which is the universal church. This will of course happen in one local situation, but that does not mean that you are baptised into being a Methodist, or a Pentecostal, etc.

 It is helpful to group together some of the other common requirements of follow-up by looking at one passage in detail: Acts 2:42-47. Read this passage now and look for four things which the believers did together (v.42). What was their attitude (v.46)?

The Christian life is not designed to be lived alone. If you can help a new believer become a part of a local church then you will be going a long way towards helping them become a disciple. But just being in the church is not enough, and you may need to think of ways of working positively towards the kind of Christian living described in the Acts 2 passage. There are many good resources (e.g. books, study courses, . . .) which can help people understand discipleship more, and to grasp the essentials of the Christian life.

 Are you near or part of a local church? In what ways does your evangelism seek to integrate people into the body of Christ? If it does not, what changes could you make in the near future?

Memory Verses

Romans 6:23
1 John 5:11-3

Unit Eight
Communication

Outline and Notes

We may know a great deal and have the right motives in what we do, but sometimes we stumble at the point of how to communicate it all with others, whether those we are working with in local churches or in evangelistic situations.

Aims

The Global Action training program goals include the aims that at the end of their Global Action training the student will:

- communicate with kindness, respect and genuineness
- be able to recognise and evaluate the strengths and weaknesses of his/her own culture
- be able to recognise symptoms of culture shock and be able to handle stresses of cultural adjustment
- have come to respect and appreciate other cultures and denominations, both within and outside the team
- have consistently maintained an accountable relationship with his/her home church, prayer and support partners
- show an attitude of respect to local church leadership

Study Objectives

As well as laying the foundation for the above training goals, this unit will enable you to:

- speak in public with greater confidence

- follow some basic guidelines in writing a prayer letter
- assess whether you should be involved in language learning where you are

Unit Outline

1 About Communication

1A   Introduction
1B   Communicating with People: Showing Respect
1C   Technique and Honesty
1D   Case Studies: Two Biblical Examples
       (1) Moses Receives the Law at Sinai (Exodus 19)
       (2) Nathan confronts David (2 Samuel 12)

2 Public Speaking

2A   Introduction
2B   Practicalities
2C   Address Your Audience
2D   Don't Include Everything
2E   Different Styles for Different Groups

3 Other Forms of Communication

3A   Everything is Communication
       Who You Are
3B   Written Communication
       Tracts
       Books
3C   Prayer Letters: Some Guidelines

4 Cross-Cultural Communication

4A   Introduction: What is Culture?
4B   Incarnational Ministry Across Cultures
       Bonding and Language
4C   Case Studies: Different Issues to be Faced
       (1) Actions Speak Louder Than Words
       (2) Children and Family
       (3) Age and Death

5 Communicating in Your Work

5A   A Special Case of Cross-Cultural Communication
5B   You and the Local Church
5C   You and Your Home Church

Additional Note on Culture Shock

1 About Communication

1A Introduction

Communication is crucial. Is what you are saying the same as what I am hearing? You may know all the right things in your head, but how are you putting them across to me? This unit is about removing unnecessary stumbling blocks which may be leaving you in situations where you have been misunderstood or misinterpreted (and not, as some might think, about learning to manipulate people).

Some miscommunication is inevitable: it is a part of life. But many times a few simple guide-lines can greatly improve how much people will understand you. This applies in many different areas, and not just in obvious ones like preaching or leading a meeting. This unit will focus on a variety of situations, some more practical, and others specifically to do with cross-cultural issues. If you worked through the material on contextualisation in unit 6 then you have already begun to think about this. The section on telling people your own story in unit 7 also involved some of the basic ideas about communication.

The remainder of this section looks at some ethical principles in communication, and concludes with a Bible study which may help you to see some of these principles at work.

 You are always communicating. Before going on, list 10 ways in which you have been communicating recently. Some may be obvious (e.g. writing a letter) and some not (e.g. you've been unhappy lately, communicating to others that something is wrong).

1B Communicating with People: Showing Respect

In almost every situation, it is *people* you are communicating with. Why bother to say this? Because sometimes even Christians forget this. You write a strong letter in the heat of the moment, and by the time it gets there you have cooled off and the other person is thrown into turmoil thinking you are still angry. You may have had good points to make, but you forgot that you were making them to another human being, someone worthy of respect. (A hint: once you have taken out your anger by writing such a letter, throw it away. Never, ever send it.)

This problem is particularly becoming clear with e-mail: what you may have intended as a light-hearted remark written quickly sounds very heavy and unfriendly when it turns up on someone else's computer screen.

The basic thing to remember in all communication is that it is a person you are dealing with, and not an idea, or a proposal, or a job, or an office. You may wish to disagree entirely with what someone is saying, but you should make it as clear as possible that in rejecting their idea you are not rejecting them as a person.

✍ Compare Galatians 3:1-5 with Galatians 5:2-12. Is Paul successful in following the advice we have just given?!

1C Technique and Honesty

Ever since Vance Packard wrote *The Hidden Persuaders* in 1957 (subtitled *An introduction to the techniques of mass-persuasion through the unconscious*) in which he showed some of the ways in which advertisers manipulate their audience, there has been the suspicion that any carefully crafted message which uses communication skills is in some way suspect: you can't believe what you see on TV or read in the papers, people often say. And perhaps we become suspicious of any well-packaged message.

Of course, this is an over-simplification. Yet some Christians almost reinforce this idea by drawing a false distinction between human effort and the work of the Holy Spirit: preparing a sermon, for instance, is seen as unspiritual compared to 'letting God speak to you' as you preach. But this is a ridiculous idea. It misunderstands how God works *through* us, using our abilities, as well as occasionally giving some supernatural insight or message.

> God can and does use unskilled people with no preparation, but his overruling of an unsatisfactory situation is no excuse for not working for something good. The good is worth aiming at. However, the good isn't everything. The good without God is groundless.
> James Rye, *The Communicator's Craft: Getting Your Message Across* (Leicester: IVP, 1990), pp.14-15.

Following on from this, an important principle is:
Do not distort the truth for the sake of a good impression. A good technique should not compromise your honesty. Do not exaggerate for the sake of effect. Do not manipulate people so that

they do what you want. Instead let people hear you properly and make their own decision to respond.

 The New Testament is full of spontaneous sermons and excited public debates. But, especially in Acts, God seems to have used such occasions in spite of the disorganisation rather than because of it. In Acts 14 people thought Paul and Barnabas were gods. In Acts 17 Paul's message about 'Jesus' and the 'resurrection' was thought to be about two new gods with those names. In what ways did Paul overcome these problems?

1D Case Studies: Two Biblical Examples

(1) Moses Receives the Law at Sinai (Exodus 19)

We pick up this story in verse 8, where Moses has managed to receive a commitment from the people to obey God, and he has passed this back to God. God's instructions to Moses in vv.9–13 build a tremendous sense of expectancy. Verses 16–23 describe what actually happened on the 'third day', the day that Moses received the law. God could of course have just announced the words of the law. But this episode is much more dramatic, and would undoubtedly have left an astonishing impression in the minds of all who were there.

The first two questions below are the most important. Spend the most time on these:

- What are some of the ways in which God makes the occasion memorable?
- What kind of attitude would the Israelites have had as they watched what was going on on the mountain that day?
- You certainly won't want to criticise God for what he did. Does this mean that there are times when an overpowering audio-visual impact is acceptable to bring home the actual message forcefully?
- Does it work here? See Exodus 24:3.
- How well does it work? See Exodus 32:1 (!)

(2) Nathan confronts David (2 Samuel 12)

This passage is one of the clearest in the whole Bible for showing how someone thought through the process of communication in order to make their message have the required impact.

If you do not know the context, read through chapter 11, where David commits adultery with Bathsheba (making her pregnant), and then has her husband killed to cover his tracks. David eventually makes Bathsheba his wife and they have the child (11:27), 'but the thing David had done displeased the Lord'. God's response is to send Nathan, a prophet (see v.25) with a message of condemnation.

- What does Nathan do? The actual message is given in v.7b-12, but Nathan would have seen that the likely response of David would have been to reject him and probably have him killed for daring to accuse the king.
- How does Nathan get round this?
- What is David's own judgement on himself? (v.5)
- How did Nathan manage to get David to see he was wrong?
- What does this incident show about communicating?

In many ways this is the best example of a parable in the Old Testament. Jesus' own use of parables reflects some of the same principles: telling a story in such a way that the listeners are drawn in and come to a judgement about themselves which they would never make if they were just thinking directly about themselves. (Luke 10:25-37 is an example of this, and slightly different, perhaps more complicated, so is Luke 20:1-8, where you can see a typical way in which Jesus communicated with those who were trying to trap him.)

2 Public Speaking

2A Introduction

In this section we focus specifically on public speaking, which does not just mean preaching, but could mean giving a report in your home church about mission work you may have been involved in, leading a short time during a prayer meeting, or giving an introduction at a Bible study. After looking briefly at some principles, most of your time will be spent actually preparing a short talk, giving it (perhaps to a group of others doing the same) and giving each other feedback on how it went.

Some people are gifted speakers, and you may or may not be one of them. Whether you are gifted in this way or not, some things can be learned just by practice and a little thought beforehand, and will help you present your talk much more clearly.

Not many people today are accustomed to sitting and listening to someone talk for a long time with no **visual accompaniment**. Most people do much better when there is a visual back-up to what they hear. If you have to do a talk without visuals, then what you say can be at different levels. It is relatively easy to hear someone tell stories; and quite difficult to follow a complicated argument with many points.

One other thing to say at the outset is this: every talk should have a clear **structure**, with a beginning, a middle and an end. One famous piece of advice for giving a talk is this:

• tell them what you are going to tell them
• then tell them
• and finally tell them what you've told them.

That way, people know where you are going, they can follow you as you present your main points, and when you reach the end they have a clear sense of what has been covered.

It should go without saying that you cannot give a talk like this without planning it carefully beforehand. Do not be at all surprised if a 5 minute talk takes an hour or two to prepare if you are new to public speaking.

2B Practicalities

The first, and most general, piece of advice is simply this: observe how public speaking is done in the culture where you are and see what makes for effective communication to the people around you. Why is it done the way it is?

Many of the difficulties people face in public speaking are of a practical nature, and not to do with content at all. Here are some basic points to remember:

• plan your opening two or three sentences well. Write them out. Then you will be well underway before you even have to worry about what you are saying.
• likewise, plan your closing sentences carefully. Often people carry on talking at the end of their talk because they can't quite find the way to stop, reducing the impact and clarity of what they have said.
• before you start, breathe deeply and take pauses as you go. Beginner speakers often experience breathing difficulties and they keep talking through nerves and tension.

- work out in advance where you are likely to have difficulties, e.g. a point which you think may be disagreed with, or a reference to something you may have to explain more fully, and prepare for it. You might be presenting mission work in Tajikistan. The obvious question from many will be: 'Where is Tajikistan?' Have a map ready.
- if you are given a time limit, stick to it. Always. No exceptions (unless it is cultural to ignore a time limit . . .)

2C Address Your Audience

Never start a talk by saying 'I had hoped there would be more here tonight . . . ' — how will that make those present feel? Don't apologise for who you are, either. 'Jim couldn't come tonight and I'm standing in for him: I don't really know much about it . . . ' is guaranteed to make people expect an absolutely worthless session.

Once you start, you must simply accept that it is you talking, and that it is the particular people in front of you who are listening. It is pointless to think about the group you may have wished to have had.

And be realistic about what your particular audience will know. For instance, if you are reporting back to your home church after a year away, they will probably not remember every detail of your past year. 'As you will recall from January's newsletter, Gustav had once been visited by a Jehovah's Witness . . . ' will lose most of your listeners. In general, don't assume that people know everything you know, even, or especially, when it comes to the Bible. If you say 'Of course you all know the story of Hezekiah and the shadow on the stairs . . . ' then those who don't will feel that it is somehow their fault and will probably feel ignorant.

Don't talk about the challenge to go overseas in an old people's home. Don't try and be academic with a group of people who are not academics. Don't use 'in-jokes' to people who won't understand what you are talking about (and generally avoid jokes if speaking cross-culturally). Avoid student humour if you are not addressing students. These points, all obvious, are simply examples of being appropriate to the audience you have.

2D Don't Include Everything

A particular temptation for a new speaker is to cover everything. In a gospel presentation this can involve going into unnecessary detail on topics that are way beyond your average listener (e.g. 'Of course we must remember here that our free response to God's offer is in fact predestined in eternity by his sovereign will, and the topic of predestination and free will needs to be elaborated briefly before we go on . . . ').

You can hear speakers making this mistake when they start going back over things they have already said and begin to add in extra stories, or points, or balancing viewpoints, etc. Careful planning will usually help you avoid this kind of error.

Many people, even those who would say 'I couldn't talk in public like that . . . ', actually like the sound of their own voice, or do not know how to stop talking or control what they are saying, and once they get going they will carry on too long. Better to be invited back again because you left people wanting more, than to outstay your welcome.

2E Different Styles for Different Groups

The particular aspect of this question of different styles that we have in mind here is to do with the *size* of the group you are addressing; in other words: the number of people present.

You have probably discovered already that sometimes a great preacher can be really frustrating in a small group where they do all the talking and do not let you discuss the subject or ask any questions. Or that someone who can lead a team worship time very helpfully seems insecure and uncomfortable doing it at the front of a large church. This is because **different styles of speaking are appropriate to different group sizes.**

Peter Cotterell has distinguished between four basic group sizes, as follows:

- **G1 familiar**: 4–6 people; like a family, everyone is involved; informal language
- **G2 small group**: 8–16 people; like many house groups; one leader but all are involved; varies between formal and informal
- **G3 large group:** 25–80 people; like an average church; usually led by one 'speaker', little interaction; those who contribute have to 'make a speech'
- **G4 celebration:** 100+ people; large churches or special meetings (e.g. conferences); very formal, only one person speaks, and they must speak with authority, and often use gifts of rhetoric and public speaking in the process

Adapted from Peter Cotterell, *Look Who's Talking*, Eastbourne: Kingsway, 1984, p.83

As you reflect on your experiences in different size groups you may see a pattern here. For example, a relaxed and joking style for the leader may suit a G2 group, but be inappropriate in a G3 group (although, if done with flair, it may be useful again in G4). Preachers accustomed to large congregations may be surprised to find their rhetorical questions being answered if they speak at a housegroup (e.g. 'How could we call this unfair?!' gets the response 'I think it's totally unfair' from someone, and throws the speaker off guard completely since he was about to explain why it wasn't).

Note also that some group sizes fall between these numbers. Often in groups which are between these categories there is a slight tension about the best way to run the group. A group of 20, for instance, is caught between having one person lead it and having an open discussion. Often the solution for such a group is to either grow or split in two.

 Study the list briefly and think about how it applies to the situation facing you as you speak.

Exercise

Prepare and present a 5 minute talk on any topic to your team. This could be a short presentation 'Mission work in X', or a short devotional talk, ('Encouragement from Psalm 23' for example) or an extract from a longer talk you might be giving somewhere else (the first five minutes of a sermon, or a sketchboard message; or your story of how you became a Christian). Explain clearly what context your talk fits.

Listen to each other's talks, and offer *sympathetic and constructive feedback*. Remember: the aim is to learn together about speaking, not to be competitive. You should find it a valuable experience both to be criticised by others, as well as to critique your friends' talks.

Note: Some of you may find yourself in the situation of talking to a group **with a translator**. Try and go through your talk beforehand with the translator, noting difficult words and phrases, illustrations that don't translate well, and so on. On a practical level: try and speak in short sentences, and be careful of stopping half-way through a longer sentence. For example, the translator may not be able to translate half a sentence because he needs to know a verb you haven't yet used, or the subject of the sentence which you haven't yet mentioned. There is no point in having a brilliant message in your own language which makes no sense once translated.

3 Other Forms of Communication

3A Everything is Communication

Everything you do communicates. Even not speaking is a form of communication: why are you being silent? Advertising provides a clear example of just how seriously the smallest details are considered as part of the overall message.

Here are just some of the ways in which you communicate without perhaps thinking it through:

- facial expression
- tone of voice
- accent
- clothing and dress style
- hairstyle
- what you eat
- the camera around your neck
- the kind of car that you drive
- your big black Bible
- a pile of tracts in your hand
- your jewellery
- your willingness or your refusal to drink alcohol
- sharing a house with members of the opposite sex

Obviously this list could go on forever. Especially in a cross–cultural situation you may be totally unaware of what it actually is you are communicating in any of the above ways. And it is not true that your primary concern is to avoid giving the wrong impression in these areas, although it is one concern.

 How far is your aim to 'give the right impression'? If what you are doing is not wrong, but just 'different', then is it OK to carry on and make sure you try to explain to friends why you are the way you are? (If this question is vague consider some of the specifics from the list above.)

Who You Are

That last question leads directly on to this difficult area: how much of what you communicate is just who you are? Is it right to try and be someone you're not just to give the right impression?

Let's take an example: you are a very sociable person who likes to talk and finds it natural and easy to start conversations with strangers. You move to a culture where that is considered impolite. What do you do?

This becomes a major issue in cross-cultural communication, so we will return to it later in this unit.

3B Written Communication

Rumours of the death of reading and writing have been greatly exaggerated. Bill Gates, founder and leader of Microsoft, recently publicised his ideas about the future of human (particularly Western) society and gave the opinion that we would soon be leaving behind us the massive printed output of recent years and moving to new forms of technology. In order to say this he wrote a book.

Likewise we have heard for many years of the paperless office. But when working with computers it is very easy to print off multiple copies, draft copies and working copies of any and every document, resulting in a general *increase* in paper output!

So we should expect that writing skills will remain essential for good communication. We look now at various different types of written material.

Tracts

Many missions and Christian organisation's make use of tracts. In general, the idea of a 'tract' goes back to a time when they were common from all sources, not just Christians. People would put their ideas on to a short piece of paper, run off a few hundred copies, and distribute them on the street or door-to-door. This is quite a rare practice in many parts of the world today, and much distributed literature especially in Western cultures is more usually called 'junk mail'. There is some evidence to suggest that papers distributed free are often seen as worthless.

So you should probably draw a distinction between giving someone a tract as some kind of reminder of a conversation, and giving someone you have never met or talked to a tract. Many Christians give out tracts without thinking this through, as if assuming that it is automatically a good thing.

If you are using tracts then work through the above points to assess how suitable your current approach is.

Books

It is also worth thinking about good books, especially evangelistic ones, which you could use with people you know. Here, you might need to think through how beneficial it is to give someone a free book unless there is clearly some desire to read it. On the one hand it is great to be able to give a good book. On the other hand, unwanted free books may just sit untouched on a shelf for years.

When a good book is sold or given in the context of a friendship, there may be several advantages:

- it will be written in the language of your friend, whereas you may be struggling to express yourself clearly in their language
- it will be there for your friend even when you are not, and perhaps long after you have left the country
- it will (hopefully!) be a carefully thought-out discussion of an issue, or a well-told story, and, unlike you, will not later think of what it should have said

Sadly, we must acknowledge that a vast amount of terrible Christian literature also exists. So please check carefully any book you distribute. In general, do not give out a book you do not know.

3C Prayer Letters: Some Guidelines

Most of us either write or read prayer letters. By 'prayer letter' we are referring to the standard way in which missionaries communicate in writing with friends and churches who are or will be supporting them in prayer, or financially, or just taking an interest in their ministry. As the name suggests, the purpose of a prayer letter is to encourage and enable people to pray, although it can equally function as a newsletter. This short section is for those faced with the task of *writing* a prayer letter.

The following guidelines are drawn from Alvera Mickelsen's *How to Write Missionary Letters. Practical tips to make your words come alive* (Bloomingdale, Illinois: Media Associates International, Inc., revised 1995). This is a very useful resource on the subject.

Many of the points Mickelsen makes are similar to our discussion of public speaking, such as the need to plan ahead, the importance of a good and clear first sentence, the need for a definite and punchy ending (instead of rambling on trying to include everything), and the need not to take for granted that the reader will remember all the details you mention from any previous letter. The following checklist may prove useful:

Writing guide-lines

Here are questions to ask yourself as you write and rewrite your letter:

1. Have I committed this letter to the Lord in prayer?
2. Does my beginning sentence and paragraph grab the reader's attention?
3. Did I write the way I talk? Does my letter sound like me?
4. Did I share what I really wanted to say?
5. Is my letter interesting and informative as well as truthful? Can I make the facts of my story more interesting by writing poignantly, dramatically, humorously or in another style?
6. Will people, places and events mentioned be clear to my readers?
7. Is my letter concise? Do I need to cut unimportant or unnecessary details?
8. Is the ending to my letter memorable? Will it call my reader to action?
9. Did I check grammar, punctuation and spelling?
10. Is my full name and mailing address on my letter?

The answer to all these questions should be yes. If any answer is no, you'll know what to work on.
Source: Alvera Mickelsen's *How to Write Missionary Letters,* p.30

She also discusses technical aspects of your prayer letter, such as making it look good on the page; taking advantage of computer facilities, varying the layout from time to time, etc..

Always remember what it is like to receive prayer letters yourself: which ones stand out to you? How often does it seem appropriate to hear from people? Every month is probably too often. If you are in voluntary training or ministry for one year then try every two months. If longer, every three months may be better. You must find a way of doing your letter which is appropriate to you, but more importantly is appropriate to those receiving it.

Finally, even though you are writing to many people, your letter will be read by one person at a time. This is obvious, but is often forgotten. So write as if you were writing to a friend: it will save you from being abstract and impersonal.

Exercise

If you are at the point where you are about to write a prayer letter, the exercise should be obvious! If you have just done one, think through it now in the light of the above guidelines. This section of the unit is for your practical help, so put it to the best use you can in a way that will help you.

4 Cross-Cultural Communication

4A Introduction: What is Culture?

In this section we can only make a start to this huge topic. Hopefully you will be able to pick up ideas from it which you can take further wherever you are. Cross-cultural communication is always raising questions about our assumptions. It is always challenging us to check if we are understanding each other: if our view of a situation is the same as the other person's. We have encountered examples of this throughout this manual, in almost every area.

We begin by asking 'what is culture'? Many definitions have been offered, ranging from a broad 'design for living' and 'the silent language that we all speak' to more technical definitions:

Paul Hiebert has defined it as 'the integrated system of learned patterns of behaviour, ideas and products characteristic of a society' (Paul Hiebert, *Cultural Anthropology*, Grand Rapids: Baker Book House, 1983 (orig. 1976), p.25). More broadly, the whole way people act, think, believe, and *are* make up their culture. We do not mean 'the arts' or 'a high level of upbringing' when we use the word in this sense.

For as long as you only mix with people from your own background and world view you will probably not think about this so much. But this is increasingly uncommon, and certainly if you have any cross-cultural experience then you will find yourself dealing with a whole variety of world views, and you will (or at least *should*) become very much aware of your cultural assumptions and background.

We should state clearly at this point that as a general rule every culture is a mixture of good and bad and that no one culture is more valid than any other. *Ethnocentrism* is the name given to a view of the world that assumes that your own culture is the best or most useful. This is a view which is easy to fall into (because you understand your own culture better and often find other ways of doing things 'strange') but which must be avoided. The need to avoid ethnocentrism is especially strong in multi-cultural contexts, such as international team work, or some student situations.

Exercise

This exercise is especially relevant for those who have changed cultures. Consider your home culture where you grew up. Have you recently noticed areas which distinguish it from the culture where you now live? Write down five of these distinguishing features. There *will be* several things to notice, so if you can't think of any then stop and think harder! And perhaps ask someone who knows you and is not from your culture. This exercise is a good way of thinking through how these issues may apply to you.

4B Incarnational Ministry across Cultures

Incarnational ministry refers to the process by which the gospel is not just preached but lovingly lived out with cultural sensitivity especially (but not only) in cross-cultural situations. 'Bonding' is one way to describe how missionaries initially attach themselves to the culture where they are working. It has become a popular theoretical concept, probably as a reaction to the cultural insensitivity of some missionaries in the past, and still today (see the section on contextualisation in the Mission unit for further discussion). It has however been noted that many people who write about it do not or have not practised it, which makes it easy to be idealistic.

Furthermore, it is generally over-simplistic to talk about 'bonding' or 'incarnational lifestyle' as if it were one well-defined idea. The challenge is to hold on to its key insight, that we must follow Jesus' example of identifying with those he came to serve and to save, while finding how to do it in a realistic way.

Harriet Hill has argued that there are at least three different models of 'incarnational ministry' and that some of them are more helpful than others:

1. Understand the people by adopting their lifestyle
2. Understand the people and adopt their lifestyle as possible
3. Understand the people and select the most appropriate lifestyle

(See her very useful article, 'Lifting the fog on incarnational ministry', *Evangelical Missions Quarterly* 29:3 (July 1993), pp. 262-69.)

This brings us back to the discussion on 'Who You Are' in the previous section. As a foreign missionary you must accept that you will never *be* one of the people of your new culture. Perhaps following their custom is not actually respected by them, and raises all kinds of unexpected problems, precisely because you are actually a foreigner:

> While visiting a remote mission station in northern Kenya, Jon Arensen says, local elders asked the missionary if they could rent the mission Land-Rover. They had heard that about 100 miles away a white lady had come to study their customs. In an effort to be accepted, she had built a house out of skins and was wearing the same clothing (or lack of it) as the local women. These elders thought this was so curious that they were willing to sell a camel to raise the cash to go have a look at this strange phenomenon. The missionary turned down their offer.
> Hill, *Lifting the Fog*, p.268, n.3

As so often is the case, the issue is more complex than right/wrong and good/bad in terms of lifestyle. Option 3 in the above list is by far the most difficult, since it involves making judgements about what you find in your new culture, but it would seem to be the most appropriate way to respond to what you find.

Exercise (for those living cross-culturally)

List five lifestyle decisions you have made since arriving in your new culture and for each one consider the cultural thinking which helped make your decision. As you think through your list you may of course find that you change your mind in some areas!

'Bonding' goes very deep. A most helpful summary of our discussion is given by one writer reflecting on Paul Hiebert's comments.

> [There are three levels of] Paul Hiebert's model for missionary identification:
>
> (1) deep-level-attitudes (e.g., ethnocentric feelings of cultural or racial superiority);

(2) mid-level roles (e.g., master-servant);

(3) surface-level cultural practices (e.g., food, houses, clothes, lifestyles).

Hiebert warns that if missionaries identify only at the surface level of lifestyles, they can miss identifying at the deeper levels.

Kenneth McElhanon, 'Don't give up on the incarnational model', *Evangelical Missions Quarterly* 27:4 (October 1991) p.391.

Bonding and Language

One area which may be a part of *appropriate bonding* is learning the language of where you are living. Again this will probably vary from place to place, and the decisions involved may be difficult where, for instance, several local languages compete with a trade language for priority, and perhaps English or French is the official language anyway.

But, although any language can express anything given enough time and effort, some things are much easier to say, and come with certain connotations, in one language rather than another. (Note: just because a language lacks a word for something doesn't mean that the idea can't be expressed. There is no Greek word for 'family', for example, in the New Testament, but related words like *oikos* (household) allow the NT writers to say things which we can see as relating to the family.)

For this reason, language learning has become an established part of mission work, and you should very seriously consider ways of pursuing it, either through language school or using some less formal method (such as E. Thomas Brewster and Elizabeth S. Brewster's *Language Acquisition Made Practical*, or *LAMP* for short, Colorado Springs: Lingua House, 1976).

The following famous story may perhaps help you see more clearly some reasons for all of the hard work it will take:

> Soon after the end of World War II one group of missionaries began intensive evangelism in Japan through the use of interpreters. They were enjoying such outstanding results that it seemed necessary to take advantage of the unique opportunity to communicate Christ. The time of reaping might soon pass. Language study could come later . . . They used various interpreters according to availability. Imagine the chagrin of one such missionary when, one day, his Japanese-speaking missionary friend (with a candour possessed by few Japanese – even your best friend won't tell you!) informed him how his invitation had been interpreted. While the missionary speaker had spoken of God's love and provision in Christ, the necessity of repentance and faith, and the urgency of making

an immediate decision for Christ, the interpreter had given short shrift to the missionary's words, but had augmented them with his own invitation which went something like this:

'These American missionaries have demonstrated their concern for us Japanese by coming thousands of miles to tell us about God. Certainly we dare not be so discourteous as to disregard their appeal. Let us show them how grateful we are by doing as they say.'

David J. Hesselgrave, *Communicating Christ Cross-Culturally* (*Grand Rapids: Zondervan, 1978, p.249*)

4C Case Studies: Different Issues to be Faced

We close this section by thinking of some actual subjects you could explore to make our discussion seem less abstract. One way of using these sample studies is actually to sit down with someone from another culture and discuss the topic with them.

(1) Actions Speak Louder Than Words

Proximity:

• how near is it polite to be when speaking with someone?
• does it differ with different age groups, between sexes, cultures?
• how much eye-contact should there be when people speak together?
• who may you touch? or not touch?
• Jesus touched people. How does his example apply in this culture?

Non-verbal Communication (Gestures):

• how do people express strong negative emotions non-verbally?
• are there any gestures or facial expressions the culture finds unacceptable?
• what body-language expresses greetings or respect?
• what standards are there for physical beauty in women or handsomeness in men?

Style:

• are there accepted customs? (e.g. only criminals have beards, or females must have pierced ears and long hair)
• dress styles: what is acceptable for male and female? is there a formal dress, or a special dress for church-going?
• are certain colours significant in dress for special occasions?
• are there any banned colours?

(2) Children and Family

- do people normally marry to have children, for sexual pleasure or for companionship?
- what happens if they are unable to have children?
- how many is a normal number of children in a family?
- do people hope for boys or girls?
- how do people regard a child born outside marriage?
- who normally would care for or discipline the child?
- what do you permit a child to do (e.g.: is a baby allowed to cry himself to sleep? do you smack children? what for . . . ?)
- how do Christians in your area interpret 'Honour your father and mother'?
- are certain children more valued than others? (e.g. disabled)
- when is a child treated on the same level as an adult?

(3) Age and Death

- does the culture put more value on youth than old age?
- how do these values show?
- do people mistreat the young/old? how?
- is it acceptable to ask someone their age? if not, why not?
- do people try to disguise their advancing years? how?
- is death a subject you would discuss openly in the culture?
- are people told if they are suffering terminal illnesses?
- have you ever seen someone die?
- at what age, if ever, did you first see a dead person or participate in a funeral?
- does the average person plan in advance for death? (make a will; arrange the funeral service; go and choose a plot for a grave . . . ?)

Exercise

Go through *at least one* of these subjects with someone from a culture new to you. The more you can do the better, since it will help you understand the people around you.

5 Communicating in Your Work

(Note: this section is especially for those working in one culture but being supported by friends or a church in another culture, eg in mission work or training.)

5A A Special Case of Cross-Cultural Communication

Our study in section 4B above showed that your situation is culturally complex as a missionary: not only are you adapting from a home culture to a new (or 'target') culture, but many of you are doing so via an international culture, and furthermore trying to fit in to a kind of Christian culture both in your sending church/country and perhaps also in the local church or mission where you are working.

In this section of the unit, we focus on this particular area of cross-cultural communication: the various aspects of your role as a missionary.

 Friends and people you meet in your new location will ask you, if they haven't already, questions like 'Who do you work for?', 'What are you doing here?'; 'How are you paid/Where do you get your money from?', etc.. There may not be one right answer for you in your circumstances, but you must know what you will say, otherwise it will look very strange indeed to be unable to answer these questions. What will you say?

5B You and the Local Church

This is a particular case of the 'bonding' issue we looked at earlier. In general, missionaries agree that the aim of cross–cultural mission is not to export cultural ways of doing things, and on the level of church structure and leadership this is important.

Ethiopia, for example, is a country where it has been possible more than usual to avoid unnecessary foreign influence. Ethiopian believers were encouraged to choose their own approach to the question of church buildings. They decided to meet in buildings which were constructed in the same simple way (and to the same basic design) as their houses. This had an unforeseen benefit after the revolution of 1974 when missionaries were thrown out and the church persecuted, in that it was a simple matter to reconstruct new church buildings.

Now this example, as with most mission examples, raises as many questions as it answers, but hopefully sets us thinking along the right lines.

Consider the following questions about church leadership and structure:

- should a church have one leader?
- should a church have a leadership team which has authority over the rest of the congregation?
- should a church vote on issues which affect its members?
- should a church have an official membership?
- should a leader undergo any training before becoming a leader (whether formal or informal training)?
- should a church or a leader or a special sub-leadership team decide who to support as a missionary and how much?
- what authority does a church body have over a missionary?
- or over a member?

There may be a wide variety of answers to these questions (although this is sometimes wrongly taken as discounting the views of those who have specific answers for perhaps very good, biblical reasons). And you may be caught between a supporting church which sees things one way and a local church on the field with a very different view.

Exercise

Here are some practical scenarios which illustrate the importance of knowing where you stand in all this:

(1) You are church planting in town X. But in the meantime you are attending an existing church there. What should your attitude be to the leadership of that church if they feel that it is more important to concentrate on the growth of their own congregation, at least for a short time, until it is sufficiently established itself?

(2) You are working in a town where none of the existing churches exactly reflects your ideal of a good evangelical church. A friend of yours becomes a Christian. What is your advice about the importance for them of attending a church?

(3) You are working in a country where you think the government is corrupt, but the local church, to your amazement, collaborates with it. What should your attitude be to the local church leadership?

Be especially sensitive to situations where you may import one understanding of different denominational stances only to find that in your new country the same names stand for something different. Evangelicals are particularly prone to doing this with regard to Catholic and Orthodox believers, as if heaven will be populated only by evangelicals. But it happens within Protestant denominations as well.

Discuss these different case studies with your mission team or church and also discuss any situations which you may actually have come acrossand where you now realise that these kind of questions are in fact the issue.

Alternative Exercise

Paul and Frances Hiebert's *Case Studies in Missions* (Grand Rapids: Baker Book House, 1987) contains many case studies on these kinds of issue. See especially part 8, 'Church-Mission Relationships', pp. 182-208. If you have access to this book then feel free to do one of these case studies as an alternative exercise.

In mission work, there should be a commitment to showing an attitude of respect to local church leadership, even though this does not dictate what that will mean in practice in your situation. In general, the principles of sensitivity and holding individual leaders in esteem will always be a good starting point.

 A mission organisation is an expression and instrument of the church (i.e. the world-wide body of Christ), although its structure is not the same as a local church or assembly of believers. It is often argued that the only reason that such mission groups exist is because local churches around the world have failed to play their role in mission. Do you agree with this? Why or why not? How would this idea affect your role with other churches: e.g. are you trying to motivate them to get on with the job, or trying to go ahead and do it instead of them?

5C You and Your Home Church

Finally, you should bear in mind some of these communication issues with regard to your home church. Remember that in many cases your home church does not fully understand what it is like to be living cross-culturally, and neither does it understand what it is like to be a missionary (although hopefully someone there will know something about this). Some of the points made earlier about prayer letters are relevant here.

Look out for issues which may appear strange to those 'back home'. If you come from a town where your church works in close co-operation with a Catholic church, for instance, there will be a lot of unintended signals if you write back an enthusiastic 'I've been out converting Catholics' letter.

All kinds of issues sound strange to those who haven't made the transition you have, from your new enthusiasm for 'gospel card tricks' to your practice of 'praying in the money for our team to go to X' (which may sound like a watered down prosperity doctrine if you aren't careful) to your adoption of a different set of Christian habits just because you are now in a different kind of church to the one which is supporting you. (How *will* they react if you've left a rather conservative church and write home that you've been filled with the Spirit, or received the gift of healing, or been making contacts in the local bar or have been fasting every second day?)

There are no simple rules for dealing with this, except to maintain respect, and show love and sensitivity at all times. You may be able to consider your current work as an indirect ministry to your home church: perhaps you will excite them to have a broader vision for mission, or to think about how they could apply some of the things you have been doing. But expect this to come through interaction with them, not because you have gone off and found a 'better way', which is hardly likely to leave them feeling valued.

 As a practical step, you could make an extra effort to write personally to your church leaders if you are not already doing so, keeping them in touch with your situation, and letting them know how much you appreciate their support, and perhaps even inviting their comments on what you are doing.

Additional Note on Culture Shock

Culture shock is not really the topic of this unit, but it is very much related to it, and experience shows that it is a frequent struggle for missionaries (at home and abroad). This brief discussion is taken from Louis Luzbetak's excellent *The Church and Cultures*, which contains many helpful illustrations of culture shock.

He offers the following four-step analysis of the different stages of cultural adjustment:

(1)   The 'Tourist Stage' – (sometimes called the 'honeymoon period') where everything is exciting and interesting, and people make an effort to welcome you in, and don't mind that you are different

(2)   The Disenchantment Stage – the novelty wears off, people become tired of you being different and just want you to fit in to their normal life, and you frequently say 'Help – I want to go home' (or 'Oh no – I'm not going home for ages yet')

(3)   The Resolution Stage – where you begin to face up to the difficulties of (2) above

(4)   The Adjustment Stage – where you begin the process of working out how to fit in appropriately.

A diagrammatic sketch of a possible form of adjustment to a new cultural environment:

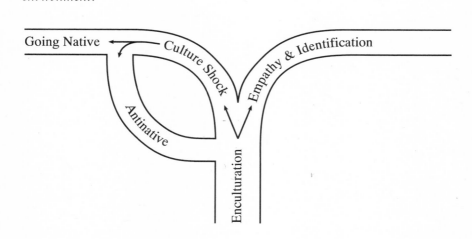

The diagram above shows what happens when, usually during stage (2) of this process, we fail to (or refuse to) adapt to various situations which surprise us, and react into culture shock. When this happens, we either react against the culture (going 'antinative' in the diagram) which forces us back to the conflict again and again; or we over-react and 'go native', which is the process of rejecting your own prior standards (your home culture, and possibly your Christian standards too) and just doing whatever is expected locally. In extreme cases this can involve serious moral compromise and sin. It is, in Luzbetak's words, 'jumping from the frying pan into the fire', in the desperate hope of being accepted. It is never the answer.

This note on culture shock has been adapted from Louis J. Luzbetak, *The Church and Cultures. New Perspectives in Missiological Anthropology* (Maryknoll, NY: Orbis Books, 1988), A different, but very good, resource for this subject is Ted Ward, *Living Overseas: A Book of Preparations* (New York: The Free Press, Macmillan Co. and London: Collier Macmillan Publishers, 1984).

Memory Verses

Colossians 4:5-6
1 Corinthians 9:22b-23

Afterword
Living as the People of God

A few reflections at the end of this study manual:

As with almost all Bible study, and thinking about mission and the Christian life, this book has probably raised as many questions as it has answered. It has suggested things you would like to look into but haven't had time to. It has encouraged you to go further in areas you already knew about. Probably there has been more material here than you have been able to fit into 120 hours of study time. Perhaps team discussions have been times of disagreement and unexpected differences of opinion. Or perhaps they have been stimulating and inspiring. Perhaps neither. Perhaps only now will you be able to go back over some of the material and really get to grips with it, and we would encourage you to do this if possible.

A key part of Christian study is to hold together theory and practice. We do not study just for what we can *know*. But what we know will work itself out into every aspect of our lives: our understanding of the Bible, our knowledge of God and of ourselves, the foundations of Christian discipleship, the many challenging aspects of mission, including evangelism and communication, and ultimately everything we understand of following Jesus.

We are called to live as God's people, playing our part in God's plan as he recreates the universe and brings together all things in Christ. Not all will come to him, and along the way mission will be a messy and tiring business, but it is all we can do to respond to the great God who has made and remade us. May we, with Paul (in Ephesians 3:14–21), kneel before the Father in heaven and ask to be strengthened with power through his Spirit in our inner being, so that Christ may dwell in our hearts through faith.

Appendix
Suggestions for Further Study

Introduction

The reading lists and notes provided here are to help students who perhaps have already done the basic kind of study envisaged in the manual, or who are particularly interested in taking things further after finishing a unit. These notes may help you to have some idea of where to start with the mass of Christian literature that is available on any topic. These are brief suggestions and fall far short of being comprehensive guides to any of the topics mentioned.

Another possible use of this appendix is to give suggestions for some further reading which may be more culturally appropriate in some ways than some of the main discussions in each unit.

Unit One: Bible Survey

Some of these books were introduced at the appropriate place in the unit, but are gathered here for the sake of convenience.

A good **one-volume commentary** on the whole Bible is:

New Bible Commentary: 21st Century Edition by D.A. Carson, R.T. France, J.A. Motyer and G.J. Wenham (eds.) (Leicester: IVP, 4th edition, 1994).

Earlier editions of this were translated into other languages, and so this may become available in other languages too. [3rd edition = *Nouveau Commentaire Biblique* (Emmaus)]

It is often helpful to supplement a one-volume commentary with a good **introduction** to the Old or New Testament. The following are all excellent for their respective areas:

The Lion Handbook to the Bible by D. Field *et al* (eds.) (Oxford: Lion Publishing, 2nd edition, 1983;

Old Testament Survey by W. LaSor, F. Bush and D. Hubbard (Grand Rapids: Eerdmans, 1982) (Revised edition, 1995) [= *Das Alte Testament: Entstehung - Geschichte - Botschaft* (German ed. H. Egelkraut, Geiseen: Brunnen, 1989)]

An Introduction to the Old Testament by R.B. Dillard and T. Longman III (Grand Rapids: Zondervan and Leicester: Apollos, 1994);

An Introduction to the New Testament by D.A. Carson, D.J. Moo and L. Morris (Grand Rapids: Zondervan and Leicester: Apollos, 1992);

Dictionary of Jesus and the Gospels by J.B. Green, S. McKnight and I.H. Marshall (eds.) (Downers Grove and Leicester: IVP, 1992);

Dictionary of Paul and his Letters by G.F. Hawthorne, R.P. Martin and D.G. Reid (eds.) (Downers Grove and Leicester: IVP, 1993).

The companion **Bible dictionary** to the earlier edition of the commentary mentioned above is still the best one-volume Bible dictionary for the reader who wants everything accessible in one place:

New Bible Dictionary by J.D. Douglas *et al* (eds.) (Leicester: IVP and Wheaton: Tyndale House, 2nd edition, 1982);

It is available as a 3-volume illustrated set, with the same text but many helpful diagrams and photographs, entitled *The Illustrated Bible Dictionary*. [= *Das grosse Bibellexikon* by H. Burkhardt *et al* (eds.), 6 vols, (Geissen and Wuppertal: Brunnen & Brockhaus, 1996)].

Most major translations come with their own **concordance**. For the NIV this is:

The NIV Complete Concordance by E.W. Goodrick and J.R. Kohlenberger III (eds.) (Grand Rapids: Zondervan, 1981).

Theological dictionaries tend to be for the more advanced student. The most useful will probably be, on the New Testament:

The New International Dictionary of New Testament Theology by Colin Brown (ed.) (Grand Rapids: Zondervan and Carlisle: Paternoster, 4 volumes, 1975-78) [= *Theologisches Begriffslexikon zum Neuen Testament*, 2nd edition, by L. Coenen and K. Haacker (eds.) (Wuppertal: Brockhaus, 2 volumes, 1996-97)].

There are many study Bibles around which combine good insights from all these different types of study aids. For the NIV the most common one is:

The NIV Study Bible by K.L. Barker *et al* (eds.) (Grand Rapids: Zondervan and London: Hodder & Stoughton, 1985).

Unit Two: Introduction to Hermeneutics

The best introduction, with the advantage that it is available in many languages, is:

How to Read the Bible for All Its Worth by Gordon D. Fee and Douglas Stuart (Grand Rapids: Zondervan and London: Scripture Union, 2nd edition, 1993) [= *Effektives Bibelstudium* (Asslar: ICI, 1990); = *Nouveau Regard Sur La Bible* (Vida)].

This also contains a guide to good Bible commentaries.

Slightly more comprehensive, and an excellent next step for those interested, is

Introduction to Biblical Interpretation by W.W. Klein, C.L. Blomberg and R.L. Hubbard jr. (Dallas: Word, 1993). This contains a lengthy bibliography of many more different types of Bible study tools, helps, reference works, and other useful books on biblical studies, which you should consult for further guidance than is possible here. (See pp.459-91.)

For those who would struggle with the English in these books then, more basic, try:

Unlock the Bible by Stephen Motyer (London: Scripture Union, 1990).

Bibellesen mit Gewinn: Handbuch fuer das persoenliche Bibelstudium by H.G. and W.D. Hendricks (Dillenburg: Christliche Verlagsges, 1995).

An approach from a different angle, stressing how Bible study can change us, is:

Transforming Bible Study by Walter Wink (Nashville: Abingdon Press and London: Mowbray, 2nd edition, 1990). A companion volume to this is Patricia van Ness, *Transforming Bible Study for Children* (??)

Unit Three: Knowing God

General

Originally written in 1973, but still in a class of its own for the serious reader who wants to know God, is:

Knowing God by J.I. Packer (London: Hodder and Stoughton, 2nd edition, with study guide, 1993) [= *Gott erkennen: Das Zeugnis vom einzig wahren Gott* (Bad Liebenzell: VLM, 1977)].

From a different angle, but a book which fits with the emphasis in our unit on being changed through our study of God, is:

Desiring God by John Piper (Portland: Multnomah Press, 1986)

Attributes of God

Packer's book deals with many of God's attributes. On a more popular level there is:
The Knowledge of the Holy by A.W. Tozer (Bromley: STL, 1976).
A brilliant study of one particular attribute, written in a lively and clear way, is:
The Holiness of God by R.C. Sproul (Wheaton: Tyndale House, 1985).

Useful Reference Works

We do not usually recommend particular background reference works, but two commentaries which may be particularly helpful if you wish to go further with the detailed Bible study of some of the key passages, are:
Exodus (Word Biblical Commentary 3) by J.I. Durham (Waco: Word, 1987), which actually sees Yahweh's presence as the key theme of Exodus, and thus relates very much to our study;
The Gospel According to John by D.A. Carson (Leicester: IVP and Grand Rapids:
Eerdmans, 1991), which is very helpful on the many verses and passages from John which are relevant to our topic.

On the Trinity

Packer's book contains some reflection on the Trinity, and the next best place to go is to a general work of reference such as a theological dictionary (see the recommendations at the end of this appendix). For the more adventurous reader:
The Promise of Trinitarian Theology by C.E. Gunton (Edinburgh: T & T Clark, 1991)

Unit Four: Understanding Ourselves

General

It is rare to find books on this subject which combine practical insights with a solid biblical foundation. Helpful books which offer insight in certain areas are:

John White, *The Shattered Mirror*, (Downers Grove and Leicester: IVP, 1987);

Floyd McClung, The Father Heart of God, (Eastbourne: Kingsway, 1985) [= Das Vaterherz Gottes, new edition, (Wuppertal: One Way, 1994)];

Joanna and Alister McGrath, *The Dilemma of Self-Esteem*, (Wheaton and Cambridge: Crossway Books, 1992);

G. Smalley and Trent, *Bitte segne mich* (Marburg: Francke, 1989);

Henry Cloud and John Townsend, *Boundaries* (Grand Rapids: Zondervan, 1992).

A useful practical work book for study is Josh McDowell, *His Image My Image* (San Bernadino: Campus Crusade for Christ, 1984).

Larry Crabb has written several helpful books in this area. Although some of them are presented as counselling books they may be helpful more generally about understanding how we function and relate as people:

Effective Biblical Counselling (Grand Rapids: Zondervan, 1977) [= *Die Last des andern: Biblische Seelsorge als Aufgabe der Gemeinde* (Basel: Brunnen, 1988)]

Understanding People (Grand Rapids: Zondervan, 1987);

Finding God (Grand Rapids: Zondervan, 1993) demonstrates his concern that we do not get caught up in introspection but focus on God in the whole subject.

On the will:

Garry Friesen with J. Robin Maxson, *Decision Making and the Will of God* (Portland: Multnomah Press, 1980) is a deep and thoughtful presentation on one particular side of the discussion;

Haddon Robinson, *Der Wille Gottes und die Freiheit underer Entscheidungen* (Marburg: Francke, 1992);

Good for integrating this discussion into Christian lifestyle in general is Dallas Willard, *In Search of Guidance* (Grand Rapids: Zondervan, 1993).

Unit Five: Discipleship

Note: Reading a book is part of the work for this unit itself (see the end of section 1 in the unit).

General

A good general book on discipleship from a biblical perspective is N.T. Wright, *Following Jesus* (London: SPCK, 1994). It combines Bible study with practical reflection.

One of the great books which helped build Operation Mobilisation in its early days was:

Roy Hession, *The Calvary Road* (Alresford, Hants: Christian Literature Crusade, 1995, originally 1950) [included in Roy Hession, *Der Weg der Erneuerung* (Wuppertal: Brockhaus, 1995)];

A good view from within OM is George Verwer's *No Turning Back* (Carlisle: OM Publishing, 1983) [included in George Verwer, *Von Dir beschenkt* (Neuhausen: Hänssler, 1990)];

Alister McGrath, *Beyond the Quiet Time: Practical Evangelical Spirituality* (London: Triangle, 1995) is also good for getting you to think about your spirituality.

Prayer

A lot of books on prayer in fact only focus on intercession. Two excellent general works are:

O. Hallesby, *Prayer* (Leicester: IVP, 1948) [= *Vom Beten* (Wuppertal: Brockhaus, 1996 reprint)];

Richard Foster, *Prayer. Finding the Heart's True Home* (London: Hodder and Stoughton, 1992);

Very good for looking at prayer in the Bible and applying it to today are:

John White, *People in Prayer* (Leicester: IVP, 1977) [= *Du darfst zu ihm kommen Menschen im Gebet* (Marburg: Francke, 1983)];

Eugene H. Peterson, *Answering God. Learning to Pray from the Psalms* (London: HarperCollins, 1989).

Worship

Graham Kendrick, *Worship* (London: Hodder and Stoughton, 1981) is basic and good. [= *Anbetung* (Wiesbaden: PJ, 1988)].

Many of A.W. Tozer's books are also helpful for reflecting on the place of worship in the Christian life.

Lifestyle

A good book to make you think about the issues is Robert McAfee Brown, *Spirituality and Liberation* (London: Spire Books, 1988). It will make you think in ways which will equip you for life, even if you don't agree with all of it.

Good for considering how to adapt what you are learning on mission work to a daily lifestyle outside it is: Mark Greene, *Thank God It's Monday* (London: Scripture Union, 1994) which especially focuses on how to relate your faith to your workplace.

Relationships

Charles Swindoll's *The Grace Awakening* (Dallas: Word Books, 1990) is powerful in this area. [= *Zeit der Gnade* (Weisbaden: PJ, 1994)];

Also excellent is Floyd McClung's *Father Make Us One* (Eastbourne: Kingsway, 1987) [= *Vater mach uns eins* (Biehl: JmeM, 1989)].

Unit Six: World Mission

General

The book we have recommended in the unit as best for understanding different aspects of Christian mission is the recently reprinted work of John Stott:

John Stott, *Christian Mission in the Modern World* (originally: Downers Grove and Leicester: IVP, 1975, reprinted 1995) [= *Gesandt wie Christus: Grundfragen christlicher Mission und Evangelisation* (Wuppertal: Brockhaus, 1976); = *Mission Chretien Dans Le Monde* (Groupe Missionaire en Suisse)].

Other useful **introductions to mission**, at different levels, are:

Stephen Gaukroger, *Why Bother With Mission?* (Leicester: IVP, 1996), basic and concerned with practical issues;

John Piper, *Let the Nations Be Glad* (Leicester: IVP, 1993), looks at God in relation to mission;

Ken Gnanakan, *Kingdom Concerns. A theology of mission today* (Leicester: IVP, 1993, originally published in India in 1989), a good introduction to mission thinking.

Other books which may be of use in this unit:

Bruce Nicholls (ed.), *The Unique Christ in our Pluralist World* (WEF; Grand Rapids: Baker Book House and Carlisle: Paternoster; 1994);

J. Sanders (ed.): G. Fackre, R. Nash and J. Sanders, *What About Those Who Have Never Heard?* (Downers Grove: IVP, 1995);

Rolf Hille and Eberhard Troeger (eds.) *Die Einzigartigkeit Jesus Christi* (Wuppertal and Giessen: Brockhaus and Brunnen, 1992);

Vincent Donovan, *Christianity Rediscovered* (London: SCM Press, 1978) is a fascinating account of how one missionary was forced to rethink his assumptions;

Roland Allen, *Missionary Methods: St. Paul's or Ours?* (Grand Rapids: Eerdmans, orig. 1912) which is still, remarkably, the best book for a look at biblical methods in mission;

Vinoth Ramachandra, *The Recovery of Mission* (Carlisle: Paternoster, 1996) is a good view from Asia of current thinking in mission. Challenging.

Mission history

The classic work is Stephen Neill, *A History of Christian Missions* (Middlesex: Penguin Books, 1964) [= *Geschichte der christlichen Mission* (Erlangen: Ev. Luth. Mission, 1990)]. Briefer, so perhaps easier to start with, is J. Herbert Kane's *A Concise History of the Christian World Mission* (Grand Rapids: Baker Book House, 1978).

A different perspective, coming from a biographical angle, is provided by Ruth A. Tucker's *From Jerusalem to Irian Jaya. A Biographical History of Christian Missions* (Grand Rapids: Zondervan, 1983) [= *Bis an die Enden der Erde: Missionsgeschichte in Biographien* (with some entries replaced by German and Swiss entries, by K. Rennstich (ed.) (Metzingen: Franz, 1996)].

Ethics

Particularly as ethics relates to mission, *the* outstanding work is:

Bernard T. Adeney, *Strange Virtues. Ethics in a Multicultural World* (Leicester: Apollos, 1995).

A good book on some biblical basics for such an understanding is:

Chris Wright, *Living as the People of God* (= *An Eye for an Eye* in the USA) (Leicester and Downers Grove: IVP, 1983)

Current Issues in Mission

Good all-round resources are:

R. Winter and S. Hawthorne (eds.) *Perspectives on the World Christian Movement, A Reader* (Pasadena: William Carey Library, revised edition, 1992) which also comes with a *Perspectives* study course which would be a good way of doing further study in this area;

D. Hesselgrave and E. Rommen, *Contextualization: Meanings, Methods and Models* (Grand Rapids: Baker Book House, 1989).

For those who would like to go deeper into the thinking behind mission, two excellent, but demanding books, are:

D. Senior and C. Stuhlmueller, *The Biblical Foundation for Mission* (Maryknoll, NY: Orbis Books, 1983);

David Bosch, *Transforming Mission* (Maryknoll, NY: Orbis Books, 1991).

Unit Seven: Evangelism

On Evangelism

A superb general work on many aspects of evangelism which is very good at setting it within the context of the church and its ministry is Michael Green, *Evangelism through the Local Church* (London: Hodder & Stoughton, 1990).

Less concerned with overall context, but especially good on the content of a gospel presentation, is Will Metzger, *Tell the Truth: The Whole Gospel to the Whole Person by Whole People* (Downers Grove: IVP, 1981).

A different approach, with a rare willingness to explore biblical models rather than common modern 'methods' is Walter Brueggemann, *Biblical Perspectives on Evangelism. Living in a Three-Storied Universe* (Nashville: Abingdon Press, 1993).

Evangelistic courses are common, and several have become books which you can use as a series of Bible studies, or just to learn about evangelism. Nicky Gumbel, *Questions of Life* (Eastbourne: Kingsway, 1993) is a widely used recent example which has clearly had a big impact in many countries (as has the *Alpha Course*).

A detailed gospel presentation is included in James Kennedy's *Evangelism Explosion* (Wheaton: Tyndale House, 3rd edition, 1983).

This is particularly strong on the area of follow up and leading people to make an actual commitment to Christ.

There is a whole range of books on making evangelism part of your lifestyle, which is a helpful balance to the strategy-orientated books which are around. Very close to this unit in outlook and thinking are Jim Petersen's two books: *Evangelism as a Lifestyle* and *Evangelism for our Generation*, combined as *Living Proof* (Colorado Springs: NavPress, 1989) [= *Der lebende Beweis: Evangelisation als Lebensstil* (Marburg: Francke, 1991)].

On Apologetics

A good general introduction to apologetics is by Alister McGrath, *Bridge-Building. Effective Christian Apologetics* (Leicester: IVP, 1992).

Michael Green's book listed above is also helpful in this area, with his second section being given over to apologetics (see especially chapters 5 and 8).

Josh McDowell has written several books along this line, although they focus less on reasons for apologetics and thinking about why you would use it, and more on things you could actually defend. His *Evidence that Demands a Verdict* (San Bernadino: Campus Crusade for Christ, 1979 revised edition) (sometimes called *Vol. 1* to distinguish it from a more technical follow-up book) is a good place to start on thinking about the resurrection and the Christian faith [= *Die Bibel im Test: Tatsachen und Argumente fuer die Wahrheit der Bibel* (Neuhausen: Haenssler, 1992)].

Church Planting

The unit does not focus on church-planting, but there is a growing amount of literature available which looks at evangelism as part of a wider goal of starting new churches. Some of this may be relevant to your work. Good overviews combining practical help with some theological reflection are:

David Hesselgrave, *Planting Churches Cross-Culturally: A Guide for Home and Foreign Missions* (Grand Rapids: Baker Book House, 1980);

Martin Robinson and Stuart Christine, *Planting Tomorrow's Churches Today. A Comprehensive Handbook* (Tunbridge Wells: Monarch, 1992).

Unit Eight: Communication

This unit is primarily practical and not much further reading is necessary unless you really want to study in depth. All the titles mentioned in the unit are good resources.

A good **general** book on communication for Christians, although it focuses quite heavily on speaking, is: James Rye, *The Communicator's Craft: Getting Your Message Across* (Leicester: IVP, 1990).

Equally helpful, and taking the discussion from general communication into preaching at some depth, is: J.D. Baumann *An Introduction to Contemporary Preaching* (Grand Rapids: Baker Book House, 1988).

Peter Cotterell's different books look helpfully at communication from several angles, including how to adjust to different group sizes:

Look Who's Talking (Eastbourne: Kingsway, 1984);

Church Alive! (Leicester: IVP, 1981);

Small Groups, Big Results: All About House Groups (Eastbourne: Kingsway, 1993).

On **prayer letters** see:

Alvera Mickelsen, *How to Write Missionary Letters. Practical tips to make your words come alive* (Bloomingdale: Media Associates International, Inc., revised 1995).

On **cross–cultural communication** *the* Christian book is:

David J. Hesselgrave, *Communicating Christ Cross-Culturally* (Grand Rapids: Zondervan, 1978) (2nd edition, 1994).

Focusing on the related, but broader, area of world–views, David Burnett, *Clash of Worlds* (Crowborough: MARC, 1990) is a helpful guide.

Many of the books mentioned in the unit on mission will also contain useful insights.

For those wishing to go further, the area you need is usually called **'cultural anthropology'**, i.e. the study of what culture is, how humans function within it, and (for our purpose) how the task of Christian mission fits into the picture. This is a complicated subject, and most of the worthwhile books on it are quite heavy, but if you're prepared for that, then try:

Louis J. Luzbetak, *The Church and Cultures. New Perspectives in Missiological Anthropology* (Maryknoll: Orbis Books, 1988).

Paul G. Hiebert, who can be tackled on several levels:

Cultural Anthropology (Grand Rapids: Baker Book House, 2nd edition, 1983);

Anthropological Insights for Missionaries (Grand Rapids: Baker Book House, 1985);

Case Studies in Mission (co-edited with Frances F. Hiebert) (Grand Rapids: Baker Book House, 1987);

Anthropological Reflections on Missiological Insights (Grand Rapids: Baker Book House, 1994).

Many of the issues discussed in this unit are regular topics in *Evangelical Missions Quarterly*, which is available from:

EMQ
Box 794
Wheaton, IL 60189
USA

You might like to consider subscribing to this as a team, or perhaps at least as a field, and making it available to all on your team.

Other Recommended Resources

We close with a few recommendations of a more general nature, which may help you to supplement the more specific reading listed above. These are general reference books which will always be of use.

Evangelical Dictionary of Theology by W.A. Elwell (ed.) (Grand Rapids: Baker Book House and Carlisle: Paternoster, 1984);

New Dictionary of Theology by S.B. Ferguson and D.F. Wright (eds.) (Downers Grove and Leicester: IVP, 1988);

Evangelisches Lexikon fuer Theologie und Gemeinde by H. Burkhardt and U. Swarat (eds.), 3 volumes, (Wuppertal: Brockhaus, 1993);

The History of Christianity: A Lion Handbook by T. Dowley *et al* (eds.) (Tring: Lion Publishing, 2nd edition, 1988?);

The Lion Handbook of Christian Belief by Robin Keeley *et al* (eds.) (Tring: Lion Publishing, 1982);

Foundations of the Christian Faith by James Montgomery Boice (Downers Grove and Leicester: IVP, revised edition 1986, orig. 4 vols 1978-81);

Systematic Theology: An Overview by Wayne Grudem (Grand Rapids: Zondervan, 1994);

Biblical Christianity in African Perspective by Wilbur O'Donovan (Carlisle: Paternoster, 1996).